For Novette
with best wishes

16 february 2000

Political Economy and the New Capitalism

Political Economy and the New Capitalism examines key developments in capitalist economies at the end of the twentieth century and brings together essays by leading economists in honour of the late Sam Aaronovitch, the veteran left-wing economist.

In his work, Sam Aaronovitch emphasized the need to take into account the most recent developments in capitalist economies. In this spirit the essays in this volume focus on key issues raised by contemporary trends, including: how the apparent triumph of capitalism reflects on Marxism, the role of the collapse of Communism in undermining the post-war Keynesian settlement, and the relevance of Keynesianism to contemporary capitalism.

Political Economy and the New Capitalism also examines the relevance of Sam Aaronovitch's pioneering empirical studies of British capitalism in the light of modern developments. A wide range of problems are reviewed from industrial concentration today to the co-ordination of economic policies in Europe. Aaronovitch's work on the role of finance in the British economy is the subject of sustained reflection. Individual chapters examine orthodox and left-wing criticisms of finance, exchange rate instability, and employment, growth and regions in the context of European Union. This work concludes with a bibliography of the published writings of Sam Aaronovitch.

This volume collects the reflections of some of the most distinguished thinkers in economics today including: Meghnad Desai, G. C. Harcourt, Pat Devine, Egon Matzner, Malcolm Sawyer, Sir Alan Budd, Jan Toporowski, Philip Arestis, Eleni Paliginis, Victoria Chick and Ben Fine.

Political Economy and the New Capitalism provides a vital and critical survey of key issues in political economy at the end of the twentieth century and will be of interest to students and researchers in political economy, the British and European economies, international, financial and industrial economics.

Jan Toporowski is Reader in Economics, South Bank University and is the author of several works including, *The End of Finance: The Theory of Capital Market Inflation, Financial Derivatives and Pension Fund Capitalism* (Routledge 1999).

Routledge Frontiers of Political Economy

Political Economy and the New Capitalism

Essays in honour of Sam Aaronovitch

Edited by Jan Toporowski

London and New York

First published 2000 by
Routledge
11 New Fetter Lane, London EC4P 4EE

Simultaneously published in the USA and Canada
by Routledge
29 West 35th Street, New York, NY 10001

Routledge is an imprint of the Taylor & Francis Group

Typeset in Baskerville by
BOOK NOW Ltd
Printed and bound in Great Britain by
St Edmundsbury Press, Bury St Edmunds, Suffolk

British Library Cataloguing in Publication Data
A catalogue record for this book is available
from the British Library

Library of Congress Cataloging-in-Publication Data
Political economy and the new capitalism : essays in honour of Sam
   Aaronovitch / edited by Jan Toporowski.
      p. cm. (Routledge frontiers of political economy ; 26)
   1. Capitalism. I. Aaronovitch, Sam. II. Toporowski, Jan.
III. Series.
HB501.P627 1999
330.12'2 dc21   99–22500
                                                       CIP

ISBN 0-415-20221-3

Contents

Figures

Tables

Contributors

A. Haroon Akram-Lodhi teaches rural development at the Institute of Social Studies in The Hague, The Netherlands.

Philip Arestis is Professor of Economics at the University of East London.

Alan Budd is Provost of The Queen's College, Oxford.

Victoria Chick is Professor of Economics at University College London.

Meghnad Desai is director of the Centre for the Study of Global Governance at the London School of Economics and Political Science.

Pat Devine is Senior Lecturer in Economics at the University of Manchester.

Ben Fine is Professor of Economics and Director of the Centre for Economic Policy for South Africa at the School of Oriental and African Studies, London University.

G. C. Harcourt is Emeritus Reader in the History of Economic Theory, University of Cambridge, Emeritus Fellow, Jesus College, Cambridge, and Professor Emeritus, University of Adelaide.

Jörg Huffschmid is Professor of Political Economy and Economic Policy at the University of Bremen.

Paul Levine is Foundation Fund Professor of Economics at the University of Surrey.

Egon Matzner is Fellow at the Max Weber Centre at the University of Erfurt, Germany.

Eleni Paliginis is Principal Lecturer in Economics at Middlesex University.

Malcolm Sawyer is Professor of Economics and Head of Economics Division at the University of Leeds.

Ron Smith is Professor of Economics at Birkbeck College, London University.

Jan Toporowski is Reader in Economics at South Bank University, London.

Introduction

This volume of essays honours the late Sam Aaronovitch (1919–98). Sam was perhaps the last autodidact in economics to make any impression on the profession. Like the great autodidacts of the past, the Classical Economists of the eighteenth and nineteenth century, and Michał Kalecki in this century, he was driven to study economics by a social, political and moral purpose, rather than to please his teachers or to satisfy personal ambition. In his case, like that of other survivors of the inter-War depression, that higher purpose was the elimination of unemployment, which he believed could only be done through the establishment of socialism. Of the many projects that he initiated, the last was a Europe-wide network to discuss practical ways of achieving full employment.

Sam was proud of his basic schooling at Cable Street School in the East End of London, and in the Communist Party. It was the Communist Party which, in a bid to influence the post-War Labour Government's colonial policy, set him to write his first book, co-authored with his first wife Kirstine, *Crisis in Kenya*, published in 1947. The book contained the first national income accounts for Kenya. During the 1950s, along with his work as an industrial organizer for the Party, Sam developed an interest in industrial economics, and the elite which controlled British industry at that time. The outcome of his studies was *Monopoly*, published in 1955, followed by *The Ruling Class*, which came out in 1961. In 1964, he published a handbook in economics, *Economics for Trade Unionists*.

By the mid-1960s, in the late middle age of his life, Sam decided that some formal training in economics would be useful. He won a place at Essex University to study for a degree in Economics. However, the historian Christopher Hill, then Master of Balliol College and a fellow-Party member, told Sam that there was not much that he could learn from academic economics, and invited him to further his studies by researching for a doctorate in economics. In 1972, Sam completed a thesis on the determinants of mergers and acquisitions in British manufacturing. This was combined with work by Malcolm Sawyer, and came out as *Big Business: Theoretical and Empirical Aspects of Concentration and Mergers in the United Kingdom*.

Sam started on an academic career in his late 50s, with an appointment as a lecturer at South Bank Polytechnic in 1974. He now broadened his industrial interests and, in the 1980s, recognizing the increasing dominance of finance over industry, worked on studies of insurance and finance. His academic employment also gave him a more secure position independent of the Communist Party.

Sam was now able to put forward his own very open form of left-wing politics. Already in the early 1960s, he had been arguing in Party circles for dialogue with all who shared its concerns over poverty, racism and inequality. He recognized that this could not take place as long as individuals were required to make ideological commitments before entering into any discussion. If they could not agree on the kind of society that they preferred, or their analytical pre-suppositions, they could at least discuss what was happening in the capitalist economy, and how this constrains economic policy. His political approach was therefore based on careful examination of how the capitalist economies were evolving. For him, capitalism was always exhibiting new features and changing its structures. He used this knowledge to make critical contributions in two directions. In the discussions of the Broad Left's 'Alternative Economic Strategy' he criticized those economic policies, on the Right and the Left, which he felt did not take into account the real situation in which the economy was at the time. He was also dismissive of academic economists whose work was abstracted from economic realities, whether because it merely extrapolated unreal axioms, or because it extrapolated the work of past economists, even a past economist like Marx, whose profound insights into the capitalism of his time could not encompass the capitalisms of all times.

The essays included in this volume therefore reflect not only Sam's interests in economic policy, industrial economics and finance, placed in the context of the 'new capitalism' at the end of the twentieth century. They also indicate the range of political outlook with which Sam was only too willing to engage in discussion.

In his modest way, Sam was bowled over when he found out that the authors of these essays wished to pay tribute to him in this way. I regret most deeply that he is unable to accept this expression of my appreciation for his assistance in contacting contributors, and putting together the bibliography of his publications. Editing this volume has also been made easier by the help which I have received from Bernard Corry, Philip Arestis, Paul Sweezy, Victoria Chick, Ron Smith, Gabrielle Reid, Stuart Wilkes-Heeg, Irene Breugel, Wiesław Toporowski, Anita Prażmowska and the librarians of the British Library of Political and Economic Science and the British Library. I am grateful to them for their assistance. An earlier version of the essay by Geoff Harcourt was printed in the *Cambridge Review*. Thanks are due to Nigel Spivey for permission to publish the essay here.

Part I

Economic policy and the nature of contemporary capitalism

1 Rejuvenated capitalism and no longer existing socialism

A classical Marxist explanation

Meghnad Desai

There is an apocryphal story that, after the Cuban Revolution, Fidel Castro got his associates together to form the cabinet. He asked whether there was an economist among them. Che Guevara put up his hand and so became the first person in charge of the Cuban economy. When after a while things were not going so well for the Cuban economy, Fidel admonished Che and asked why things had gone wrong and how as an economist he would explain this. Astonished, Che replied that he knew nothing of economics. Fidel asked, 'why then did you put up your hand when I asked at our first meeting who was an economist among us?' Che said 'Oh, I thought you asked who was a communist among us, not an economist!'.

It is difficult to be a communist as well as an economist, and few have managed it so well as Sam Aaronovitch. But, as the century nears its end, one cannot wonder whether anyone could have, or even did, predict that capitalism would be alive and well 80-plus years after the October Revolution, and even worse, that the Bolshevik Revolution would be reversed not only in spirit but also that its legal and political manifestation – the USSR – would be no more. The death of the USSR and the continued survival of capitalism are the two most urgent questions of inquiry for all those who ever rejoiced at the prospect of a forthcoming Communist Revolution.

There are, of course, ad hoc, contingent explanations for the disappearance of the USSR – Star Wars, the burden of defence budgets, the personalities of Gorbachev or Brezhnev or Reagan. After the event there are many who claim to have predicted the event. But, if so, neither the Western defence establishment, nor yet the financial markets took any of these predictions seriously. Indeed, the fighter aircraft of the Strategic Air Command went on circling the globe on a 24-hour basis years after. For all I know, they are still doing so.

Endogeneity of Western Marxism

Any explanation of these two shattering events has to be based on some serious theory in which social formations are taken as objects of study. Only political economy – in the sense that Marx and Marxists have used the term – has any hope of explaining these events. This is so, despite the vulgar who think that when the USSR died, Marxism died with it. But even as we use Marxian political economy to explain these twin events, we cannot consider our tools to be outside the explanation, as that playful ex-Marxist Imre Lakatos reminded us long ago. Marxian political economy was itself shaped (some would say distorted) by the course of capitalism and the Soviet Union. As one waxed and the other waned, say in the 1930s, a style of political economy came into fashion that was economistic as well as mechanical. This continued during the 1940s – the pinnacle of the popularity of USSR in the West – and the 1950s when its economic achievements caused many anti-Marxists (W. W. Rostow, for instance) to take it seriously. The Kremlinologists, who became influential in US administrations, took the USSR very seriously as a threat until, that is, it dissolved. It was all rather like Dorothy and the Wizard of Oz.

But Marxian political economy was also a tool for those who were engaged in a struggle against capitalism and fascism in the 1930s, or against imperialism in the colonial and post-colonial struggle. To them, the Soviet Union was, for a long time, the beacon of liberation. As these hopes were dashed – especially in the West after the Hungarian Revolution and Khrushchev's revelations at the XXth Party Congress – a new effort was made at rescuing Marx and Marxism from the clutches of Stalinist orthodoxy. Marx's work was subjected to endless analysis. As some old and abandoned manuscripts began to be published, they were scoured for new signposts of a liberating ideology. Engels was now raised above, now cast below, his comrade – blamed for having been a reductionist or praised for being far sighted, as in his essay on *The Origins of the Family*. Marx's work was found to be wanting in not having a theory of class, of the State, or of spontaneity of the proletariat, or of gender.

Western Marxism – as this enterprise came to be called – became a continuing feast after 1956. It entered academia as higher education expanded in all Western countries – after they had recovered from the effects of the Second World War – and the twin pressures of full employment and the baby boom made such education both affordable and demanded. For about 30 years after 1956, we were all engaged in a curious enterprise. There was not the remotest hope of a Workers' Revolution in the West, and the one Revolution that had been the beacon of hope was, by now, much tarnished. Indeed, a critique of the Bolshevik Revolution was a major part of the enterprise of Western Marxism. For a while, hope rested on the East. But, despite the Chinese Revolution and Vietnam's successful struggle against USA, we have no idols of the Left surviving at the end of the twentieth century.

Western Marxism is dead. Some day its history will have to be written, but for the present, I wish to argue that while Western Marxism is dead, Classical Marxism is not. In trying to understand the trajectory of capitalism, Western Marxism is an obstacle, because it was predicated upon capitalism being crisis-ridden and near its death. Ernest Mandel's characterization of late twentieth century capitalism as its '*Triosième Age*', says it all (Mandel 1975). Old decrepit capitalism was fated to die in the astrology of Western Marxism.

But it did not. Marxists must explain why, within their theory, such an outcome is likely though not inevitable. An explanation that is not predicated upon either eternal life for capitalism nor imminent death. It must probe the reproduction of capitalism as a global system – just as it was in the nineteenth century, albeit on a different scale in the post-colonial, post-industrial and post-Keynesian late twentieth century (Desai 1995). In what follows, I shall attempt a short critique of the inadequacies of Western Marxism (WM, hereafter) as far as its economic theory was concerned. I shall then try to construct a classical Marxist explanation of the persistence of capitalism. Both will be short sketches which I hope to expand in a full-length treatment in a forthcoming book yet to be written.[1]

The faulty analytics of Western Marxism

As far as economic theorising goes, WM in its 1956–86 phase innovated very little. Much of the apparatus that it took as given comes from the debates in Marxism in the 40 years following the death of Marx. But after the advent of Stalin, the debate not only declined in its range but also a monistic view of Marx's theory was popularized. This view was based on the notion of monopoly capitalism – an amalgam of Hilferding and Lenin reworked in the late 1930s and 1940s in terms of Neoclassical theories of imperfect competition (Chamberlin, Joan Robinson, Kalecki) and Keynesian macroeconomics. The word monopoly changed its meaning between its Marxian origins in Class monopoly of means of production, to the Hilferding–Lenin idea of a finance/industry collusion, to a neoclassical definition of monopoly power as excess profits co-existing with excess capacity. Dynamics was exchanged for comparative statics, a general disequilibrium theory for partial equilibrium.

Along with this switch from dynamic general disequilibrium notions to partial comparative static equilibrium notions, the grounding of profits in monopoly power severed any link between prices and labour values. At about the same time, however, Paul Sweezy introduced the Western world to the debates on the Transformation problem in his scholarly introduction to works of Bohm Bawerk and Bortkiewicz (Sweezy 1948). That, however, was modelled as a macroeconomic two-sector or three-sector exercise. While it fascinated a generation of academic economists (see Desai 1991a for a survey) it meant that no connection could be made between the rhetoric of monopoly profits and monopoly capitalism and Marxian theory of values and prices. Even for Marxists, the Transformation problem became an esoteric exercise. Rather like Keynesian macroeconomics, the Marxian economics also had a gap between its micro and its macro aspects.

The theory of monopoly capitalism, if one can so describe the ragbag of elementary Keynesian macroeconomics and Chamberlinian microeconomics, was static and hence could not within itself generate any theory of cycles. It had also no monetary aspects, rather like neoclassical microeconomics and even the neo-Keynesian compromise which ruled the roost in the 1950s and 1960s (see Desai 1974, concluding chapter, for a critique). Even post-Keynesian economics as it fed into Marxist economics did so via Kalecki's work which was deeply static in its treatment of monopoly profits. This meant that, in the 1970s, as inflation and unemployment became simultaneously a problem, against the prediction of neo-Keynesian economics, neither Keynesians nor their Marxist cousins had any explanation. As the monetarist tide swept all before it, Marxists could only follow in its train (see Mandel 1978 as an example). After all, the monetarists did not blame inflation on worker militancy but on State profligacy. Unproductive labour became the scapegoat, as much on the Left as on the Right (O'Connor 1973).

But at least here was a crisis of capitalism. Could it lead to its demise or could capitalism renew itself? Monopoly capitalism searched for evidence of a rising concentration of industry (here again marrying with an empiricist tradition in industrial economics – see Aaronovitch and Sawyer 1975 and Aaronovitch and Smith 1981 for empirical and theoretical analysis in this tradition at its best) and found it, but could conclude little about the dynamics of profitability from that evidence. It had no theory of innovation, nor of capital mobility either within a country as between industries, or between countries. Thus, the theory said that investment was financed by internal funds and not through equity markets. Capital mobility was ruled out from having any impact. Any theory of multi-national capital was based on a purely extractive and exploitative description of the multi-national mode, and the innovative nature of the multi-national mode was not foreseen by the Western Marxists as it was, for example, by Stephen Hymer (Hymer 1972).

Thus, within Western Marxism, capitalism remained a crisis-ridden system but without any dynamics. It was perpetually in crisis and about to break up. Ernest Mandel searched for a cyclical explanation in the theory of long swings, but again it was not integrated into any theory of value (Mandel 1995).[2] There was much useful work done on an ad hoc basis criticising life under capitalism, its tendency to waste surplus, to have high levels of unemployment later extended into the theory of social structure of accumulation by American Marxists (Bowles *et al.* 1984).

What was missing, in a dialectical sense, was a theory of the strengths of capitalism as well as its weaknesses in a dynamic interactive manner. It was capitalism's reliance on the creative destruction of innovations and its ability to destroy old industries and build new ones, its ability to search for profits anywhere, its capacity to overcome political restraints endogenously in the politics of Ronald Reagan and Margaret Thatcher, its tendency to reproduce through the circuit of money and credit as well as 'real' capital, that took Marxists and even Anti-Marxists by surprise. Monopoly capitalism could not have explained the demise of US Steel as it became USX, the near-bankruptcy of IBM as it faced the PC revolution and Microsoft, the fierce competition that US Auto industry – the epitome of monopoly capital – faced from Germans, Japanese and Koreans, the cross-industry mergers, the emergence of holding companies, the shift in power from manufacturing to services, from concrete goods to abstract ones (Auerbach *et al.* 1988; Desai 1997). It could not, above all, say how profitability had revived after declining in the late 1960s and 1970s.

Classical Marxism: A suitable programme for revival

Now who could have predicted that capitalism would be alive and well a century after Marx's death and 75 years after it had reached its highest phase, in Lenin's words? Karl Marx, that is who. Ironically, it is in the crudest and most simplistic theories of capitalism – as outlined in *Capital* and elsewhere in books published in Marx's own lifetime – that the key lies to understanding capitalism. It was a fatal error of the generation of Marxists between 1883 and 1923 to repair Marx's economics, which needed no such repair, but neglect to build up a political theory of democratic action in an era when the proletariat were beginning to win the franchise. I wish to argue that Marx's economic theory is a good point to start with, and such repair as it may need is not to rejig it for monopoly capital, but by filling the gaps left by Marx in his magnificent edifice (see Desai 1991b for a discussion of these 'gaps').

Since it was thought that Marx had predicted the imminent demise of capitalism (which he had not) or that revolutions will happen in the most developed capitalist countries (he kept changing his mind on this, especially after the failure of the Paris Commune), it became de rigeur in Western Marxism to say that Marx was not into prophecies, lest he be rejected for his failure to predict accurately.

Marx did, however, have a model, a framework of the evolution of modes of production, tersely and perhaps too schematically described in his *Preface to A Contribution to a Critique of Political Economy* (CCPE). This is the famous passage in which Marx first lists seriatim various modes of production and then goes on to give a succinct sentence or two about how a transition might take place from one mode to another. He then says how long a mode of production may last before it is ripe for transition. This is the famous line:

> 'No social order ever perishes before all the productive forces for which there is room in it have developed; and new, higher relations of production never appear before the material condition of their existence have matured in the womb of the old society itself.'

It could not be clearer. The words 'ever' in the first sentence and 'never' in the second should have warned Marxists. Here after all is Marx's own summary of the basic thesis argued in a book which he and Engels had consigned to 'the gnawing criticism of the mice'. While people have ever since tried to revise, correct and elaborate practically everything in this short preface, the simple and clear message has been overlooked. Capitalism could not end until its potential had been exhausted. Note that there is nothing here about inequity, or poverty, or revolt of the masses. It is an issue of the productive potential of a mode of production. The material preparations for the future mode also have to be there. The questions then are:

1. Had Capitalism exhausted its productive potential?
2. Had the higher relations appropriate to socialism begun to mature in the womb of the Capitalist order?

Death of Capitalism/Harbinger of socialism?

This is the interconnectedness of the two questions I started with. Was there ground to believe that Capitalism had exhausted its productive potential during the twentieth century, and if so how could one tell, within the Marxian model? On the second question, could we say that preconditions of a higher mode of production – of socialism, though not yet of communism – had been developing within the capitalist mode so that the new mode was ready to emerge? Again, how could one, within the Marxian model, tell?

To put the matter in this way at all is contrary to the spirit of Western Marxism. It had trashed the Preface as a simple enumeration of modes of production, decried the exclusive emphasis on productive forces in the Preface as one-sided and mechanistic, extolled relations of production, and given them as much non-economic garb as possible. My argument is that it is precisely the model denounced as crude and simplistic, the model put forward by Marx – in his first full-length publication published during his lifetime – which is capable of facing up to those two questions in a serious and non-contingent way.

Even in Classical Marxism (CM), there are unreconciled, if not contradictory views on the trajectory of capitalism. In *Capital* Volume I, Part 7, we have the classic model of accumulation with cycles, but without any discussion of a Falling Rate of Profit. In *Capital* Volume II, Chapter 21, The Scheme for Extended Reproduction is presented which sketches a Two-Sector model of Balanced Growth (in modern economic jargon) with value rates of profit which across sectors are unequal, but constant across time. There are no cycles, no crises. This is the scheme that led to a long debate in European Marxism after the publication of Volume II in 1884 (Luxemburg 1913/1953). This debate is well-summarized in Rosa Luxemburg's *Accumulation of Capital*. In *Capital* Volume III, we have the section on Falling Rate of Profit. Marx never had the time to blend these various strands into a single theory of the reproduction of capitalism over the long run (Desai 1979, 1991b).

The debate on breakdown between 1883 and 1923 got off on the wrong footing. Somehow those who became active in the Socialist movement after Marx and Engels were alive and active, thought that Marx had predicted the imminent collapse of capitalism. They derided Bernstein for pointing out the adaptive capacities of capitalism (Gay 1952). Somehow capitalism had to be a mode which could not learn nor adapt, but must follow supra-human inexorable laws. But, rhetoric apart, Luxemburg offers as much a theory of the continuation of capitalism as Bernstein, except that she has a better theory grounded more securely in Marx's value theory (Desai 1979). She endogenizes imperialism, but does not invoke either finance capital or monopoly power to explain the sustained reproduction of capitalism. Her revolutionary activity therefore focused on the class struggle in the metropolis as a way of deflecting capital from its self-reproduction and expansion.

Hilferding and Lenin start, in my view, with the wrong question. They are already surprised that a revolution has not brought capitalism to an end.

Hilferding with youthful impatience, and Lenin during the War, with anger, attributed capitalism's survival to elements not in Marx's theory – finance capital and monopoly power. But in one sense, there is no need to pose the question this way. In a millennial sense, previous modes of production had lasted centuries and the transitions to their successor modes had also spanned centuries. Thus, Western European Feudalism could be said to have begun during the fall of the Roman Empire, and lasted at least up to the Black Death at the earliest, and the French Revolution at the latest. So the mode lasted between 600 to 1,000 years and the transition from it took up to 300–400 years. (See Hilton 1978 for an account of the transition to capitalism debate in which Sweezy, Dobb and others took part.)

Given that capitalism had superior forces of production (through the growth of knowledge so well described in Volume I of *Capital*), one would have expected that it would last as long, at the very least, as Feudalism. If that sounds terribly pessimistic, think another way. By 1914, capitalism had not even covered the globe; the visionary prose of the *Communist Manifesto* had sketched out a global phenomenon, but all that was yet to come. Not only Asia (except Japan), but also Africa and South America were untouched, as was much of Eastern Europe and Russia, as Luxemburg and Lenin well knew having written so eloquently on Polish and Russian capitalist development. The impatience of the 1883–1913 phase of this debate is hard to comprehend.

It is also peculiar that what were signs of the progressive development of the forces of production – the so-called Third Industrial Revolution of Steel, Chemicals and Electricity with the emergence of large industrial units – should have been seen as a sign of decadence rather than growth. The pattern of symbiotic co-operation between finance and industry in Germany was not sinister; it was not a faithful reproduction of the mid-nineteenth century British pattern, that is all. Capitalism was spreading from Britain to Western Europe and North America and taking different forms, but remaining a self-expanding accumulation system based on profit transformed from surplus value. Marx's fascination with new industrial processes, Engels's poring over new scientific developments, disappear in the 1883–1913 generation. The question posed is a negative one; not what makes capitalism reproduce itself, but why has it not yet collapsed.

The impatience of that first post-Marx generation seemed to be rewarded in the 1914–1923 period. There was a bloody war and, in the middle of the War and for a while after, a series of uprisings inspired by Marx's writings. Even though by 1923 only the Russian Revolution had been undefeated, there had been encouraging flare-ups in Germany, Hungary, Austria and Italy. Perhaps Marxists thought that this mode of production could be the shortest lived of all. For the next 30 years, capitalism remained beleaguered and militaristic. Fascism, depression and war followed hyperinflation and post-war depression. The colonies were rising up. It looked as if capitalism was subject to its most serious challenge from Communism.

But again, with hindsight of course, one wonders. Taking the second part of the statement on transition from the Preface to CCPE quoted above, were there elements of a higher social order being prepared in the womb of the old order? Was the USSR the harbinger of a socialist mode of production? The debates within Russia in the 1920s had centred on accumulation strategies, on the development of the forces of production. Having been the weakest link in the capitalist chain may have made the revolution easier to foment, but as a laboratory of the new order (the Webbs notwithstanding), Russia was inadequate. The compulsion to accumulate in face of the blockade and then the Second World War was such that, far from new relations of production developing between living and dead labour, there was a retrogression. This is of course not an incontrovertible statement. My critique is not about socialism in one country, as there was little possibility of doing anything else. But as social orders go, when the propaganda is seen through, the basic relationship of extracting surplus from living producers was, if anything, more savage than metropolitan capitalism had achieved. This may have been justified by the circumstances but it began to dawn on many socialists that the USSR was, perhaps, not a beacon of hope for a new order after all.

The New Order was thus failing on account of the social relationships within that Order. For a while, in the 1950s, it looked as if it could succeed in the race for the development of productive forces. Soviet growth rates were higher than those in the West; its military and space technology was better. Income distribution was no worse, and, if you count health and education in a human development-type measure it was, if anything, better. It seemed by the end of that decade, as Khrushchev boasted, that in material productivity the New Order will bury the Old.

WM, which was born from disillusionment with the USSR after 1956, was faced with a double dilemma. It did not like its domestic capitalist order, but nor did it believe that a Revolution was on the cards at home. What was worse, it did not like what it saw in the putative New Order and did not want a revolution which led to any outcome like that in USSR. Briefly it flirted with Chinese- and Cuban-type revolutions, but that was all. Thus it did not expect a revolution at home, nor could it figure out what type of order it would like if a revolution was imminent. The May 1968 Paris uprising and its echoes in other European countries reflect this tension.

The reasons for this tension were there – deep down the New Left liked the level of development of productive forces it enjoyed as well as the bourgeois liberties which had been won in the metropolis. The periphery was a romantic attachment but not somewhere the New Left wished to live. Unlike in the Spanish Civil War, few actually went to fight on the other side in Vietnam or Nicaragua. The reasons for this are explained perfectly within the CM framework. Along with the development of the productive forces – the base as it were – the superstructure develops as well. If you want your bourgeois freedoms, you had to live in advanced capitalism. And only by outdoing advanced capitalism in the sphere of productive forces, could there be any hope of going beyond bourgeois freedoms. WM refined the crude model by trying to see a variety of superstructures for each base. But the crude model was eventually right.

As fascist regimes fell in Portugal, Spain and Greece, liberal democracy and advanced capitalism became symbiotic by the late twentieth century.[3]

During the 25 years after May 1968, events were to turn the world of WM upside down. Capitalism won back its lead in the development of productive forces; profitability was restored through the State reneging upon/renegotiating the social contract in the advanced capitalist democracies. The innovative urge was still active in Capitalism while the USSR failed to keep up the pace. It had been fashionable among economists to downgrade Schumpeter's emphasis on the individual entrepreneur and claim that all invention/innovation was corporate R&D-led. Had that indeed been the case, then socialist countries could have done just as well in innovation as capitalist countries. But Silicon Valley disproved this anti-Schumpeterian thesis, and corporations were restructured or grew like topsy from small beginnings. The capacity of capitalism for reproducing itself at a higher level of productive forces – through cycles and mass unemployment and restructuring of firms and labour markets – was proved again. The Master had been right all along. No social order ever fell before it had exhausted its productive possibilities.

Capitalism as a social order between 1968 and, say, 1993 demonstrated its potential for expansion of productive forces. But how had it done it and can we explain it within the CM context? The basic CM model relies on the fluctuations in the rate of profit (as transformed surplus value) as the motor for cycles. This simple *Capital* Volume I Part 7 explanation – the crudest version of CM – is sufficient to explain what happened. While WM was trying to explain what did not happen and blaming, revising, refurbishing Marx, right under its very nose as it were, reality was behaving according to CM rules. It was the cycle in the rate of profit that held the key to the trajectory of capitalism. Two decades of a high level of employment sustained by Keynesian policies and high levels of unionization had created the conditions for a squeeze in the share of capital in national income. Add to that two international conditions – the Bretton Woods Dollar Exchange Standard plus Cold War military expenditure, which squeezed government budgets and eased the transmission of shocks from the USA to other OECD countries – internationalized the threat to the share of capital in national income in OECD countries generally, but especially in USA and UK (Glyn and Sutcliffe 1971; Nordhaus 1975). This appeared as inflationary pressures as each side of the struggle for shares jockeyed for position. As the 1970s opened, there were further pressures – partly due to Vietnam but also due to the renewed ability of fixed capital to be geographically mobile. The abandonment of Bretton Woods by the USA, the subsequent depreciation of the dollar, and the consequent oil shock led to stagflation, deindustrialization, the demise of official Keynesianism, and the rise of monetarism and libertarianism (Desai 1996).

The Reagan/Thatcher/Kohl regimes effected the restoration of profitability by repulsing union power, deflating the economy and de-regulating the domestic and the foreign capital markets. The restoration of profitability could now be at a global level. Capitalism in one country was sustained by the Bretton Woods restrictions on capital movements. Globalization had arrived fulfilling the vision of The Communist Manifesto; the Chinese Walls had been literally battered by the flow of commodities. China was the first to succumb to this onslaught, with USSR and Eastern Europe following a decade later. As the capitalist system had developed its productive forces, the socialist camp had stagnated. Not having developed new social relations in the previous 70 years, it fell behind even in the race for material prosperity. The system failed to shift from absolute to relative surplus value; its total factor productivity growth (in modern economic parlance), was low or negative. Despite being despotic, it failed to exploit enough.

Thus, a new and higher social order had not grown in the womb of the old order and the old order rejuvenated itself. Despite high levels of industrial concentrations and manifestations of monopoly power in a neoclassical and WM sense, capitalism stayed competitive in Marx's sense by having a dynamic technological drive which devalorized products and people's skills constantly. The circuits of capital spread out of their national confines and began to span the globe. The pursuit of profitability, the constant search to restore the rate of profit became a versatile race round the globe which ranged from exploiting new products and processes fresh out of R&D laboratories, to transferring old and mature products to countries of the periphery where there was still absolute surplus value to be realized. The pursuit of profits harnessed new financial products and new generations of bond dealers, working round the clock, around the globe, super-exploited at super salaries.

This is not just rhetoric. Data on profitability, although available only at national levels in the USA and UK, show a clear decline and revival of profitability during the 1965–95 period (Desai 1997; Dumenil and Levy 1997). The stagnation of the USSR economy in the 1970s is also well-established (Easterly and Fischer 1995).

This is not to say that capitalism is utopia or that it has changed its spots. Marx never argued that the inequity, poverty or waste were accidental to capitalism. But critical political economy must recognize that capitalism is a mode of production, whose sole aim is accumulation via profitability. As long as the system generates profits by absolute or relative exploitation, it will survive. If it produces high levels of employment, growth and welfare state benefits – these are all by-products, unintended or not. It is neither a kind nor a cruel system. It is a mode of production and its survival depends on its efficiency.

Conclusion and consolation

Has nothing come then from the 75 years or more of 'No Longer Existing Socialism'? Was it all in vain – all that selling of newspapers at factory gates, all those marches, those petitions, facing police batons, those endless meetings and fighting funds? I would say no. Not just to please Sam, but that is precisely where a new and higher order was being created. Not in the citadel of socialism itself, certainly not after about 1925. But in the democratic countries, the forces that defended the Revolution, that fought their own ruling orders, succeeded in sowing seeds of a higher order. They advanced free speech and rights of free association. They fought for and made possible full employment, economic safety nets for the poor, growing social entitlements and the beginnings of non-discrimination against Black people, women, the colonized and native tribals. This movement struggled for and won human rights and the right, yet unfulfilled, of people to a humane society. Even as some of these gains are threatened, the fight has established a beachhead and it is from here that future generations will start. That is something to be proud of.

Notes

1 I denote Western Marxism as comprising: all the work done in the non-Communist West since the death of Marx, i.e. in North America and Europe from 1883 to 1923 and, after 1923 (or rather the death of Lenin), outside the USSR and, after 1948, outside Eastern Europe. After 1923, the debate petered out (except perhaps for the Frankfurt School) and resumed vigorously after 1956.
2 Mandel's writings on long swings deserve a separate and detailed treatment. While he was, in many ways, prescient in his Marshall lectures, published in 1980, his revisions of his lectures in 1995 fail to address the two central questions I am asking here.
3 Poulantzas was very open in registering his surprise at the peaceful demise of fascism in Western Europe in the 1970s. Given the debate over the previous 20 years in WM, this was unpredicted.

References

Aaronovitch, S. and Sawyer, M. (1975), *Big Business: Theoretical and Empirical aspects of Concentration and Mergers in the UK*, London: Macmillan.

Aaronovitch, S. and Smith R. (with Gardiner, J. and Moore, R.) (1981), *The Political Economy of British Capitalism: A Marxist Analysis*, Maidenhead: McGraw-Hill Book Company.

Auerbach, P., Desai, M. and Shamsavari A. (1988), 'The Dialectics of Plan and the Market: On the Transition from Actually Existing Capitalism', *New Left Review*, No. 170, September/October.

Bowles, S., Gordon, D. and Weisskopf, T. (1984), *Beyond the Waste Land: A Democratic Alternative to Economic Decline*, London: Verso.

Desai, M. (1974), *Marxian Economic Theory*, London: Hamish Gray.

— (1979), *Marxian Economics*, Oxford: Blackwell.

— (1991a), 'The Transformation Problem: A Survey', in G. Caravale (ed.), *Marx and Modern Economic Analysis* Vol. I, Aldershot: Edward Elgar.

— (1991b), 'Methodological Problems in Quantitative Marxism', in Dunne, P. (ed.), *Quantitative Marxism*, Oxford: Polity Press.

— (1995), 'Global Governance' in M. Desai and P. Redfern (eds), *Global Governance: Ethics and Economics of the New World Order*, London: Pinter.

— (1996), 'Marx-Hayek Cycle and The Demise of Official Keynesianism', in Baranzini, A. and Cencini, M. (eds), *Inflation and Unemployment, Contributions to a New Macroeconomic Approach*, London: Routledge.

— (1997), 'Profitability and the Persistence of Capitalism', in Bellofiore, R. (ed.), *Marxian Economics A Reappraisal: Vol.2 Essays on Volume III of Capital Profit, Prices and Dynamics*, New York: St. Martin's Press.

Dumenil, G. and Levy, D. (1997), 'The Dynamics of Historical Tendencies in Volume III of Capital: An Application to the US Economy since the Civil War', in Bellofiore, R. (ed.) *Marxian Economics: A Reappraisal; Vol. 2 Essays on Volume III of Capital: Profits, Prices and Dynamics*, New York: St. Martin's Press.

Easterly, W. and Fischer S. (1995), 'The Soviet Economic Decline', *World Bank Economic Review*, Vol. 9, No. 3, September.

Gay, P. (1952) *The Dilemma of Democratic Socialism*, New York: Columbia University Press.

Glyn, A. and Sutcliffe R. (1971), 'The Collapse of UK Profits', in *New Left Review*, No. 66, March/April.

Hilton, R. (ed.) (1978), *The Transition from Feudalism to Capitalism*, London: Verso.

Hymer, S. (1972), 'The Multi-national Corporation and the Law of Uneven Development', in Bhagwati, J. (ed.), *Economics and World Order from the 1970s to the 1990s*, New York: Collier Macmillan.

Luxemburg, R. (1913/1951), *The Accumulation of Capital*, translated by A. Schwarschild. London: Routledge and Kegan Paul.

Mandel, E. (1975), *Late Capitalism* (Le Troisième Age du Capitalisme, in original), London: Verso.

— (1978), *The Second Slump*, London: Verso.

— (1995), *Long waves in Capitalist Development*, London: Verso.

Nordhaus, W. D. (1975), 'The Political Business Cycle', *Review of Economic Studies*, Vol. 42, No. 2, April.

O'Connor, J. (1973), *The Fiscal Crisis of the State*, New York: St Martin's Press.

Sweezy, P. (ed.) (1948), *Karl Marx and the Close of His System*, London: Augustus Kelley.

2 Contemporary capitalism and Keynes's *General Theory*[1]

G. C. Harcourt

The year 1996 is 60 years on from the publication of *The General Theory of Employment, Interest and Money* of J.M. Keynes. There are definite signs that the profession is becoming interested again in the approaches, theories and policies which flow from his magnum opus, following the abortive attempts of the past 20 years or so to destroy Keynes and all his ways by conservative elements in the profession and body politic. In the advanced capitalist countries, mass unemployment has again emerged as a sustained and disgraceful problem, not least because so much of it was created deliberately by government actions in the first place. The need for a combination of policies and the creation of appropriate institutions with which to tackle this blight, to which Sam devoted his last months, is at least being recognized, even if the political will to act is still largely conspicuous by its absence. All this is the background to the present essay.

Some years ago, Professor Peter Riach of De Montfort University suggested to me that, following the example of unfinished musical compositions sometimes being finished by others after the deaths of the composers concerned, we ought to consider making a 'second edition' of *The General Theory*. We were also inspired by Keynes's letter to Ralph Hawtrey in August 1936 (*The Collected Writings of John Maynard Keynes*, hereafter *C.W.*, vol. XIV, 1973, p. 47) in which he mentioned that he was thinking of writing some 'footnotes' to *The General Theory* once he had absorbed his own new ideas and the critics' reaction to them. His heart attack in 1937, the Second World War and his untimely death soon after the end of the war, on Easter morning 1946, meant that he never did get to write those 'footnotes'.

Peter and I therefore decided to approach a group of Keynes scholars, ranging from the Golden Oldies to the up-and-coming, to ask them to write chapters setting out what they thought Keynes might have written in, say, 1939 on particular aspects of *The General Theory* and then why have they done what they have on those aspects in the post-war period. *A 'Second Edition' of The General Theory* (two volumes, hereafter G.T.[2]) was published by Routledge in 1997. The chapters in the first volume of G.T.[2] broadly track the chapters of *The General Theory* itself; those in the second volume contain overviews, extensions and new developments under the rubric of the economics of Keynes and comparisons of Keynes's contributions with those who have followed similar paths. The present essay gives, I hope, a tantalising overview of how today's scholars of Keynes see contemporary capitalism.

Sixty years on there need inevitably to be major changes to the foundations of the system set out in the original *General Theory*. The first is the necessity to have more explicitly imperfectly competitive microeconomic foundations. This is still a controversial issue. Both Paul Davidson and Jan Kregel are sceptical, to say the least, of the necessity for them in a theory of effective demand, not least because Keynes himself took as 'given' the degree of competition (*The General Theory*, p. 245). Robin Marris (1991, 1997) is an outstanding pioneer here. He argues that only when we allow imperfectly competitive market structures to rule (he takes as an example what he calls 'imperfect polipoly') is it possible to set up simple yet believable models which produce Keynes-type results, in particular sustained involuntary unemployment of labour due to a lack of overall – effective – demand in the product market. In G.T.[2] his chapter is followed by a thoughtful one by Nina Shapiro (1997), who argues against this viewpoint. Her principal point is that the failure of the economic system *when left to itself* to be able to signal appropriately to decision-makers operating in necessarily uncertain environments means that investment expenditure (even on average) by business people may not be sufficient to absorb the saving that would be made voluntarily from full employment incomes. This implies that markets structures are in principle irrelevant for this central proposition. She argues, I think correctly, that matters would be worse – there would be higher average levels of unemployment and greater fluctuations in prices, output and employment – in a competitive economy than in an imperfectly competitive one.

Secondly, financial innovation means that we have endogenous money processes rather than a given money supply, i.e. the quantity of money is more determined by demand from its users than by the monetary authorities as its supplier. Sheila Dow (1997) is a notable innovator on this issue. She reminds us that, while Keynes was essentially an endogenous money person for all of his life, in *The General Theory* he had, for expositional and possibly for tactical purposes, taken the quantity of money as given, not exogenous in any absolute sense. Keynes usually concentrated his arguments on one set of issues at a time. He therefore took as provisionally *given*, values of variables which ultimately would have to be explained when all the arguments concerning all the issues were brought together. Dow shows that Keynes's theory of liquidity preference may be used in an endogenous money world because demand as well as supply factors play key roles in determining the patterns of rates of interest.

Thirdly, the assumption of a constant *long-term* price level has to be replaced by the assumption of 'rising prices for ever' as a reasonable (if not a rational) expectation. Arthur Brown (1997) and Brian Reddaway (1997) have written eminently sensible evaluations of the consequences of this assumption. Interestingly Brown, like Keynes, is more wedded to the goal of attaining a constant general price level than is Reddaway. Reddaway feels that there is enough flexibility and innovation in society's institutions and practices to allow adjustments for rising prices to be made, rather than to have a single over-riding goal of a constant price level which almost certainly would unnecessarily damage both employment and growth. Brown, like Keynes, gives more weight to the role of money as a unit of account and, I suggest, to having the operations of the economy consistent with the conventions of historical-cost, double-entry book keeping, an innovation which was essential for the rise of capitalism in the first place.

Finally, the open economy aspects of the functioning of economies needed to be emphasized more explicitly and systematically than in the first edition, and the design of international institutions and policies had to be rethought accordingly. Paul Davidson (1997) has made a notable start on this. Having observed that with both fixed and floating exchange rates, there are inbuilt contractionary and deflationary biases in the operation of the world economy, Keynes set about designing institutions to offset them. The key objective was to gain time for economies which tended to run into deficits on their current accounts (in a fixed exchange rate regime) and continuing devaluations (in a floating exchange rate regime) to make the structural and cost adjustments needed to correct these faults: otherwise they were forced to impose measures which led to contracting output and employment, declining investment expenditure, and so a cumulative downward spiral in their external competitive position. Those countries which were blessed in the other direction, so that surpluses accumulated or exchange rates appreciated, were not subject to powerful forces which made them take corrective actions and so behave in a socially beneficial way. Hence, the contractionary biases in the working of the system as a whole were reinforced. At Bretton Woods, Keynes tried to overcome this but his suggestions were not accepted; the seeds of the ultimate destruction of the system were planted at its inception.

Davidson has the same aims as Keynes but advocates different measures in order to fit in with the changed climate of the 1990s. Sensing that the political time is not yet ripe for the world economy to have either an international mechanism whereby to finance international trade and capital movements, or a World Central Bank, Davidson designs a half-way house instead. The main features are institutional pressures which would serve to make creditor nations behave in a socially responsible manner at a world level, a 'currency' between Central Banks to provide liquidity, and the creation of an environment wherein all countries can aim for full employment without running into external constraints. The overall aim is to reduce the contractionary bias in the world's operations without running into inflationary pressures which spread world-wide. This will allow the economies of the world to advance steadily with each allowing the others 'free lunches'. It is a scheme fittingly in the spirit of Keynes and only the dark forces of ignorance and self-interested greed stand in the way of discussion of its principles and details – and its implementation.

In recent years the link between Keynes's philosophical contributions and his economics has been the subject of some outstanding research work. It relates to both the nature and the method of theorising in a subject such as economics. A number of contributors to G.T.[2] have written about this issue. In the second volume we have a chapter by Rod O'Donnell who wrote the seminal work (1982, 1989) on this aspect of Keynes's contributions. In his chapter, O'Donnell

(1997) puts to rest for ever (I hope) the canard that Keynes was a techniques luddite as far as the use of mathematics in economic theory and of econometric techniques in applied work were concerned. Another chapter is by John Coates who draws on his profound researches into the relationship between Keynes and the Cambridge philosophers, especially Wittgenstein, and what he has dubbed 'ordinary language economics'. He discerns in Keynes's philosophy at the time of the writing of *The General Theory* an anticipation of the modern work on fuzzy logic and fuzzy sets. Coates (1997) conjectures that these recent developments may allow a bridge to be erected between the complex, multi-dimensional yet often vague concepts of economics and the powerful analytical procedures of mathematics. Fuzzy sets evidently allow us to handle in a precise analytical manner vague concepts such as 'baldness' – a contribution appreciated by the editors of the G.T.[2] to whom the notion of membership or non-membership of a category which is gradual rather than abrupt gives comfort.

Keynes sensed the conflict between precision and relevance due to the omission of crucial factors which was often associated with the former. Keynes also sensed what the recent developments allow. Furthermore, he understood the rich and widely ranging fund of common knowledge on which economists, by using ordinary language as much as possible, could draw.

One consequence of the findings on method has been a re-thinking of the nature and implications of uncertainty in the Keynesian system. This had led to a re-appraisal of the possibility of ever fitting Keynes's ideas satisfactorily (or even at all) into the dominant neo-Walrasian framework of modern economics because it cannot handle either historical (calendar) time or money itself. Peter Howitt (1997) has contributed a courageous account of this and of his own change of mind, writing of Keynes's intuitive and innovative mind and of his refusal ever to be constrained by past intellectual capital, and certainly not by his own.

Finally, Keynes's intuitions still have to be related back to his predecessors – especially Marx, but also to other 'heretics' under the rubric of under-consumption. John King (1997) has summarized this admirably. In 1987, Claudio Sardoni published a fine book on Marx's and Keynes's theories of effective demand and crisis. It was based on thorough research into what the two authors actually wrote. Reading his account, it could quickly be realized that, after allowing for differences in terminology and attitudes to the survival of the capitalist system and its accompanying institutions as such, whenever these two great analysts of capitalism tackled the same questions, they came up with broadly the same answers. Yet it is known that Keynes had a very low opinion of Marx. We think that this tells us more about Keynes than Marx, and Sardoni's chapter in the second volume of G.T.[2] confirms our view.

Sardoni does not think that Keynes would have changed his opinion of Marx, despite Joan Robinson's attempts to make him see that coming at Keynes's puzzles through Marx's approach was a more rewarding way to tackle them. Sardoni shows how, initially, as Keynes moved towards *The General Theory*, he found Marx's emphasis on the circuits of capital, and the fact that entrepreneurs want to make money profits rather than produce commodities as such, were clues both to understanding how capitalism works (well and poorly) and to the critique of 'classical' economics, especially of Say's Law. These arguments were contained in the sections on the co-operative, neutral and entrepreneur economies which did not make it to the published version of *The General Theory*.

Keynes's contributions to the understanding of capitalism must also be related to those of his contemporaries, most of all to Michał Kalecki; Peter Kriesler (1997) has done this. Kriesler is the author of the definitive book on Kalecki's microeconomics (Kriesler 1987). He has prepared himself admirably for the task of comparing and contrasting the 'General Theories' of Kalecki and Keynes and of comparing them in turn with the system of their classical/neo-classical rivals. Kriesler is more partial to Kalecki's solution to the realization problem of deficient demand than to that of Keynes. The only aspect of their respective analyses in which he argues that Keynes is superior concerns the role of expectations, financial matters and especially the determination of the rate of interest. Of course Kriesler admires Keynes, but he thinks that Kalecki's approach, which derives from Marx and the classical economists (in the non-Keynes sense) so that Kalecki's version of *The General Theory* emphasizes accumulation and cyclical growth, and the role that distribution between classes plays in these processes, is a more natural way to analyse modern capitalism.

We ended G.T.[2] with a consideration of the relationship of Keynes's contributions to those of his successors. We took Axel Leijonhufvud as a foremost example. Bruce Littleboy (1997) looks back on the Keynes–Leijonhufvud saga nearly 30 years on from Leijonhufvud's great book, *Keynesian Economics and the Economics of Keynes* (1968). Since that date a huge literature has emerged and Leijonhufvud himself has backed off from some of his major suggestions, especially on the reversal of quantity *versus* price movements in Marshall (and Keynes) and Walras. Littleboy is one of the most insightful surveyors of these developments. His doctorate on the topic was the basis of a well-regarded book published in 1990. In his chapter in the second volume of G.T.[2] he compares and contrasts Leijonhufvud's views on Keynes then and now with those of some leading post-Keynesians, especially Shackle, whose views are discerned to be at odds with those of Leijonhufvud. Littleboy argues persuasively that in many instances this is not the case, and that when it appears to be so, it is largely because the post-Keynesians or Leijonhufvud or, most of all, Keynes have themselves been misunderstood.

It is also fitting that Leijonhufvud's own mentor, Robert Clower (1997) should have written a deeply thought-out evaluation of the nature of Chapters 2 and 3 of *The General Theory* and that James Tobin (1997) has set out his own thoughts nearly 60 years on from his first encounter with *The General Theory* as a freshman at Harvard in the year it was published. Clower rewrites Chapter 3, 'The Principle of Effective Demand' as he thinks Keynes would have (up to 1946) so as to make crystal clear the outlines of the new system as Keynes saw them – in Keynes's own words actually. (A feature of several of the chapters is that parts at least are written by 'the authors as J.M.K'.). Clower next sets the scene by suggesting that Keynes was more preoccupied with existence problems than with stability ones, in particular, the existence of a rest state with unemployment. He then examines the Marshallian base of Keynes's system. He argues that it grew straight out of Marshall's partial equilibrium demand and supply analysis, with quantity leading to price rather than price leading to quantity, as in Walras. (Clower nevertheless identifies Walras as belonging, when Keynes was learning his trade, to the same tradition as Marshall.) Clower next works through the various ways Keynes has been interpreted, usually in terms of the Keynesian cross, relating these analyses back to Marshall's models. Clower 'does a Marshall on Keynes', that is to say, not so much taking literally what exactly Keynes wrote but instead interpreting him so as to mean what Clower argues he needed to say and mean. Finally, Clower quotes from Chapter 18 the passage which other commentators have taken to be evidence for a long-period interpretation of *The General Theory*.

'In particular, it is an outstanding characteristic of the economic system in which we live that, whilst it is subject to severe fluctuations in respect of output and employment, it is not violently unstable. Indeed it seems capable of remaining in a chronic condition of sub-normal activity for a considerable period without any marked tendency either towards recovery or towards complete collapse.' (*C.W.*, vol. VII, 1973 p. 249.)

Clower, though, argues that Keynes's vision – as set out now by Clower – is the basis for a research programme which, if successful, will constitute a second Keynesian revolution that actually does for economics what Keynes intended to do by publishing the 'first edition' in February 1936.

In the opening chapter of the second volume of G.T.[2], Tobin sums up a lifetime of reflecting on the messages of *The General Theory* and presents his considered judgements, many of them based on his own outstanding contributions to the development of Keynesian economics.

First, in the guise of John Maynard Keynes, he amends the original definition in Chapter 2 of involuntary unemployment in order to make it more simple, operational – and convincing: if people want to work at existing conditions of employment and cannot get jobs, they are involuntarily unemployed. Otherwise, as both Keynes *and* himself, he remains unrepentant: demand deficiencies rather than supply constraints bite most of the time in capitalist economies; policy can do something about this without having radically to change either institutions or political systems; money is integrated in the workings of the system as a whole; it is *not* a veil; price and wage flexibility are beside the point theoretically, as far as determining the levels of activity and unemployment are concerned, though there is much to be said for relative money-wage stability if we want a stable economy overall; wage-earners do not, and do not have to, 'suffer' from money illusion to make Keynes's system 'work' – their behaviour is perfectly consistent with sensible behaviour, with the balancing of pros and cons, so that it is sensible for wage-earners to resist cuts in money-wages in order to protect relative positions but not to go in for industrial unrest every time the prices of wage goods go up a little.

When we come to the mid 1990s and Tobin writes as Tobin, he argues that we have to come to grips with what we mean by equilibrium when there is unemployment. He tells us that he prefers to use the phrase 'rest state' because, clearly, the labour market is *not* clearing at the given price if, as is usually the case, there is involuntary unemployment present. He then tackles head-on the disequilibrium interpretation of Keynes. Keynesian rest states are centres of gravitation for short-period flow equilibria, given inherited stocks of capital goods, labour supplies and technical knowledge. But clearly all these change over time, some from the very attainment of short-period flow equilibrium. So we must consider the characteristics of the next period's centre of gravitation, taking into account what has happened in the previous period(s) and the implications for stocks, short- *and* long-term expectations and so on, for this period. It is an open question whether, either in fact or in theory, the disequilibrium dynamics so released will produce a succession of short-period equilibria which, left to themselves, will converge on a long-period, full stock and flow equilibrium. Tobin, like Keynes, is not sure that this is a very interesting or relevant question anyway.

These are some of the themes and chapters to be found in our G.T.[2] volumes. Space and time prevent me from discussing John Cornwall's and Robert Skidelsky's very different evaluations of the social philosophy and policy measures which, originating in *The General Theory*, have now been updated by our two scholars; or referring to the intricate analysis by Jan Kregel, Ingo Barens and Volker Caspari, and Colin Rogers and Tom Rymes of that most difficult of all chapters in *The General Theory*, Chapter 17, on interest and money; and much else besides. I must, though, mention the two chapters on investment by Robert Eisner (1997) and Luigi Pasinetti (1997). In essence, these two scholars accept Keynes's formulation. Eisner by stressing recent empirical findings, Pasinetti by making a subtle argument which both defends Keynes and holds off a critique of Keynes's formulation. The critique is based on the results of the capital theory debates of the 1950s to 1970s: see Harcourt (1972). In any event I hope I have written enough to show that there is in these volumes a Keynesian understanding of capitalism relevant to Sam's concerns, and to tempt my readers to browse through the volumes in the U.L. or the Marshall, or even to have them on their own book shelves.

Note

1   I thought it a great privilege to be asked to contribute to this volume for Sam, and to be invited to his splendid 78th birthday party. I am grateful to Jan Toporowski for his helpful comments on a draft of the paper and to the editor of *The Cambridge Review* for allowing me to reprint a second version of the article that appeared there in May 1997.

References

Brown, A. J. (1997), 'The inflationary dimension', Chapter 27 in Harcourt, G. C. and Riach, P. A. (eds), *A 'Second Edition' of The General Theory*, Vol. II, London: Routledge.

Clower, R. W. (1997), 'Effective demand revisited', Chapter 3 in Harcourt, G. C. and Riach, P. A. (eds), *A 'Second Edition' of The General Theory*, Vol. I, London: Routledge.

Coates, J. (1997), 'Keynes, vague concepts and fuzzy logic', Chapter 35 in Harcourt, G. C. and Riach, P. A. (eds), *A 'Second Edition' of The General Theory*, Vol. II, London: Routledge.

Davidson, P. (1997), '*The General Theory* in an open economy context', Chapter 30 in Harcourt, G. C. and Riach, P. A. (eds), *A 'Second Edition' of The General Theory*, Vol. II, London: Routledge.

Dow, S. C. (1997), 'Endogenous money', Chapter 28 in Harcourt, G. C. and Riach, P. A. (eds), *A 'Second Edition' of The General Theory*, Vol. II, London: Routledge.

Eisner, R. (1997), 'The Marginal Efficiency of Capital and Investment', Chapter 12 in Harcourt, G. C. and Riach, P. A. (eds), *A 'Second Edition' of The General Theory*, Vol. I, London: Routledge.

Harcourt, G. C. and Riach, P. A. (eds.) (1997) *A 'Second Edition' of The General Theory*, 2 vols, London: Routledge.

Howitt, P. (1997), 'Expectations and uncertainty in contemporary Keynesian models', Chapter 15 in Harcourt, G. C. and Riach, P. A. (eds), *A 'Second Edition' of The General Theory*, Vol. I, London: Routledge.

Keynes, J. M. (1936), *The General Theory of Employment, Interest and Money*, London: Macmillan. *The Collected Writings of John Maynard Keynes*, Vol. VII (1973).

Keynes, J. M. (1973), *The General Theory and After. Part II: Defence and Development. The Collected Writings of John Maynard Keynes*, Vol. XIV, London: Macmillan.

King, J. E. (1997), 'Underconsumption', Chapter 23 in Harcourt, G. C. and Riach, P. A. (eds), *A 'Second Edition' of The General Theory*, Vol. I, London: Routledge.

Kriesler, P. (1987), *Kalecki's Microanalysis: The Development of Kalecki's Analysis of Pricing and Distribution*, Cambridge: Cambridge University Press.

Kriesler, P. (1997), 'Keynes, Kalecki, and *The General Theory*', Chapter 38 in Harcourt, G. C. and Riach, P. A. (eds), *A 'Second Edition' of The General Theory*, Vol. II, London: Routledge.

Leijonhufvud, A. (1968), *On Keynesian Economics and the Economics of Keynes: A Study in Monetary Theory*, London: Oxford University Press.

Littleboy, B. (1990), *On Interpreting Keynes: A Study in Reconciliation*, London: Routledge.

Littleboy, B. (1997), 'On Leijonhufvud's economics of Keynes', Chapter 39 in Harcourt, G. C. and Riach, P. A. (eds), *A 'Second Edition' of The General Theory*, Vol. II, London: Routledge.

Marris, R. L. (1991), *Reconstructing Keynesian Economics with Imperfect Competition*, Aldershot: Edward Elgar.

Marris, R. L. (1997), 'Yes, Mrs Robinson! *The General Theory* and imperfect competition', Chapter 4 in Harcourt, G. C. and Riach, P. A. (eds), *A 'Second Edition' of The General Theory*, Vol. I, London: Routledge.

O'Donnell, R. M. (1982), *Keynes: Philosophy and Economics, An Approach to Rationality and Uncertainty*, PhD. Dissertation, University of Cambridge.

O'Donnell, R. M. (1989), *Keynes: Philosophy, Economics and Politics. The Philosophical Foundations of Keynes's Thought and Their Influence on his Economics and Politics*, London: Macmillan.

O'Donnell, R. M. (1997), 'Keynes and formalism', Chapter 31 in Harcourt, G. C. and Riach, P. A. (eds), *A 'Second Edition' of The General Theory*, Vol. II, London: Routledge.

Pasinetti, L. (1997), 'The Marginal Efficiency of Investment', Chapter 13 in Harcourt, G. C. and Riach, P. A. (eds), *A 'Second Edition' of The General Theory*, Vol. I, London: Routledge.

Reddaway, W. B. (1997), 'The changing significance of inflation', Chapter 26 in Harcourt, G. C. and Riach, P. A. (eds), *A 'Second Edition' of The General Theory*, Vol. II, London: Routledge.

Sardoni, C. (1987), *Marx and Keynes on Economic Recession*, Brighton, Sussex: Wheatsheaf Books.

Sardoni, C. (1997), 'Keynes and Marx', Chapter 36 in Harcourt, G. C. and Riach, P. A. (eds), *A 'Second Edition' of The General Theory*, Vol. II, London: Routledge.

Shapiro, N. (1997), 'Imperfect competition and Keynes', Chapter 5 in Harcourt, G. C. and Riach, P. A. (eds), *A 'Second Edition' of The General Theory*, Vol. I, London: Routledge.

Tobin, J. (1997), 'An overview of *The General Theory*', Chapter 25 in Harcourt, G. C. and Riach, P. A. (eds), *A 'Second Edition' of The General Theory*, Vol. II, London: Routledge.

3 The 'Conflict Theory of Inflation' re-visited[1]

Pat Devine

Introduction

In the first three decades after the Second World War, the period of the developed capitalist world's 'long boom' (Purdy 1976) or 'golden age' (Glyn *et al.* 1990), relatively full employment was accompanied by continuous and gradually accelerating inflation, culminating in the price explosion of the 1970s. By the end of the 1970s the explicit or implicit policy commitment to maintaining full employment that had been adopted by most governments in the period following the war had been replaced in most countries by an explicit prioritization of anti-inflationary policy. This ushered in two decades of stagflation during which low growth rates were accompanied by high levels of unemployment and still high rates of inflation. By the mid-1990s, however, inflation had fallen to levels not seen since before price explosion of the 1970s and some commentators had begun to talk of the 'death of inflation' (Bootle 1996).

From the 1970s onwards the dominant theory of inflation in academic and business circles has been some variety of monetarism in which: (i) inflation is caused by excess growth of the money supply, brought about by government failure; and (ii) inflationary expectations play a crucial role. The policy implication of this analysis is that the central bank should be independent of the government in order to establish the credibility of its anti-inflationary stance and thus reduce inflationary expectations and the costs of transition to a non-inflationary equilibrium. In some versions, credibility is further enhanced by commitment to a fixed exchange rate, preferably re-inforced by membership of an international currency system such as the Exchange Rate Mechanism and the single European currency.

Alongside this orthodoxy, however, there have been alternative theories which have emphasized influences determining the strength of cost pressures, such as labour market conditions, the degree of unionization or the extent of market power, or more generally have sought to explain inflation as the outcome of underlying distributive struggle. This paper is concerned with one version of the latter which came to be known as the 'Conflict Theory of Inflation'. It emerged during the 1970s in the context of a controversy over the cause(s) of inflation that developed within the Communist Party of Great Britain's Economic Advisory Committee, of which Sam Aaronovitch was a prominent member, and in the columns of its theoretical journal, *Marxism Today*. The context was the attitude the Party should take towards wage claims and incomes policies. At stake was whether the Party should continue with the militant economism which had characterized its approach during the 1950s and 1960s or whether it should adopt a Gramscian strategy of seeking to create a hegemonic consensus through the promotion of a prices and incomes policy that would challenge the prerogatives of capital (Purdy 1974). The principal contending theories of inflation in this controversy were a form of Marxist monetarism and the conflict theory of inflation.[2,3]

The purpose of this paper is to assess how well the conflict theory has stood up to the experience of the past 20 years. In the next section, the theory as developed by the author (Devine 1974) is briefly summarized. The following section (p. 26) reviews subsequent theoretical developments, with particular reference to the work of Burdekin and Burkett (1996), after which an account is given of experience since the 1960s in terms of the conflict theory of inflation (p. 30). The final section (p. 35) draws some conclusions, in particular that the low levels of inflation prevailing in the mid to late 1990s reflect a historic defeat for the working class in the period of new right, neo-liberal hegemony which began to be created at the beginning of the 1980s, and presents some thoughts for the future.

The conflict theory of inflation, 1974

The theory proposed by the author in 1974 was that the continuous inflation that had characterized the period since the Second World War was the result of a situation in which: (i) workers could not be prevented from seeking real wage increases in excess of productivity growth; (ii) the only means available for them to do this was through money wage increases; (iii) capitalists could not be prevented from increasing prices in order to offset the pressure on profits from money wage increases in excess of productivity growth; and (iv) the state pursued an accommodating monetary policy in order to maintain full employment. The argument advanced was that the post-war settlement and the 'long boom' or 'golden age' that followed had fundamentally altered the balance of power between labour and capital. The Second World War had been fought on the basis of an implicit social contract that once the war ended there would be no return to the mass unemployment of the inter-war years (Addison 1975). In addition, the challenge presented by the Soviet alternative appeared to have been greatly strengthened by the detachment from the capitalist world of Eastern Europe and China, and the continued existence of capitalism in the long run was perceived as being under increasing threat. In this context, relatively full employment was seen as a political necessity. However, by transforming conditions in the labour market and abolishing the industrial reserve army of the unemployed, full employment fundamentally altered the *modus operandi* of the capitalist economic system.

Working class aspirations came to include first an expectation of a continuing rise in real income, subsequently an increased share of real income, and finally a share in decision making. In a capitalist economy workers can only bid for real income through increased money income, since they have no direct influence on prices, which are set by capitalists. In a context of oligopolistic rivalry among capitalists, in which competition takes primarily non-price forms, capitalists confronted with common wage cost pressures can offset these by increases in prices without their relative competitive position being affected. If the state pursues an accommodating monetary policy aggregate expenditure increases sufficiently for the full employment output to continue to be bought at the higher prices. Thus inflation is the outcome of a situation in which the power of capital and labour is relatively equally balanced and the claims made on real output exceed the real output available to meet them.

To this analysis of the fundamental reason for the appearance of chronic inflation after the Second World War, three further considerations were added. First, once the existence of continuous inflation had become generally recognized both compensation for past inflation and expectations about future inflation had to be taken into account when determining the money wage increase that would result in the target real wage increase. Second, since the real wage consists of the social as well as the private wage (public goods and social services as well as private goods and services), the analysis was expanded to take into account public expenditure and taxation. To the extent that workers – or more generally the competing interests making up society – demand higher levels of social and other forms of public expenditure than they are willing to pay for through taxation, the result is a budget deficit which has to be financed. Finally, the real income available in a country is, in part, determined by its terms of trade with other countries. If these alter, due to differential domestic inflation rates or changes in the external value of the currency, this will have an effect on the extent to which the competing domestic claims on real income can be met.

The generalized version of the conflict theory of inflation as set out in the 1974 paper was summarized as follows:

> The competing claims of private consumption, investment, public provision, military expenditure, the foreign balance, have exceeded the availability of resources. Efforts to commandeer resources for one use, if not acquiesced in by those from whom the resources are to be taken, call forth responses designed to frustrate them which for the most part manifest themselves in higher prices. Thus, if the state increases direct taxation on personal incomes or indirect taxation, in order to increase social provision or to stimulate private investment *via* reductions in corporate taxation or to make room for a shift of resources into the balance of payments, workers will seek to offset the effect of this on their private consumption through higher money wages; if capitalists raise prices in order to raise profits to finance increased investment or if the terms of trade deteriorate and prices

rise, workers will again seek to offset this through higher money wages; if workers obtain higher money wages, in order to offset increased taxes or increased prices or simply to assert their claim to a higher standard of living and a larger share of what is produced, they will commandeer a larger proportion of resources for private consumption than would otherwise be the case and the state or capitalists will seek to offset this through higher taxes or higher prices. Chronic inflation is the result of a situation in which available resources are insufficient to meet claims on them and claimants cannot be prevented from bidding – workers *via* higher money wages, capitalists *via* higher prices, the state *via* higher taxes or borrowing from the banking system.

(Devine 1974, pp. 85–6)

Subsequent theoretical developments

Three years later, an influential paper by Rowthorn (1977) set out a formal model of the conflict theory of inflation incorporating an explicit role for expectations and monetary policy within an expectations augmented Phillips curve framework. In the basic model conflict occurs only between capital and labour, with the relative strength of each being determined by the historically evolved institutional, political and ideological context. However, the extent to which power can be exercised is affected by conditions in the labour and product markets, and therefore by demand. Below a threshold level, future inflation is not anticipated in the sense that capitalists and workers do not take it into account when determining their behaviour. As demand increases and unemployment falls, conflict intensifies and unanticipated inflation increases. The redistribution of real income that results from this unanticipated inflation is not accepted by those who lose out and their attempts to restore their position intensify the inflationary pressure. The model also incorporates a role for taxation and the terms of trade, which influence the amount of real income available to meet the claims of capitalists and private sector workers, so that increased taxation or adverse shifts in the terms of trade, whose real (private) income effects are not accepted, also intensify inflationary pressure. However, once the threshold level of inflation is reached future inflation is anticipated, capitalists and workers take it into account when determining their behaviour and the trade-off between inflation and unemployment ceases to operate. In this new situation an explosive hyperinflation sets in which can be stabilized only by policies which reduce demand and increase unemployment to a level at which 'the claims of the rival parties become mutually consistent. Demand functions as a regulator of class conflict' (Rowthorn 1977, p. 237).[4] Monetary policy is introduced into the model through its effect on demand and therefore the intensity of conflict and the extent of inflationary pressure resulting from that conflict. Although Rowthorn recognized that there may be circumstances in which monetary policy is rendered ineffective by private sector financial behaviour, he regarded these as exceptional, arguing that in general 'money plays a more active role and monetary factors may exert an independent influence on economic activity' (p. 230).

In 1981, Rosenberg and Weisskopf published a paper using an accounting framework, similar to that used in Devine (1974), which provided an empirical analysis of US inflation from a conflict theory perspective for the period 1954–79, divided into three sub-periods. They distinguished four 'classes' – workers, capitalists, transfer recipients, and beneficiaries of government programmes other than transfers – with each class formulating a real income aspiration and acting to achieve this to the extent that it is able. Available real income depends on productivity and the terms of trade. Since classes anticipate expected inflation when formulating the money claims that will realize their real income aspirations, an excess of real income claims over real income available explains only unanticipated inflation. However, they argue that their conflict model 'can also explain overall inflation insofar as the anticipated component is itself based upon past price behavior and hence on past unanticipated inflation' (Rosenberg and Weisskopf 1981, p. 43). Although the authors conclude that their empirical analysis provides support for a conflict theory interpretation of post-war US inflation, in two significant ways their emphasis differs from Rowthorn's position. First, they assume that 'the supply of money adjusts passively to accommodate price increases rather than posing an independent constraint on price inflation, for the conflict theory approach treats government policy in general and the money supply in particular as endogenous to the forces being modelled' (p. 43). Second, they suggest that 'current economic conditions' (p. 47) – Rowthorn's level of demand and rate of unemployment – are relatively less significant than stable patterns of behaviour shaped by historical, sociological, demographic and political factors in influencing the real income claims of the contending classes.

The most substantial and sustained work on the conflict theory of inflation to have appeared to date, however, consists of a series of papers by Burdekin and Burkett starting in the late 1980s and culminating in their 1996 book, *Distributional Conflict and Inflation: Theoretical and Historical Perspectives.* Burdekin and Burkett (1996) draw a distinction between a conflict *approach* to the analysis of inflation and particular models or theories using a conflict approach but originating from 'a quite diverse array of economic and social paradigms' (p. 2). They argue that inflation is always the result of the monetization of conflicting income claims, without prejudice to the source(s) of the claims or the mode(s) of monetization which have to be analyzed 'in terms of particular historical and institutional settings' (p. 14) to which specific models have to be shaped. Drawing on a comprehensive study of the literature, including early contributions by Davidson (1972), Desai (1973), Furtado (1967), Kalecki (1943), Nuti (1972) and Sunkel (1960), they provide an excellent and succinct summary of the conflict approach:

The conflict approach attributes inflationary pressure to an excess of real income claims (by labor, capital and government) over the real income available to satisfy these claims. Causes of excess claims' growth may be specified in terms of the historical-institutional factors conditioning workers' perceptions of their 'relative deprivation' compared to other householders (Baxter 1973) and corresponding 'aspirations gaps' positively related to these perceived income and life-style inequalities both domestically and internationally (Panic 1976). Excess claims may also be driven by distributional conflicts between capital and labor (Devine 1974, Rowthorn 1977). Here, inflationary pressure stems from organized efforts by capitalists and workers to increase their shares in the limited income available. Such conflicts may occur in the private sector (through wage bargaining and the pricing policies of firms), through the state (for example, increased demands by labor for social expenditures and by capital for investment subsidies, accelerated depreciation allowances, and so on), and *via* the feedback effects between these private- and public-sector conduits for the assertion of claims on national income. . . . A key implication of the conflict approach is that even a 'non-activist' monetary policy rule in reality entails a particular stance by the central bank toward the accommodation or non-accommodation of conflicting income claims. . . . from a conflict perspective, the transition to a low and stable inflation regime cannot be reduced to the lowering of rational agents' inflation expectations *via* a credible commitment to a non-activist rule. Rather, such a transition requires a removal of the sources of inflationary pressure *via* a reduction in the power of particular sectors to register claims on income and have those claims monetized by the central bank and/or the financial system.

(Burdekin and Burkett 1996, pp. 38–9)

Building on earlier work, Burdekin and Burkett develop the conflict approach to inflation in important new ways, identifying and analysing significant theoretical links and extending both the historical coverage and the methods of empirical analysis used. Their distinctive contributions may be summarized as follows:

1   The development of models that incorporate simultaneously exogenous inflationary pressure, arising from both conflict within the private sector and competing claims on government mediated through the budget deficit, and endogenous or inertial inflation due to inflationary expectations.
2   The modelling of monetary policy (the extent of accommodation) as a function of both private and public sector pressure.

3   An insistence that monetary accommodation may occur both through central bank monetary policy and through private sector credit creation.
4   A focus on the conditions necessary for successful stabilization programmes and a transition to long-term non-inflationary regimes.
5   An analysis of the effects on the inflationary process and stabilization programmes of exchange rate changes and international capital flows.
6   Econometric estimates of models of: (a) the inflationary process in the German hyperinflation after the First World War and the US economy after the Second World War; and (b) the determinants of monetary policy in the US after the Second World War and in Europe before and after the formation of the European Monetary System.
7   A qualitative evaluation of secondary sources on Latin American inflation from the conflict inflation approach perspective.

On the basis of their empirical results and historical analysis, Burdekin and Burkett (1996) find evidence that monetary policy in Germany and the US in the periods studied responded both to private sector conflict pressures and to budget deficits, and also that in both countries private sector financial institutions responded independently of the central bank to private sector pressures. However, their main conclusion is that technical stabilization programmes based on non-activist rules-based approaches or fixed peg exchange rate regimes are in themselves insufficient to effect a transition from high to low inflationary regimes. For this to be possible there must also, and more fundamentally, be a resolution of the underlying socio-economic distributional conflict giving rise to the irreconcilable real income claims. In all the cases studied this resolution, not surprisingly, is found to have been on terms favourable to capital, representing a defeat for the working class, dramatically in the cases of hyperinflation Germany (pp. 176–7) and Latin America (p. 200) but no less surely in the cases of the US (pp. 153, 158) and Europe (p. 216). In their examination of the determinants of monetary policy in Europe before and after the formation of the European Monetary System (EMS) in 1979, Burdekin and Burkett find no evidence that member countries pursued a less accommodating policy than non-members nor any significant change in policy stance after the EMS was established. Noting that inflation and real economic performance both declined markedly after 1979, they conclude:

> To the extent that wage growth declined over time, this phenomenon . . . is surely more attributable to the role of unemployment in disciplining labor claims and union power . . . than it is to EMS arrangements inducing credibility-based reductions in inflation expectations and nominal income claims. . . . In the final analysis, the post-1979 economic events in Europe must be interpreted in the light of the political changes and apparent shift to the right. . . . In light of soaring unemployment and stagnant output growth, it is actually quite significant that monetary policy did not ease.

Indeed, our estimated monetary policy reaction functions show limited signs of a tightened stance after 1979 but no signs whatsoever of a looser policy stance. It is perhaps this apparent willingness to stay the course that separates the post-1979 period from the preceding decades.

(Burdekin and Burkett 1996, pp. 216–17)

The conflict theory of inflation and capitalism since 1970

In the concluding section of Devine (1974) it was claimed that 'an important determinant of the outcome of struggles over incomes policy will be coherent argument relating inflation to the fundamental characteristics of modern capitalism and exhibiting it as a central present day manifestation of the basic contradiction of that system – the conflict between capital and labour. . . . the existence (or absence) of a convincing Marxist theoretical analysis of inflation will surely play an increasingly important part in determining the context in which such struggles are fought out, as well as contributing to a growing consciousness of the urgent need for socialism' (pp. 91–2). Such was the optimism of that era! In fact, the 1970s were the decade in which distributional struggle intensified dramatically and conflicting and incompatible claims resulted in a price explosion. In the absence of a historic bloc pursuing a hegemonic strategy designed to strengthen labour's structural position at the expense of capital, this unsustainable situation, resulting from the relatively even balance of power between capital and labour that had been created by the post-war settlement and full employment, was resolved on capital's terms by the rise of the neo-liberal new right and the reintroduction of mass unemployment.

An account of the course of distributional conflict in the UK in the 1950s and 1960s was offered in Devine (1974). However, it was the 1970s that turned out to be the decade in which distributional conflict reached its high water mark, as is evident from the contrast between the 1960s and 1970s in Table 3.1, which sets out summary data for the UK for the 1960s, 1970s, 1980s and 1990s, together with annual data for the 1990s.

In the 1970s, GDP and GDP per employee increased at a slower rate than in the preceding or following decades and the terms of trade (not shown in Table 3.1)[6] worsened dramatically, due to the increased price of oil and other commodities. This meant that there was less scope than in the previous decade for increases in investment, government expenditure and private consumption taken together. However, although the rate of increase of investment fell sharply, that of government expenditure rose and the rate of growth of private consumption fell only slightly. The refusal by workers to accept the burden of slower growth and worse terms of trade is reflected in the 16.0 per cent average annual increase in nominal compensation (money income). Capitalists inevitably sought to offset wage increases by increasing prices, which resulted in a 13.9 per cent average annual rate of inflation and an annual rate of increase in real income of 2.4 per

Table 3.1 UK 1961–96: selected economic indicators (annual percentage change at 1990 prices unless otherwise stated)[5]

Period	Inflation indicator (GDP deflator)	GDP	GDP per worker (employee)	Investment (gross fixed capital formation)	Government expenditure (public consumption)	Private consumption	Nominal income per worker (employee)	Real income per worker (private consumption deflator)	Unemployment (% of civilian labour force)	Adjusted wage share (% of GDP at factor cost)
1961–70	4.2	2.9	2.6	5.2	2.1	2.4	7.1	3.0	1.7	72.7
1971–80	13.9	2.0	1.7	0.4	2.4	2.3	16.0	2.4	3.8	73.8
1981–90	6.2	2.6	2.1	4.1	1.1	3.5	8.6	2.5	9.8	73.3
1991–96	3.5	1.4	2.3	-0.6	1.1*	1.4*	4.6	0.7	9.3	73.6*
1991	6.5	-2.0	1.1	-9.5	2.6	-2.2	8.6	1.1	8.8	76.7
1992	4.4	-0.5	1.4	-1.5	-0.1	-0.1	5.2	0.5	10.1	76.0
1993	3.2	2.2	3.7	0.6	0.3	2.6	4.3	0.8	10.4	73.8
1994	2.1	3.8	3.8	3.7	2.0	3.0	3.5	1.0	9.6	72.1
1995	2.4	2.4	1.8	-0.1	1.0	2.0	2.9	0.3	8.8	71.7
1996	2.6	2.3	1.9	3.7	0.9	2.9	3.3	0.7	8.3	71.0

Source: European Commission (1997), Annex, Tables 3, 10, 11, 16, 18, 20, 24, 29, 31, 32, 98.
* Author's calculations.

cent. Although the rate of increase of real income was lower than in the previous decade, the adjusted share of wages in GDP rose to an average of 73.8 per cent and profitability (not shown in Table 3.1)[7], set at 100.0 for 1961–73, fell to 76.5 for 1974–85, reflecting the relative strength of labour at this time. Of course, these average figures conceal wide fluctuations, swings in policy, periods of sharp industrial conflict and the start of the era of rising unemployment in the second half of the decade as the Labour Government abandoned the post-war commitment to full employment and adopted deflationary policies, with the average annual rate of unemployment increasing from 1.7 per cent in the 1960s to 3.8 per cent in the 1970s.

It was the victory of the Conservatives in the 1979 general election, however, that ushered in a decade in which the new right consolidated a neo-liberal hegemony, with the return of mass unemployment and the partial restoration of discipline in the labour market and the workplace, as the distributional conflict was increasingly resolved on terms favourable to capital. Unemployment in the 1980s averaged 9.8 per cent, the average wage share in GDP fell to 73.3 per cent and profitability (1961–73 = 100) rose from an average of 76.5 for the period 1974–85 to an average of 91.5 for 1986–90. Distributional conflict, however, was not easily suppressed. The industrial unrest, high rates of unemployment and low rates of real income growth that prevailed in the first half of the decade made the Conservatives deeply unpopular and in an attempt to offset this unpopularity the government engineered an electoral boom. This resulted in the average annual rate of increase of investment over the decade as a whole reaching 4.1 per cent and that of private consumption rising to 3.5 per cent. The average rate of increase of government expenditure over the decade, however, fell to its lowest of the three decades covered in Table 3.1. Nominal income rose by an annual average of 8.6 per cent, but this was offset by an average annual rate of inflation of 6.2 per cent, less than half that of the 1970s but still significantly higher than in the 1960s. The outcome was that real income grew at an average annual rate of 2.5 per cent, slightly faster than in the 1970s.

The stabilization on capital's terms that was achieved in the 1980s began to bear fruit in the 1990s. Over the period 1991–6 unemployment remained very high, averaging 9.3 per cent per annum, real income grew more slowly than at any time since the Second World War, at 0.7 per cent per annum, and profitability (1961–73 = 100) recovered further to an average of 99.2. Although the electoral boom of the late 1980s proved unsustainable, with GDP during 1991–6 growing at an average of only 1.4 per cent per annum and investment actually falling at an average rate of –0.6 per cent per annum, it is evident from the year by year data for the 1990s in Table 3.1 that the defeat of labour, the increased 'flexibility' and insecurity in the labour market, and the ideological ascendancy of neo-liberalism, had for the time being created the conditions for a relatively successful capitalist economy. Unemployment and inflation rates fell, GDP and investment growth picked up, the rate of growth of real income showed no sign of recovering from its postwar low, and by 1996 profitability (1961–73 = 100) had increased to 109.8.

The history of the major capitalist economic regions since the 1960s followed a broadly similar pattern to that of the UK. Table 3.2 provides summary data for the period 1961–90 for the UK, the European 15, the US and Japan.

The distributional conflict that underlay the price explosion of the 1970s produced a general increase in the share of wages in GDP. Although the rate of growth of real income in the 1970s fell compared with the previous decade, it more or less kept pace with GDP and the rate of growth of government expenditure exceeded that of GDP, in both cases with the exception of the US. The average rate of inflation more than doubled in the UK, the EU15 and the USA, and increased significantly even in Japan, as prices were raised in the attempt to offset the rapid growth of money income. As inflation accelerated and anti-inflationary policies replaced full employment as the political priority, unemployment began to rise and the growth rate of GDP and investment started to fall. The scene was set for the 'stabilization' programmes of the 1980s (Glyn 1992). During the 1980s the annual average unemployment rate for the UK and the EU15 was more than twice that of the 1970s and in the US and Japan it was significantly higher than in the previous decade. The share of wages in GDP fell and, with the exception of the UK, the rate of growth of real income fell sharply. The rate of inflation also fell sharply although, with the exception of Japan, it remained above that of the 1960s. In the period 1991–6 (not shown in Table 3.2; see Table 3.1 and Appendix for 1990s data) the rate of unemployment stayed at historically high levels while the rate of growth of GDP and, with the exception of the US, real income fell significantly, as did the rate of inflation.

However, although the broad pattern was similar, there were nevertheless also marked differences between the experience of the major economic regions in the capitalist world. The EU15 as a whole, despite significant differences between countries, followed the same basic pattern as the UK in the 1960s and 1970s, although with a stronger economic performance – higher rates of growth of GDP, GDP per head, investment, private consumption and real income. However, the balance of forces was more favourable to labour, as indicated by the higher share of wages in GDP, and the distributional struggle took longer to resolve on terms favourable to capital, with the result that during the 1980s the economic performance of the EU15 fell below that of the UK – higher inflation and lower rates of growth of GDP, GDP per head, investment, private consumption and real income. Indeed, the continental EU15 are still seeking a resolution of the underlying distributional conflict in the 1990s as they seek to adapt their social welfare regimes to meet the criteria for European monetary union and the imperatives of intensifying global competition (Esping-Andersen 1990, 1996).

US experience has been closer to that of the UK, except that the balance of forces has been less favourable to labour, as evidenced by the lowest rates of increase of real income recorded in Tables 3.1 and 3.2 and the lowest share of wages in GDP until the 1990s. This enabled lower rates of inflation than in the UK and the EU15 to be combined from the 1980s onwards with lower rates of unemployment. Japanese experience has, in some respects, been more like that of the EU15 than the US, with due allowance for the exceptional performance

Table 3.2 UK, EU15, USA and Japan, 1961–90: selected economic indicators (annual percentage change at 1990 prices unless otherwise stated)

Period and economy	Inflation indicator (GDP deflator)	GDP	GDP per worker (employee)	Investment (gross fixed capital formation)	Government expenditure (public consumption)	Private consumption	Nominal income per worker (employee)	Real income per worker (private consumption deflator)	Unemployment (% of civilian labour force)	Adjusted wage share (% of GDP at factor cost)
1961–70										
UK	4.2	2.9	2.6	5.2	2.1	2.4	7.1	3.0	1.7	72.7
EU15	4.4	4.8	4.6	6.0	3.7	4.9	9.1	5.1	2.2	74.3
USA	3.0	3.8	1.9	3.9	3.5	4.1	5.2	2.5	4.7	71.1
Japan	5.4	10.5	8.9	15.7	5.9	9.0	13.5	7.5	1.2	73.5
1971–80										
UK	13.9	2.0	1.7	0.4	2.4	2.3	16.0	2.4	3.8	73.8
EU15	10.8	3.0	2.7	1.6	3.2	3.4	14.0	3.0	4.0	75.4
USA	7.5	2.7	0.6	2.8	0.9	3.0	8.1	0.8	6.4	72.1
Japan	7.8	4.5	3.7	3.5	5.1	4.7	13.1	4.0	1.8	78.0
1981–90										
UK	6.2	2.6	2.1	4.1	1.1	3.5	8.6	2.5	9.8	73.3
EU15	6.7	2.4	1.9	2.4	1.9	2.5	7.7	1.1	9.0	73.1
USA	4.5	2.7	0.9	2.4	2.7	3.0	5.3	0.5	7.1	71.5
Japan	1.9	4.0	3.1	5.2	2.5	3.7	4.0	1.9	2.5	75.0

Source: European Commission (1997), Annex, Tables 3, 10, 11, 16, 18, 20, 24, 29, 31, 32.

of the 1960s. Distributional conflict in the 1970s is reflected in the fact that, although the rate of growth of GDP and GDP per worker fell by more than half compared with the 1960s, real income and private consumption fell by less than half, the share of wages in GDP rose from 73.5 per cent to 78.0 per cent and the rate of inflation reached its highest point of the three-and-a-half decades under consideration. In the 1980s, by contrast, the rate of growth of real income fell by much more than that of GDP and GDP per head, the share of wages in GDP fell, investment recovered, unemployment increased and the rate of inflation fell dramatically. However the rate of unemployment, although increasing from decade to decade, has remained remarkably low, despite the stagnation of the real economy in the 1990s. In Japan, as in the US, the underlying balance of class power has been relatively more favourable to capital than in the UK or the EU15 and Japan, like the US in the 1980s and 1990s but to a much greater extent, has experienced both lower rates of inflation and lower rates of unemployment than those that have prevailed in Europe.

Conclusion

The argument of this paper has been that in the period following the Second World War the balance of power between capital and labour, both globally, under the impact of the defeat of fascism and the detachment of Eastern Europe and China from the capitalist world, and nationally, to differing extents reflecting different national historical experiences and institutional contexts, had shifted in favour of labour. This created a situation in which distributional conflict gradually gathered strength, reaching a peak in the 1970s. The outcome was a decade of rapid inflation as the monetary expressions of the incompatible real income claims of the two major social classes resulted in a wage–price or price–wage spiral, exacerbated by the impact of an adverse shift in the terms of trade of the developed capitalist countries and contradictory claims on government for both higher expenditure and lower taxation. The rise of the new right and the neo-liberal ascendancy of the 1980s and 1990s can be seen as a historic defeat for labour and the reassertion of the power of capital. Anti-inflationary policies replaced full employment as the political priority, mass unemployment reinforced the power of neo-liberal ideology, and discipline was re-imposed in the labour market and the workplace. However, although reduced demand and increased unemployment functioned everywhere as 'a regulator of class conflict' (Rowthorn 1977, p. 237), it did so in a context structured by the underlying balance of class forces. Thus, the trade-off between inflation and unemployment occurred at much lower levels in the US and Japan, where capital was relatively more power-ful, than in the UK and the EU15, where labour was relatively more powerful.

There has been much discussion of the extent to which de-regulation, the internationalization of production and the globalization of financial markets have removed the conditions for effective full employment policies at the national level (Glyn 1995, Hirst and Thompson 1996, Rowthorn 1986). One way of thinking about this may be in terms of Polanyi's (1944) concept of the 'double movement'.

Polanyi argued that the conquest by capital and market forces of more and more spheres of social life in the nineteenth century undermined the conditions for the continued operation of the capitalist market and called forth a second movement of social regulation. The settlement following the Second World War may be thought of as a further step in the process of social regulation. However, by suspending or weakening the operation of the economic cycle, the settlement caused capitalism to begin to seize up as full employment led to accelerating inflation and the absence of severe slumps inhibited the process of re-valuing capital downwards and recreating the conditions for profitable investment. In the absence of a hegemonic left alternative project, this resulted in the eventual triumph of the new right and the neo-liberal agenda as the post-war settlement was undermined and the power of capital, increasingly global capital operating in unregulated global markets, was re-asserted. However, the cost of this process in terms of the performance of the real economy and people's welfare has been enormous – high unemployment, increased insecurity, reduced welfare provision and, in the two countries that have moved furthest in this direction (the US and the UK), increasing poverty and inequality. Indeed, as the 1990s come to an end, global instability, unemployment and the danger of generalized depression are increasingly replacing inflation as the principal concern of informed commentators. On this reading, what is now needed is a further round of social regulation, initially at the national and European levels, but increasingly also internationally.

Social regulation, however, is the outcome of theoretical work and social and political struggle in the course of which a broad consensus is created around a viable alternative. In the context of the debates in the UK in the 1970s referred to on pp. 24–26, Sam Aaronovitch (1981) played an important role in developing such an alternative. He also subsequently (Aaronovitch 1986) drew attention to some weaknesses in the alternative economic strategy he had helped to develop and that was dominant on the left in the UK at that time – its statism, national focus, patriarchal assumptions and lack of awareness of environmental issues. It was the failure of the left in the 1970s to create a hegemonic consensus around a convincing alternative that enabled the right to resolve the distributional conflict of the 1970s on terms favourable to capital. If the historic defeat of labour of the past two decades is to be transcended, progress is urgently needed in the development of institutions and social processes through which decisions over investment, the growth rate and the distribution of income can be arrived at by negotiation, thus creating the conditions for full employment to be achieved and maintained without generating distributive conflict, inflation and unsustainable growth.[8] A major implication of a conflict analysis of inflation, as Burdekin and Burkett have demonstrated, is that monetary policy is not a neutral technical instrument. The present trend towards central bank independence from governments is a manifestation of the prevailing neo-liberal ideological ascendancy. What is needed is a move in quite the opposite direction, to bring monetary policy under greater democratic control as part of a more general process of extending the control of civil society over both the state and the economy.

Appendix EU15, USA, Japan 1991–6: selected economic indicators (annual percentage change at 1990 prices unless otherwise stated)

Period and economy	Inflation indicator (GDP deflator)	GDP	GDP per worker (employee)	Investment (gross fixed capital formation)	Government expenditure (public consumption)	Private consumption	Nominal income per worker (employee)	Real income per worker (private consumption deflator)	Unemployment (% of civilian labour force)	Adjusted wage share (% of GDP at factor cost)
EU15*										
1991	5.5	1.5	1.3	−0.4	1.9	2.2	7.1	1.4	8.3	71.6
1992	4.5	0.9	2.4	−0.8	1.6	1.7	6.8	2.0	9.4	71.6
1993	3.7	−0.5	1.4	−6.6	1.2	−0.3	4.2	0.1	10.9	71.2
1994	2.6	2.8	3.3	2.5	0.4	1.8	3.3	0.1	11.3	69.8
1995	2.9	2.4	1.9	3.6	0.7	1.8	3.4	0.4	10.9	69.1
1996	2.6	1.6	1.5	1.5	1.0	2.0	3.4	0.8	10.9	68.7
USA										
1991	3.5	−0.5	0.5	−5.3	1.5	−0.2	4.6	0.8	6.7	72.3
1992	2.4	2.5	2.6	5.8	−1.0	3.0	5.3	2.4	7.4	72.4
1993	2.0	3.4	1.6	11.9	−0.8	3.5	3.5	1.1	6.8	72.2
1994	2.1	4.1	0.1	12.3	−0.9	3.5	1.8	−0.4	6.1	72.0
1995	2.5	2.0	0.6	5.3	−0.3	2.3	3.5	1.1	5.6	72.3
1996	2.1	2.4	1.0	5.7	0.6	2.6	3.5	0.8	5.4	72.5
Japan										
1991	2.7	4.0	1.9	3.3	2.0	2.5	4.6	2.0	2.1	71.6
1992	1.7	1.1	0.0	−1.5	2.0	2.1	1.3	−0.6	2.2	71.7
1993	0.6	0.1	−0.3	−2.0	2.4	1.2	0.8	−0.4	2.5	71.9
1994	0.3	0.5	0.4	−1.0	2.2	1.8	1.3	0.6	2.9	72.5
1995	−0.5	0.8	0.7	0.6	1.9	1.6	1.2	1.6	3.1	73.2
1996	0.0	3.8	3.4	8.6	3.2	2.9	2.5	2.2	3.3	72.6

Source: European Commission (1997), Annex, Tables 3, 10, 11, 16, 18, 20, 24, 29, 31, 32.

* Includes East Germany from 1991 for unemployment and adjusted wage share and from 1992 for the other indicators.

Notes

1   I should like to thank Phil Leeson, Elena Lieven, David Purdy, Roger Simon and Nick Weaver for helpful suggestions. I should also like to thank Don Bain, Allan Pred, Natalia Vonnegut and Richard Walker, Department of Geography, and Jean Lave and Carol Page, Social and Cultural Studies in Education, at the University of California at Berkeley, for making available essential facilities and a congenial working environment during the sabbatical semester at Berkeley in which this paper was written.
2   In this context, and possibly more generally, the term 'the Conflict Theory of Inflation' was first used in an article by Roger Simon writing under the name James Harvey (Harvey 1977). According to Simon (private correspondence), it was suggested to him by Sam Aaronovitch during discussion of a preliminary draft of the article.
3   I am grateful to David Purdy for the following comment made in private correspondence: 'It is perfectly true to say that in the debate within the CP in the 1970s, the principal rival to the conflict theory of inflation was a form of Marxist monetarism. But later and in a broader intellectual context, the sharp division between competing theories of post-war inflation became a little blurred. Some non-Marxist 'monetarists' . . . eventually realized that while blaming governments for monetary incompetence might make good propaganda, it was hardly social science, and they began to analyse the socio-political forces which – disastrously from their standpoint – underlay the commitment to full employment and generated persistent pressure for increased public expenditure without any countervailing pressure to contain taxes. . . . [W]here we sought to promote social negotiation and democratic planning, they maintained that inflation could only be finally defeated by insulating governments from popular pressure. Nevertheless, there is a clear sense in which the conflict theory of inflation is not the exclusive prerogative of Marxists.'
4   This is the same level as the 'natural' or 'non-accelerating inflation' rate of unemployment of mainstream monetarism, but with a very different interpretation. In Rowthorn's model, the Phillips curve becomes vertical above the threshold level of inflation, at which point full anticipation gives results analogous to those of rational expectations.
5   The data in Tables 3.1 and 3.2 are affected not only by the secular tends discussed in the text but also by cyclical movements which are in general not discussed, although they really should be in a more extended treatment.
6   For the terms of trade, see European Commission (1997), Annex, Table 28, pp. 246–7.
7   For profitability, see European Commission (1997), Annex, Table 98, pp. 378–9.
8   The term 'full employment' needs to be used with care. I do not mean by it the male family wage full employment of the post-Second World War period but rather a situation in which it is possible for everyone to live by engaging in some form of socially useful activity that is supported by society, whether through wages or some other form of income provision.

References

Aaronovitch, S. (1981), *The Road from Thatcherism: The Alternative Economic Strategy*, London: Lawrence and Wishart.

Aaronovitch, S. (1986), 'The Alternative Economic Strategy: Goodbye to All That?', *Marxism Today*, Vol. 30, no. 2, February, pp. 20–6.

Addison, P. (1975), *The Road to 1945: British Politics and the Second World War*, London: Cape.

Baxter, J. L. (1973), 'Inflation in the Context of Relative Deprivation and Social Justice', *Scottish Journal of Political Economy*, Vol. 20(3), pp. 262–82.

Burdekin, R. and Burkett P. (1996), *Distributional Conflict and Inflation: Theoretical and Historical Perspectives*, Basingstoke: Macmillan.

Bootle, R. (1996), *The Death of Inflation: Surviving and Thriving in the Zero Era*, London: Nicholas Brearley.

Davidson, P. (1972), 'A Keynesian View of Friedman's Theoretical Framework for Monetary Analysis', *Journal of Political Economy*, Vol. 80(5), pp. 864–81.

Desai, M. (1973), 'Growth Cycles and Inflation in a Model of Class Struggle', *Journal of Economic Theory*, Vol. 6(6), pp. 427–45.

Devine, P. (1974), 'Inflation and Marxist Theory', *Marxism Today*, March, pp. 70–92.

Esping-Andersen, G. (1990), *The Three Worlds of Welfare Capitalism*, Cambridge: Polity.

Esping-Andersen, G. (ed.) (1996), *Welfare States in Transition: National Adaptations in Global Economies*, London: Sage.

European Commission (1997), *European Economy: Annual Economic Report for 1997*, No.63, Brussels: Directorate-General for Economic and Financial Affairs.

Furtado, C. (1967), 'Industrialization and Inflation: An Analysis of the Recent Course of Economic Development in Brazil', *International Economic Papers*, Vol. 12, pp. 101–19.

Glyn, A. (1992), 'The Costs of Stability: The Advanced Capitalist Countries in the 1980s', *New Left Review*, September/October, 195, pp. 71–95.

Glyn, A. (1995), 'Social Democracy and Full Employment', *New Left Review*, May/June, 211, 33–55.

Glyn, A., Hughes, A., Lipietz, A. and Singh, A. (1990), 'The Rise and Fall of the Golden Age', in Marglin, S. and Schor, J. (eds), *The Golden Age of Capitalism*, Oxford: Clarendon Press.

Harvey, J. (1977), 'Theories of Inflation', *Marxism Today*, January, pp. 24–9.

Hirst, P. and Thompson, G. (1996), *Globalization in Question: The International Economy and the Possibilities of Governance*, Cambridge: Polity Press.

Kalecki, M. (1943), 'Political Aspects of Full Employment', *Political Quarterly*, Vol. 14(4), pp. 322–31.

Nuti, D. M. (1972), 'On Incomes Policy' in Hunt, E. K. and Schwartz, J. G. (eds), *A Critique of Economic Theory*, Harmondsworth: Penguin.

Panic, M. (1976), 'The Inevitable Inflation', *Lloyds Bank Review*, July, pp. 1–15.

Polanyi, K. (1944; 1957), *The Great Transformation*, New York: Farrar & Rinehart; Boston: Beacon Press.

Purdy, D. (1974), 'Some Thoughts on the Party's Policy Towards Prices, Wages and Incomes', *Marxism Today*, August, pp. 246–52.

Purdy, D. (1976), 'British Capitalism Since the War – Part One: Origins of the Crisis' and 'British Capitalism Since the War – Part Two: Decline and Prospects', *Marxism Today*, September, pp. 270–7 and October, pp. 310–18.

Rosenberg, S. and Weisskopf, T. (1981), 'A Conflict Theory Approach to Inflation in the Postwar US Economy', *American Economic Review, Papers and Proceedings*, Vol. 71(2), pp. 42–7.

Rowthorn, R. E. (1977), 'Conflict, Inflation and Money', *Cambridge Journal of Economics*, Vol. 1(3), pp. 215–39.

Rowthorn, R. E. (1986), 'Unemployment: A Resistible Force', *Marxism Today*, September, pp. 28–31.

Sunkel, O. (1960), 'Inflation in Chile: An Unorthodox Approach', *International Economic Papers*, Vol. 10, pp. 107–31.

4 The fall of the wall

A socio-economic interpretation of the end of systems competition

Egon Matzner[1]

Among the 1980s, 1989 was a year of spectacular macro-events and profound changes in what Karl Popper called the situational logic of individual behaviour (Popper 1944). This was the case for agents in politics, public administration, business and industry, in academia and the arts, as well as in the everyday life of private households. Although the macro-events, from Tienanmen to the fall of the Berlin Wall, attracted great public and intellectual interest, this cannot be said of the changes at the micro-level of decision-making. I shall argue that the end of the Cold War, which resulted from the implosion of the Soviet Empire, has brought about a dramatic change in the situational logic of our globe. That this holds true for the former communist countries is a truism. But that an upheaval has also occurred in the old Western democracies is not yet fully understood, if at all. I shall try to show that the end of the Cold War has had far-reaching consequences for decisions and actions in all spheres of public and private life in the former 'West'. This has a deep bearing on the prosperity or decline of Western institutions and policies. As the rules of the game in the 'West' are now also accepted by the former 'East', the consequences are also felt there, although not as acutely as in the 'South' of our globe.

In the first part of this chapter I sketch out the post-1989 socio-economic context in the Western world. In the second part, two factors influencing the prosperity or decline of institutions are discussed in newly adapted game-theoretic terms. The hypothesis is ventured that during the Cold War systems rivalry provided the 'West' with a strong stimulus for co-operation among countries, and within countries among political parties and interest groups. The over-riding objective of co-operation was the pursuit of a public purpose in economic growth and social welfare, reducing unemployment and providing skills and higher education. With the end of the Cold War this stimulus has gone, and so far has not been replaced by a new one. Thus, the end of the Cold War contributed to a 'thrust reversal' (Schubumkehr), i.e. a switch from the dominance of positive-sum games to that of negative-sum games. In the final part of the chapter the significance of the public purpose and of co-operation as a way of achieving it is re-stated, and the concept that co-operation should therefore become the primary objective of politics is suggested.

The new socio-economic context

To understand and explain the decisions and actions of individuals it is useful to visualize the situational logic in which they find themselves, or their socio-economic context. This consists of the following elements:

1   World Views on which the decisions, actions and interests of the dominant agents are based.
2   Institutions (in the shape of governments, enterprises, the family, but also markets, laws, decrees, norms and even habits).
3   Available Technology (ranging from simple tools to telecommunications) and the knowledge necessary to apply it.
4   Relative Prices, incomes and costs, but also relative attention, which induces individual effort.
5   Political Instruments available to influence the four previous elements (Matzner 1994).

How has the socio-economic context for public and private action changed during the past decade? Let us imagine two individual agents such as the minister of finance and the president of a central bank of an EU member country which is a net contributor to the Union. Our two agents still advocate full employment in a welfare state. Which features would strike them as significant? I shall select the five that are most pertinent to the 'Western' countries.

From systems rivalry to competition among locations and national currencies

The first and most important new feature in the current socio-economic context is the disappearance of the Soviet system with all the consequences of that system. The removal of external danger, is a basically positive development. The end of the arms race means an end to the constant danger of nuclear war at a global level. But it also has serious unwelcome consequences for 'the West'. The role of the arms race has been taken over by the scramble for arms markets in the former Soviet and Yugoslav spheres of influence. The eastward enlargement of NATO is, above all, an expansion of markets captured by Western arms producers to the detriment of the arms industry of Russia and the other post-Soviet states. There have also been cuts in arms research and research connected with security issues, which used to provide employment for political scientists and economists, particularly in the United States. While the West also viewed the Soviet Union as a serious competitor in the civilian sphere, it was possible to get many important economic, educational and welfare programmes approved (Prager 1962). The European Reconstruction Programme known as Marshall Plan, under which the United States donated a total of US$ 13 billion to the non-communist European countries[2], was a programme aimed at fighting communism. The 'Point 4 Program' directed at non-communist regimes in underdeveloped countries had the same aim.

US aid to Europe was provided under stringent conditions. Among them were requirements like the elaboration of infrastructure programmes and the obligation to participate in the multi-lateral settlement of payments, i.e. planned economy-type measures. Full employment and planned economic development in the Soviet Union and the countries within the Soviet sphere of influence, as well as recollections of the world economic crisis in the period between the two world wars, made it possible for full employment and economic growth to become recognized as desirable political aims also in the West.

Comprehensive social security in the Soviet Union facilitated the progressive elaboration of social security systems and the perfection of the welfare state in the Western countries. The development and promotion of the education system, of higher learning and of research institutions was sparked off by the 'Sputnik shock', particularly in the United States, but also in the other OECD countries. Certain excessive public expenditures must perhaps also be attributed to rivalry between the two opposed systems. Since such expenditures were considered as 'social armament' needed to compete with the rival system, it was quite easy to get political approval for them, just like for all arms expenditures during the Cold War. A programme of cuts in social welfare expenditures and the abrogation of social security legislation (for example the abolition of the ban on dismissals in enterprises with up to 11 employees) like the one presented by the German government in summer 1996 would have been very unlikely while the German Democratic Republic existed. The competition to reduce social welfare programmes, that took place between Democrats and Republicans in the US presidential election campaign 1996, could hardly have occurred two or three decades earlier. This does not mean that the welfare state could have remained as it was, if the Soviet Union had continued to exist as a rival to market societies.

In 1989 the change from systems rivalry to competition among locations ('Standort-Konkurrenz') and national currencies became clear. While the desire to surpass the (imagined) scientific and social welfare achievements of the Soviet Union stimulated the development of the welfare state, (imagined) competition with the newly industrialized countries in East Asia and with the new cheap-labour countries in central and eastern Europe is now taken as justification for attempting to dismantle the welfare state and social welfare programmes. This is happening at a time of the world economic crisis when social security programmes are more necessary than ever.

The international monetary order and de-regulation of capital markets

A peculiarity of the international monetary order established by the United States as victor in the Second World War is that its rules of the game tend to restrict the demand for products and thus keep down employment. The main purpose of the international monetary system is to enable the international settlement of payments of the countries participating in world trade. For this purpose, the member countries of the International Monetary Fund (IMF) are obliged to reduce excessive deficits in their current accounts. A country in deficit must curb its economic activity with measures such as increasing interest rates and taxes, or by reducing public expenditures. This results in lower imports, but also lower production and employment both domestically and in other countries, from where less is imported. The production, income and employment of both the country in deficit and its main trading partners are reduced by this asymmetric adaptation mechanism: the total sum or outcome is negative.[3] That such restrictive tendencies did not predominate during the post-war period must largely be attributed to systems rivalry. But, since 1989, restrictive tendencies are no longer counteracted by political efforts to offset them.

Another important restrictive impulse affecting public expenditure programmes originates in the de-regulation of national capital markets, particularly foreign exchange markets, which has become prevalent in the past 15 years. This has reduced the freedom of manoeuvre for conducting effective national fiscal and monetary policy. Fiscal and central bank policy is now guided by the need to keep domestic assets attractive for foreign investment. Foreign investors in their turn are guided by currency stability and the current and expected return on investment. Expansionary expenditure programmes, rising public debt and low interest rates aimed at stimulating growth tend to reduce the attractiveness of a national currency. Since this holds for all currencies, competition to enhance attractiveness of currencies has a restrictive influence on production, growth and employment. International investors (such as pension and investment funds, enterprises, but also private asset holders) are the jurors of such beauty contests among national currencies (in Keynes's metaphor), exerting an influence which is stronger than the preference of electorates for policies furthering active employment, social welfare, education and culture.

This situation is aggravated by the fact that such 'beauty contests' drive interest rates up. Consequently, profits on financial investment are often higher than profits on investment in production. Higher interest rates of course also mean that more interest is due on public debt. When the target of monetary stability predominates, higher interest payments will reduce or replace expenditures on other public tasks. Frequently this affects the social welfare and education expenditures benefiting the social groups which are least able to defend their case. It is remarkable that in the debate on 'Standort-Konkurrenz' (competition among locations), the higher interest paid by enterprises as a result of beauty contests among currencies has not appeared in the argument. The discussions keep revolving around the cost of labour, taxes and social security contributions, despite the fact that in the past 20 years interest rates have increased much more than the other cost factors just mentioned.

The surplus of private saving; public debt and the erosion of the multiplier effect

Circular flow analysis reveals that private household savings out of current income (i.e. current income minus consumption) by definition constitute a loss of effective demand for goods and services currently produced. However, this saving – mostly with the credit sector acting as intermediary – is absorbed by the financing of private investment and the export surplus. If private saving surpasses private investment plus the export surplus, and if nothing else happens, demand will go down by that difference or surplus of private savings. However, effective demand is not reduced to the full extent of this surplus. With lower demand, production and employment decline. With higher unemployment, government revenue from taxes and social security contributions falls as social welfare expenditures rise. The private savings surplus is then absorbed by this automatic increase in the budget deficit. In 1994, the private savings surplus of Austrian households of ATS 100 billion corresponded to the Austrian net budget deficit.

That these important inter-relations are much more than a tautology has been theoretically clarified by Steindl (1982) and empirically illustrated by Guger and Walterskirchen (1988). Keynes predicted in 1943 (Keynes 1980) that they would be a consequence of the maturity of national economies. Since private saving is relatively stable, while private investment and exports are quite sensitive to variations in interest rates and effective demand, the socio-economic context of mature national economies is one that favours rising unemployment and growing public indebtedness. Measures to 'improve the attractiveness of locations', e.g. through tax relief for higher incomes or raising interest earnings on financial investment as a consequence of beauty contests, contribute to pushing up the private saving surplus even further, thereby aggravating the original problem of excess household saving. This trend is additionally promoted by national tax policy. Income from property is taxed less and less, while the tax on income from work tends to be increased directly and indirectly. This is not only an outcome of 'Standort-Konkurrenz': to a considerable extent it is due to the changed world view and interests of the dominant agents. With increasing frequency key representatives of trade unions, or of socialist, liberal or social-conservative parties reveal themselves as private rent-seekers instead of agents of the public interest.

The rising income disparities observed in the OECD countries in recent years are an indication that the ability of national governments to exert an influence through policy measures is diminishing. This is also manifested by the weaker stimulation of demand by public expenditure: the public expenditures multiplier is losing effectiveness because rising saving rates make domestic demand go down, and also because rising import penetration rate will shift a larger share of demand to other countries.

European Economic and Monetary Union

The creation of the European Union through the Maastricht treaties, particularly the plan to introduce a single European currency, in a wider sense can be seen as a consequence of the end of the Cold War. In a narrower sense it has to be regarded as a consequence of German unification, because German political influence during the Cold War largely rested on its strong economic position.

This, in turn, resulted in the strength of the Deutschemark. As pointed out above, asymmetric adaptation and 'beauty contests' among currencies are detrimental to investment, production and employment. The substitution of national currencies by the Euro is a step towards less competition among them. There are hopes that the monetary dominance of Germany will be replaced by a more multi-national approach in negotiating EU monetary policy. The actual outcome of European Monetary Union is still an open question.

Fulfilment of the convergence criteria would heighten the dominance of monetary stability targets already enforced by the IMF and by de-regulated financial markets. The convergence criteria with respect to price levels, exchange rates and long-term interest rates are met by most EU member countries wishing to join EMU. But most of them have difficulties meeting the requirements for the respective shares of the public net deficit and of total government debt in Gross Domestic Product. In view of the circular flow relationships, one cannot be surprised that the convergence criteria are not fulfilled at a time of recession and rising unemployment. Fulfilling the fiscal criteria will delay any economic upturn and improvement in labour markets.

The political arguments for the introduction of the Euro are very strong and there are also positive economic arguments (an end to speculation and beauty contests among the currencies being replaced by the Euro, a uniform unit of account, the reduction of transaction costs), in favour of introducing the Euro as soon as possible, i.e. according to the existing timetable. After the introduction of the single European currency national monetary policies will certainly cease to exist. The governments of the member countries will become permanently dependent on capital markets to finance their deficits. Inevitably, the credit-worthiness of countries will be rated in a manner similar to that of enterprises. Freedom of manoeuvre to finance the welfare state will diminish. Its fate will be decisively influenced by European Central Bank policy. If the convergence criteria are upheld or if – as advocated by the Deutsche Bundesbank – they become even more exacting, one must expect the continuation of low economic growth and a further increase in the number of the unemployed and poor. Regional differences will become sharper, nationalisms and xenophobia will continue to rise, and the welfare state will succumb to crisis. One can only hope that under the pressure of the resulting problems EU policy-makers will gain greater insight and energy and become better able to solve their problems than is the case at present.

The revival of laissez-faire ideology

Thanks to Albert O. Hirschman we know that citizen involvement tends to shift between private interest and public action (Hirschman 1982). A changed dominant world view is one of the new elements in the socio-economic context of such action. Until the early 1970s, the prevalent view in economics and the social sciences was that the welfare state programme could prevent economic crises, or at least mitigate them. Today, most people believe that the welfare state itself causes economic decline and unemployment. The welfare state supposedly raises the comparative costs of a particular capital location or 'Standort', thus lowering its competitiveness. In this way, the welfare state is believed to undermine the very economic base on which it rests. Consequently, it is thought that the competitiveness of a particular 'Standort' can only be maintained or regained by fiscal and monetary discipline. If negotiated settlements between the major social groups, i.e. collective bargaining agreements and labour legislation, are included in the 'welfare state', then monetary discipline must also become enforceable at enterprise level and allow wage cuts and the introduction of longer working hours without any negotiated compromise. In its radical form the 'roll back' from the welfare state (Atkinson 1995) also includes the end of social partnership.

This 'monetarist revolution' was intellectually prepared by economists during the 1950s and 1960s. Starting from Chicago, its main ideas became the dominant doctrine of the 1970s and 1980s. This doctrine managed to ensure the triumph of the monetary stability target over the aims of the welfare state in the real world. Advocates of monetarism act as advisers to influential politicians and central bank presidents. Their views dominate commentaries in the media and thus enter the world view of large numbers of people. Yet, this would not have been enough to secure the victory of the 'monetarist revolution' both in the intellectual and the political arena. De-regulation and the monetary discipline which it inspired, also favour the dominant interests of financial capital (from large enterprises, to pension funds, down to small holders of financial assets). The losers in the game, i.e. unemployed persons or unsuccessful entrepreneurs, are reminded of their personal responsibility for their own fate. In short: the power élites which dominate the economy have lost interest in the welfare of the weaker members of society (Bhaduri and Steindl 1987). The end of systems rivalry has made such behaviour possible. The economists and social scientists who are legitimising these developments have just been composing the incidental music. The play itself is acted out by political leaders.

It is questionable whether the monetarist policy of the United Kingdom and the United States has been a success. Important welfare indicators are negative, the number of destitute persons (including the 'working poor') is growing and there is economic stagnation in Europe. In the US average incomes are falling, income disparities are growing and public infrastructure is in decay. With receding state interference these negative results were foreseeable (see Matzner 1982).

In spite of all this, the political and intellectual dominance of monetarist laissez-faire ideology remains unbroken.[4] The political representatives of the welfare state, i.e. the social-democratic parties and trade unions, for a long time opposed even justified reforms of self-serving public expenditures, and injustices and malfunctioning of the welfare state itself, with clientelism, and sometimes even corruption. The reform of the welfare state has largely been neglected and alternatives to monetarist laissez-faire ideology have not been sufficiently elaborated. As Atkinson (1995) has pointed out, this is a more demanding task than making proposals for de-regulation and monetary discipline, often on the basis of unfounded theories.

The new socio-economic context

Our two agents, the imaginary minister of finance and the central bank president, today face a situational logic of full employment in a welfare state that differs profoundly from that of the year 1980. The characteristics of the situation can be captured by again referring to the four basic elements of a socio-economic context.

1   The world view today is that of the *homo oeconomicus*, able to pursue his market-oriented self-interest, unthreatened by systems rivalry, and uncontrolled by regulations or institutions.
2   Institutions, technology, knowledge. De-regulation and the increasing obsolescence of national borders due to telecommunications has brought forth enterprises active on global markets dominated by capital markets.
3   Relative prices, income, costs. Relative prices have become more important for international companies and global markets. Earning ratios are more dominant because of international competition among currencies and locations. Interest earnings make up an increasing share of higher incomes.
4   Political instruments. The political instruments of the nation state have been weakened by the factors mentioned above as well as by the influence of IMF, World Trade Organization, EU, etc. The priority accorded to monetary stability negatively affects all programmes of the welfare state.

The (probably social-democratic) minister of finance and his colleague, the central bank president, can only either act in accordance with the changed situational logic or resign.

According to Streek (1996), in the new socio-economic context, instead of using national sovereignty to tame and correct the market forces in favour of some public interest, '. . . the only political programme still implementable by globalised national economies without jeopardising the nation state . . .' would be to give up national sovereignty altogether.

If the minister of finance still wished maintain full employment in a welfare state, he should help to create a socio-economic context where this would be possible. Which considerations could guide him?

On the prosperity and decline of institutions

Which institutions survive?

What makes institutions like the state and its welfare agencies, prosper or decline? This also applies to the institutions necessary for a common European currency. It concerns relations between EU institutions on the one hand and the institutions of EU member states on the other. Such institutions could complement (both sides prospering) or substitute each other (one side winning what the other side would lose). Can the diverse processes of institutional change, continuation and decline be captured theoretically in a way that leads to new insights on future policies?

Institutional change as viewed by Karl Marx is determined by technology (the 'productive forces'). The institutional fetters ('production relations') on technology are removed by social struggle. A number of macro-developments can be explained in this way. Technical progress in communications technology made the globalization of capital markets and foreign exchange transactions possible. However, the expansion of capital markets cannot unleash productive forces. On the contrary, the dominance of financial over real capital established in this way is obstructing economic growth.

A similar argument holds for the explanation of institutional growth proposed by New Institutional Economics. According to this theory, those institutions survive which can obtain larger marginal returns than competing ones (North and Thomas 1972). However, the development of institutions, even that of private property, cannot be explained in this way. Take the case of the expansion of capital markets: it can hardly be said to be the result of applying a marginal productivity calculus. Marginal productivity may be useful in analysing already-existing material production, particularly in agriculture. But what kind of marginal productivity could explain the introduction of a new financial derivative or the non-introduction of another? The decision is more like that of a person choosing to play poker rather than scat. New players may join the dominant game or may try to play one that does not yet exist. Such a decision is not based on the calculation of marginal returns, neither ex ante nor ex post. Innovation is a matter of predilection, ability and risk appraisal within a total calculus. The expansion of capital markets, like the development of globally active enterprises, can be better explained by Adam Smith's theory of 'increasing market size'. It becomes possible through improvements in technology and cheaper means of communication. These open up new possibilities of making profits on the basis of existing interest differentials and profit margins (Kregel 1994).

In the functional analysis of the state (see Matzner 1982) the development of institutions is a response to pressure exerted by some problem. Institutional decline arises because of persistent failure to resolve problems. Those institutions survive which sustain, either directly or indirectly, larger value added (in national account terms) and greater political consent (e.g. through increased productivity because employees are cared for by the welfare state), such that this gain is larger than the (transaction) cost of maintaining the respective institutions. Institutions will suffer a decline if the gain falls permanently below that transaction cost. However, the expansion of the capital market cannot be explained in this way. As in the enterprise sector, and as Adam Smith argued, it depends on the identification and realization of profit chances.

Ultimately the rise and fall of institutions depends decisively on the social interaction of the agents constituting them, and on the (physical and legal) persons who use these institutions, according to how those persons' expectations are fulfilled. Jacob Burckhardt refers to this kind of interaction (quoted by Lendi 1992) when concluding that the rise and fall of the Italian city states depended on their citizens' commitment. If the citizens' 'inner commitment' was stronger than their simultaneous 'inner retreat', the conditions were present for prosperous development. When inner retreat was stronger than inner commitment, some 'external factor' was sufficient to set the decline of an institution in motion. Burckhardt's answer is important because it explains the evolution of institutions as a result of social interaction. This is an advantage over other types of explanation mentioned earlier which focus on motives (income opportunities) or results (development of the productive forces, larger marginal utility, a plus in value added and/or political consent). Burckhardt's explanation may be developed by game theory analysing social interactions in situations where the decision of one agent also depends on the decision(s) of (an)other agent(s). Such situations are very common and are illustrated by the game-theoretic model of the prisoners' dilemma (PD).

An (unconventional) game theory explanation

Human behaviour in social situations is almost always connected with the observing or breaking of rules (customs, habits, legal norms, or rules in games like poker). Institutions such as the state and the global foreign-exchange market are social entities characterized by rules. The following attempt at interpreting social interaction embedded in social situations and social entities is inspired by game theory but does not, in certain important points, completely follow its conventions.

Actions taking place in social situations may be divided into agents' decisions or actions that do not have any effect on other agents and decisions or actions that have either a positive or a negative effect on others. Game theory analyses social situations in which the second kind of actions occur. A further distinction is made between co-operative and non-co-operative behaviour. In the case of co-operative behaviour, the result of the action taken by the agents does not harm some common concern of the individuals involved. Co-operative behaviour would be: not to break any law, agreement or binding rule, i.e. not to steal, or selfishly harm fellow human beings or the environment, etc. It would be non-co-operative behaviour to harm the public interest.

In conventional game theory (cf. Osborne and Rubinstein 1994) a distinction is made between constant-sum games and non-constant-sum games. An example of a constant-sum game is the well-known zero-sum game: what one person wins, the other persons lose. The PD model is a non-constant-sum game: on the assumption that the pay-offs expected by the agents are additive, their sum will differ, depending on which decisions the agents take.

Following the Polish clinical psychiatrist Ryszard Praszkier (1996) and differing somewhat from the conventions of game theory we can distinguish within PD between three new sub-variants of the game.

In the *positive-sum sub-variant*, all agents co-operate and thus together contribute to the 'public purpose'. In PD (see Table 4.1), this corresponds to the sum 5 + 5. This variant is characterized as a positive-sum one because both agents end up better in this case than with all other possible decision combinations. In the *negative-sum sub-variant* the agents do not co-operate with each other and thus

Table 4.1 Pay-off matrix in a simple PD game

		Actor B	
		Co-operation	Non-co-operation
Actor A	Co-operation	5, 5	1, 8
	Non-co-operation	8, 1	2, 2

damage the 'public purpose'. In Table 4.1, this corresponds to the sum + 2 + 2, which is obtained by non-co-operative behaviour on the part of A and B. This variant is characterized as a negative-sum one because both parties end up worse than with all other decision combinations. In the *zero-sum sub-variant*, some agents co-operate and the others do not. Thus, the 'public purpose' is partly supported and partly 'damaged'. In the prisoner's dilemma game illustrated above, the non-co-operative agent achieves the best result and the co-operative one the worst of all decision combinations. The constant sum in this sub-variant is assumed to be 9.[5]

These sub-variants illustrate Burckhardt's explanation of the rise and fall of Italian city republics, which was applied to the development of other institutions by Lendi (1992). 'Prospering' of institutions as a result of 'inner commitment' by the citizens corresponds to positive-sum sub-variant within PD which results from co-operative behaviour, if not by all agents then at least by the decisive ones. It yields positive results for all agents. 'Decline' of institutions, as a result of 'inner retreat' by the citizens, corresponds to the negative-sum sub-variant of the game, caused by non-co-operative behaviour of the decisive agents. It results in a loss for all agents. Nothing in Jacob Burckhardt's or Martin Lendi's texts would correspond to the variant of the zero-sum-game. However, this variant characterizes a precarious situation where a decision is called for and where the zero-sum game may easily switch into a positive-sum or negative-sum one. If the external environment remains constant, and if a strategy of 'tit for tat' is chosen within PD, this will tend towards co-operation and thus to the positive-sum sub-variant of the game (Axelrod 1984).

The classical liberal economists thought that the pursuit of self-interest, 'if unrestrained by suitable institutions, carries no guarantee of anything except chaos' (Robbins 1978, p. 56). The classical economists' programme of economic policy started from a divergence between private and public interest. Adam Smith and the English classical liberal economists therefore attributed an active role in politics to the state. The 'invisible hand' they refer to is, according to Robbins, that of the law giver, whose task it is to create a legal framework which will exclude selfish behaviour that would harm public welfare (Robbins 1978). They wanted to influence the conditions for decision-making and action in such a way that the common pursuit of self-interest, would secure the public interest, or at least would not harm it. (A game-theoretical explication of this is found in Holler 1986.) In the language of game theory, the classical liberal economists advocated the pursuit of self-interest and competition under conditions of a positive-sum game. Adam Smith's 'moral sentiments' correspond to what is called co-operation in game theory. The classical economists' programme of social policy is: pursuit of self-interest under competition plus co-operation.

As we know from Jacob Burckhardt, besides co-operation ('inner commitment') and non-co-operation ('inner retreat'), the development of institutions depends on a third factor, an 'external factor' which may reinforce non-co-operation or co-operation, or may cause one to change into the other. 'Moral sentiments', the state and 'external factors' determined prosperity and decline in Europe, resulting from positive- or negative-sum games in the twentieth century.

The inter-war period. The Second World War; the Cold War; the end of the post-war period?

The inter-war period was one of decline, reaching its lowest point during the world economic crisis, followed by the extreme and unprecedented destructiveness of the Second World War. The magnitude of human and material destruction, makes it dangerous to explain that period in the unemotional terminology of game theory. The very name 'game' theory heightens this danger since, in everyday language, this word is associated with sport and fun. Our game-theoretical review of this period seeks to reveal how non-co-operation and negative-sum games, may start quite harmlessly, even like some masquerade, but turn into catastrophes.

At the beginning of the inter-war period of decline, non-co-operation was slowly intensifying. The advocates of the dictatorship of the proletariat, just like those of a state led by a 'Führer', demanded the (physical) elimination of their opponents. Less radical groups pursued similar competitive aims by democratic means, at least without demanding the physical liquidation of opponents. They were unable to co-operate for some 'public interest' encompassing needs they all had in common. The 'external factor' was the Soviet Union, whose followers in the European countries advocated the creation of soviet republics according to that model. Threats to eliminate 'class enemies', which actually took place in the Soviet Union, were bound to antagonize opposing groups. The 'external factor' thus re-inforced non-co-operation and speeded up the downfall of democratic institutions. The Second World War was the murderous extreme of non-co-operation, culminating in the systematic annihilation of the Jews.

The Cold War which followed immediately after the 'hot' one commenced a long period of growth in the OECD countries. Roughly five years of reconstruction preceded 25 years of steady expansion with falling unemployment, followed by slower growth and rising unemployment. The success story of the Cold War period is a story of co-operation within and among the non-communist countries, a sequence of positive-sum-games. Political, economic, social and intellectual decision-makers were motivated towards co-operation and positive-sum games by moral sentiments, which made co-operation appear desirable, and the catastrophic consequences of non-co-operation during the world economic crisis and the Second World War. Lessons were also learned from the peace treaties after the First World War and the ill-fated League- of-Nations loans. As a consequence, the loser of the war, (West) Germany, hardly had to pay reparations. Instead, like most Western European countries, it received considerable sums under the Marshall Plan to finance reconstruction.

In view of the debacle of the inter-war period, politicians and scholars approved of State intervention and regulation of the economy. Sizeable portions of the economy became state-owned. There was widespread consensus about the political and moral values of full employment, access to health services, social security and free higher education for all qualified persons. The needs of employees and farmers were voiced by their representative bodies and considered before important decisions were made.

Finally, an 'external factor' existed in the shape of the Soviet Union which had emerged stronger from the Second World War despite the great sacrifices it had had to make. After the War, the Soviet Union worked as an external threat which stimulated co-operation within the OECD countries. Under the impact of systems competition with the Soviet Union, poverty disappeared in the OECD countries. Before that period, and after it, in the traditional world view of the *homo oeconomicus*, eliminating poverty has been regarded as support for idleness. After the Sputnik shock, the mobilization of talent was considered to be part of the arms race. In the OECD countries Keynesian monetary and fiscal policies were regarded as proper instruments for the stimulation of effective demand, i.e. of production, investment and employment.

However, the Soviet Union lost the competition between systems. That became obvious when the treaty following the Conference on Security and Co-operation in Europe was signed in 1975. The treaty provided the Soviet Union with international guarantees for its sphere of influence established by the agreements of Yalta and Potsdam. After 1975, the only threat left was a military one. Accordingly, the interest in co-operation and positive-sum games among political, economic, social and research policy-makers began to diminish. A potentially attractive alternative model of society (or hope for one) no longer posed by a challenge. There now is less pressure on decision-makers, e.g. owners of capital, to improve the social conditions for which they are responsible. There is less competition for workers as well as a certain lack of 'moral sentiments' and responsibility for the 'public purpose'.

The arms race between the Soviet Union and the United States was a prisoners' dilemma situation in which the two powers played the sub-variant of a zero-sum game. It ended with the exhaustion of the Soviet Union, caused by the dominance of non-co-operation and negative-sum games in the Soviet Union itself and among countries in its sphere of influence. Large enterprises and combines in the centrally planned economies were constantly pursuing negative-sum strategies against the central authority. This involved having low target figures put in their plan, or obtaining larger allotments of raw materials, energy, machines, etc. Within enterprises, negative-sum games, low productivity, theft of resources, were played against public institutions both 'from above' by the elite nomenclatura and 'from below' by workers. The Soviet satirist Raikin vividly described this non-co-operation in a sketch entitled 'Everything depends on all of us'. The scene shows what happens to two trees, the big tree of collective property and the tiny tree of private property. The big tree belongs to everybody and thus to nobody. Everybody takes what they can grab, some even get at the roots, until the collective tree can hardly bear good fruit because too many people have snatched something from it. Meanwhile, the little private tree thrives, blossoms, sprouts. . . . This satire was told in the 1970s. This negative-sum game in the various Soviet republics and allies of the Soviet Union eroded a Soviet system which never succeeded in replacing Stalinist terror by co-operation (cf. Sen 1973).

The implosion of the Soviet Union marks the end of the post-War period.[6] 'The West', whose economic doctrine is now also shaping the former Soviet block, does not have an external factor to counteract the inherent tendency for non-co-operation. Therefore, non-co-operation and negative-sum games are becoming increasingly predominant. In the hemisphere formerly controlled by Moscow, the end of the duel between the superpowers has paved the way for a series of negative-sum 'games' in the form of wars of secession. The same is the case in former Yugoslavia, the country between the former opposing blocs. Wartime has replaced the post-war period also in Europe.

The threat to the welfare state of monetary stability targets

The reduced priority of full employment and welfare policies observed since the end of systems rivalry indicates the rise of negative-sum games. This must be added to the factors changing the socio-economic context. The asymmetric adaptation mechanism, for example, forcing solely the countries running current-account deficits to bring about its reduction (pp. 42–43), corresponds to a negative-sum game. Yet, the adaptation mechanism could also give positive sums, if governments and central banks took other economic and social policy goals, such as full employment, as targets besides monetary stability. Negative-sum games gain ground when monetary stability predominates; this reduces effective demand, and therefore production and employment.

Similar negative-sum games arise from currency competition among countries. The attraction of a currency is influenced positively by price stability, a low budget deficit, an export surplus and high interest rates, i.e. factors that adversely affect effective demand, and thus production, investment and employment. The beauty contest – like a chorus line, however ragged – forces all countries in the same direction. In the end, the world economy's effective demand is lower than it would have been without the contest. This is again the result of a negative-sum game.

'Standort'-competition among governments to attract international enterprises usually has an expansionary economic effect but influences negatively the state budget, at least in the short term. Such enterprises require a good infrastructure, which raises public expenditures, and tax concessions, which reduce public revenues. This 'competition' is itself a consequence of insufficient effective demand which is not big enough to support higher production and employment in existing industrial locations, let alone in additional new ones. The deflationary combination of the asymmetric adaptation mechanism with the Maastricht European convergence criteria, gives a negative-sum game: only a few locations can win the competition and attract internationally active enterprises; the other players get nothing (Kregel *et al.* 1995).

Attracting international enterprises by fiscal means has a negative effect on other programmes financed out of the state budget, such as welfare state benefits. More fiscal inducements have to be provided when the invested capital has paid for itself, to prevent the enterprise from moving elsewhere. However, this cannot be prevented if there are locations offering far cheaper labour costs for the same kind of production. In their turn, enterprises, are locked in a prisoners' dilemma situation vis-à-vis their competitors in a given market. As soon as one competitor moves to a low-wage country, the others must do the same. This is compounded by the convergence criteria for introduction of the Euro, another negative-sum game that lowers effective demand by squeezing directly public consumption and investment, private investment and demand for import goods, and indirectly private consumption. So far, there is no systematic compensation for this reduction in demand.

The most serious threat to welfare, however, comes from making monetary stability the over-riding political goal. This expresses the present predominance of financial capital over the production sphere. It spreads the negative-sum games to all social and cultural spheres. The absolute priority given to monetary stability over other public goals means that the latter are more difficult to fulfil when the stability targets are not met. This primarily affects the targets of full employment and economic growth. Consequently, the financial demands on the (welfare) state rise at the same time as its revenues are reduced. This triggers a chain reaction of further zero-sum and negative-sum games. For example, if more than two persons compete for one available job, this is the situation of a zero-sum game: only one can win, all others must lose. As is well known, at present the number of persons in the EU who are looking for jobs is more than ten times larger than the number of vacancies. Every cut made in social, health, education or cultural budgets due to the predominance of monetary stability gives rise to zero-sum games between those persons who barely receive what they need and those who do not make it. This discourages co-operation in the sense of pursuit of a public task, and reduces 'inner commitment'. The basis of the welfare state, like of any other institution, is co-operation allowing (expectations of) positive-sum games that will encourage and reward those taking part in it. This basis is seriously jeopardised by the inordinate growth of non-co-operation, leading to negative-sum games.

The return of positive-sum games in politics

New tasks for politics, economics and society

If negative-sum games are replacing positive-sum ones, then the over-riding political task in our time must be to stage positive-sum games. What are the consequences of non-co-operation? What are the preconditions for co-operation in different social situations? Above all, what are the conditions under which zero- or negative-sum games can be transformed into positive-sum ones? This constitutes a demanding research programme, a challenge to theory and to experimental economic and social science.

A new public agenda

Co-operative behaviour presupposes that a public interest (or 'public purpose') exists which is adopted as public task. This public interest may be harmed by the pursuit of self-interest. Behaviour is co-operative when the actors over-ride their self-interest and act in accordance with the public interest. Fulfilment of the latter will in the longer run be to the advantage of all agents or participants in the co-operative behaviour. When co-operation does not emerge spontaneously or in a self-organized way, the state should act to identify co-operative behaviour. An agenda of public tasks satisfying the public interest is needed to secure positive-sum games. This is best done by creating a socio-economic context in which the pursuit of self-interest coincides with the 'public purpose', an idea which goes back to Adam Smith and English classical political economists (Robbins 1978).

The agenda of public tasks should have co-operation as a general principle of procedure. It should be applied in carrying out the most urgent public task or tasks at any particular time. In periods of high inflation this would be currency stability; at times of high unemployment it would be the restitution of full employment. Any socially significant problem that could not be solved through self-interest and market forces, because they themselves had caused it, would qualify for inclusion in the agenda for public action. Problems of public interest for Europe as a whole would be, for example: slower economic growth, rising unemployment, increase in poverty and inequality, environmental damage, organized crime, drugs, as well as excessively high real interest rates, excessive public debt, and of course, whenever that is the case, inflation. This agenda should be open to new, as well as to old, problems and those of concern to all of Europe. The criterion for inclusion in an agenda of EU problems would be a serious divergence between private and public interest occurring in a number of EU member countries. Just as in the case of the convergence criteria, efforts should concentrate on the task or tasks generally regarded as most urgent. The absolute priority of monetary stability should only remain in force until the introduction of the Euro. Thereafter, it should become a public task besides others, whose place in the list of priorities would depend on how urgent they are.

Five difficulties with the co-operation mode

Anyone wishing to contribute to leaving the downward-sloping path of non-co-operation that leads to zero- and negative sums, and who would like to see inaugurated the co-operation mode which promises positive sums as a reward, should be prepared to encounter at least five difficulties:

1   How to make decision-makers and the large number of persons affected by them, aware of the consequences of non-co-operation, and the long-term advantages of co-operation. One can only move from non-co-operative to co-operative behaviour if the idea of co-operation and of a positive-sum game is already present in the minds of the actors. For, as the clinical psychiatrist Praszkier from Warsaw so correctly remarked, one usually desires something one knows. He observed that the mind of *homo post-sovieticus* is closed to the idea of the positive-sum game (Praszkier 1996). Unfortunately, this is also true for *homo oeconomicus* in the West. Romantic cultural pessimists are not alone in deploring the erosion of 'moral senti-ments' dating back to the stock of cultural values of pre-industrial society (cf. Hirsch 1976). Empirical investigations in the USA have revealed a rapid decline of 'social capital' (e.g. Putnam 1995), i.e. of people's ability to do something for other persons, to trust others (Davy 1995) and to enter into exchange relationships with one another that are not determined by economic advantage. This dangerous tendency is also observable in many other countries. Making (non-)co-operation understood is of universal concern.

2   How to explain for every specific social situation what are the results of non-co-operation and the preconditions for and advantages of co-operation. In this effort, the model of the prisoners' dilemma and other game-theoretical models, as well as the concept of socio-economic context, could be useful.

3   Detailing the co-operative interactions in every concrete situation and for every institution in danger of disintegration, and then to stage the respective positive-sum games. The theoretical models and concepts mentioned under item 2 above could again be helpful in practical implementation.

4   Making decision-makers and the persons affected by them accept the co-operation mode. This would not be easy, as reducing the priority of monetary stability would, overall, cause losses to capital market investors and a loss of influence to central banks. Both investors and central banks would fight to keep their advantages. Yet, one should not conclude that the introduction of the co-operation mode would be impossible. But EU banks are advocating the introduction of the Euro, even though this will make them lose most of their profitable foreign exchange business. Therefore, there is reason for hope: it is not just a necessary condition.

5   Making the co-operation mode worth reporting in the media. This will not be easy at all. There is already a lot of talk about co-operation but this term, just like the related term solidarity, is mostly used in a very vague way in

everyday political rhetoric. This is different from the concept of co-operation presented in this study, derived from the theory of strategic games and clearly defined in analytical terms. It will be hard to persuade the media, for which only 'bad news is good news' to take a serious interest in unspectacular co-operation that does not immediately promise to attract public attention. The same can be said of negotiated compromises: they are only worth being publicised in a derogatory way, as 'bad news'. The co-operation mode can hardly compete with the most radical form of non-co-operation, the duel, which seems to be the show best suited to the binary age of electronic mass media, be it in the form of a boxing contest, a TV duel between politicians or an entertainment show of the kind 'The winner takes all'. Making the truth known has always been difficult, but one should not stop trying. The rise and fall of Mr Berlusconi demonstrates that the quality of marketing, even in the media, cannot always replace the quality of what is being marketed.

Recognizing the potential of positive-sum games, their conception, staging and acceptance, was no easier during the long period after the Second World War, when positive-sum games predominated. They were then much easier to organize, as many people had personal experience of the consequences of non-co-operation ending in totalitarian dictatorship and the catastrophe of the Second World War. During that period co-operation was mostly threatened from 'outside'. Later danger emanated from the Soviet system, but stimulated various kinds of co-operation as a social defence within the threatened countries. In this period of reconstruction and expansion, co-operative behaviour was stimulated and remunerated by rapidly increasing income, investment and employment. At the end of the twentieth century the lessons learned from totalitarian dictatorship and the Second World War are losing influence. Increases in income, which are an important part of positive sums, are becoming smaller. Public values other than money or material goods are needed to replace the former goals of security. Non-material values have so far only appeared in their destructive form. For example, to the argument that continuation of the war would bring still more poverty and misery to more people, a Bosnian (or Serb or Croat) commander is said to have replied 'Even if the standard of living drops by another 50% we will still be better off if we gain our national independence'.

Would it be impossible to introduce non-monetary values to the positive sum and to make them acceptable at times when incomes having reached high levels stagnate or begin to go down? Could personal satisfaction not be derived from doing something that is also useful for other persons? It may still appear utopian today to suggest that co-operation should become the essence of politics. However, it will perhaps be possible to defend this idea in the future by recalling its origin: it can at least draw on the political and social theories of classical liberal economists like Adam Smith, on classical philosophy like that of Immanuel Kant, on the core of socialist thought (leaving aside the Marxist world of historical subjects and de-personalized collective actors), on Christian conceptions of society, on encyclicals by the Pope, as well as recently on the Communitarian 'I and We Paradigm' (Etzioni 1988).

Implementing positive-sum games in politics will not be utopian if it is based on a realistic view of current problems. The pressure of the problems at hand should establish a suitable hierarchy of tasks to be put on the public agenda. So far, after monetary stabilization, mainly deregulation and privatization have been awarded the status of public tasks. However, the recent scare over 'mad cow' disease shows how a potential catastrophe can contribute to a revival of the priority of public interest over short-term private interests.

Socio-economic factors encouraging co-operation

These suggestions could be criticised as utopian if it were not for the fact that human beings do not always act against their own interest. This is why we need a socio-economic context whose inherent logic minimizes the divergence between public and private interests. Ideally, it should include incentives to mobilize self-interest for the fulfilment of a public goals. Such a socio-economic context would have to create opportunities for the fulfilment of public tasks beyond stability targets, at the national level, but above all also at the supra-national level: through institutions such as the European Union, the OECD, The United Nations, the International Monetary Fund, the World Trade Organization, and the International Labour Office. The new socio-economic context should also facilitate and stimulate spontaneous and self-organized co-operation.

The new elements in such a context can be classified by reference to the four basic elements of socio-economic context.

In the new *world view*, the market will continue to play a central role in the fulfilment of individual and social needs. But if unrestrained pursuit of private interest increasingly harms others and thus the public interest, this world view recognizes the need for regulation. The effectiveness of regulatory institutions must therefore be restored. Monetary stability cannot be regarded as an intrinsic value, but one public task among others.

Restoring the power of national, as well as sub- and supra-national authority implies reversing the dominance of financial markets over product and labour markets. This presupposes reforms of important institutions like the IMF (e.g. change to a symmetrical adaptation mechanism) and of capital markets. The speed of financial transactions would have to be lowered (e.g. by separating the execution of a transaction from the time it begins to bear interest).

In the case of *relative prices, incomes, and costs*, non-monetary advantages (e.g. prestige, attention), should be used to fulfil other than monetary public tasks. For example, the cost of financial transactions could be raised by a 'Tobin tax' on them (Tobin 1982, and, elaborated further, Bhaduri and Matzner 1990). Political instruments must also be made more effective by a public agenda at all levels of political authority and the creation of suitable conditions for realizing that agenda.

If, as Hirschman suggests, citizen involvement shifts between private interest and public action, then the future of the welfare state could be viewed with optimism. However, we have no guarantee that such shifts will occur. The 'five difficulties' listed above make this clear. Optimism must rely on a less certain, yet quite promising argument: the future. The creation of a better socio-economic context, is not just a matter of forecasting; it is also the result of individual action.

Today, the creation of a socio-economic context conducive to co-operation transcends the possibilities of the nation state. Therefore this issue should be put on the agenda of international policy-makers. What other framework would be more appropriate to elaborate these ideas than the constitution of the European Union? In the EU research into specific subjects and problems will be as necessary as concerted political effort in which positive-sum games at various levels of decision-making and action are a priority.

We find ourselves in an era of change during which, in Schumpeter's words, old methods run into crisis, usually also manifested in financial crises. The crisis of the welfare state can certainly also be considered as a crisis of 'old methods', but not exclusively. Old and new methods practised by institutions other than the welfare state are making significant contributions.

Staging the co-operation mode and creating a socio-economic context favourable to co-operation are suggested as 'new methods' able to meet the challenges of the current period of change.

Notes

1   The author would like to thank Karl S. Althaler (Vienna), Horst Grabert (Berlin), Max Haller (Graz), Stuart Holland (London), Hardy Hanappi (Vienna), Manfred J. Holler (Hamburg), Hans Keman (Amsterdam), Gabriele Matzner-Holzer (Vienna), Sabine Mayer (Vienna), Claus Noé (Hamburg), Sylvia Pintarits (Munich), Manfred Prisching (Graz and Harvard), Sonja Puntscher-Riekmann (Vienna), Hazel Rosenstrauch (Vienna) and Gunther Tichy (Graz and Vienna) for their encouragement and critical remarks, and Silvia Plaza for translation and editing. Responsibility for the text of course rests entirely with the author.

2   In 1996 this corresponds to about US$ 50 billion. Considering the low standard of living at the time, this magnitude was of even greater significance. The largest donation per capita was made to the Austrian people. Why? Austria was threatened by communism most seriously (Kennan 1967).

3   The IMF statute lists as one of its objectives the reduction of fundamental disequilibria between countries. This would imply that countries should also reduce their (fundamental) surplus. In reality, the restriction of deficits has become the only policy accepted by the IMF.

4   It is true, however, that at present an increasing number of opposing voices can be heard (cf., inter alia, Holland 1994, Atkinson 1995, Sinn 1995, or Scharpf 1996).

5   Holler (1996) presents analytical definitions on this which largely correspond to the descriptions used here. It is interesting to note that Hayek refers to a similar social situation in the following words: 'Modern game theory has, moreover, shown while some games lead to the gains of one side being evenly balanced by the gains of the other, other games may produce overall net gain. The growth of the extended structure of interaction was made possible by the individuals' entry into the latter sorts of game, ones leading to overall increase of productivity' (Hayek 1988, p.154).

6   The writer Antonio Fian (1996) has pointed out that the expression 'end of the post-war period' may assume a terrible meaning.

References

Atkinson, A. B. (1995), 'The Economic Consequences of Rolling-Back the Welfare State'. Draft of Lectures at the Centre of Economic Studies, University of Munich.

Axelrod, R. (1984), *The Evolution of Co-operation*, New York: Basic Books.

Bhaduri, A. and Matzner, E. (1990), 'Relaxing the International Constraints on Full Employment Politics'. *Banca Nazionale di Lavoro Quarterly Review*, No. 172, March 1990.

Bhaduri, A. and Steindl, J. (1987), 'The Rise of Monetarism as a Doctrine'. *Thames Papers in Political Economy*, London: Northeast London Polytechnic.

Davy, B. (1995), 'Trust me!' in: Der öffentliche Sektor – *Forschungsmemoranden*, H. 3–4, Vienna: Institute of Public Finance, University of Technology

Etzioni, A. (1988), *The Moral Dimension. Towards a New Economics*, London: Collier Macmillan.

Fian, A. (1996), 'Sprache, Auschwitz, Kulturerbe, Unterhaltungsindustrie, Sprache – Zu unveröffentlichten Texten, Briefen und Polemiken Michael Gutenbruners' in *Hölle, verlorenes Paradies*. Aufsätze Droschel Verlag: Graz.

Guger, A. and Walterskirchen, E. (1988), 'Fiscal and Monetary Policy in the Keynes-Kalecki Tradition' in Kregel, J. A., Matzner, E. and Roncaglia, A. (eds), *Barriers to Full Employment*, Basingstoke/London: Macmillan.

Hayek, F. A. (1988), 'Play, the School of Rules', in *The Trend in Economic Thought. The Collected Works of F. A. Hayek*, Vol. III, London: Routledge.

Hirsch, F. (1976), *Social Limits to Growth*, Cambridge, MA: Harvard University Press.

Hirschman, A. O. (1982), *Shifting Involvements. Private Interest and Public Action*, Princeton N.J.: Princeton University Press.

Holland, S. (1994), *Toward a New Bretton Woods. Alternatives for the Global Economy*, Nottingham: Spokesman for Associate Research in Economy and Society.

Holler, M. F. (1996), personal letter to the author.

Kennan, G. F. (1967), *Memoirs 1925–1950*. Boston: Little, Brown.

Keynes, J. M. (1980) 'The Long-term Problem of Full Employment' in *The Collected Writings of John Maynard Keynes, Volume XXVII, Activities 1914–1946, Employment and Commodities*, London: Macmillan, pp. 320–5.

Kregel, J. A. (1994), 'Capital Flows: Globalization of Production and Financing Development'. *UNCTAD Review*, Geneva.

Kregel, J. A., Matzner, E. and Unterweger, P. (1995), 'Why the Jobs are Disappearing'. *Bulletin*, International Federation of Metalworkers, Geneva.

Lendi, M. (1992), 'Der Beitrag der Schweiz an das neue Europa', in Lendi, M. (ed.), *Bewährung des Rechts*, Zürich: Verlag der Fachvereine.

Matzner, E. (1982), *Der Wohlfahrtsstaat von Morgen. Entwurf eines zeitgemäßen Musters staatlicher Intervention*, Wien, Frankfurt/Main: Campusverlag.

Matzner, E. (1994), 'Instrument-Targeting or Context-Making? A New Look at the Theory of Economic Policy', *Journal of Economic Issues*, Vol. XXVIII/No. 2.

North, D. C. and Thomas, P. R. (1972) *The Rise of the Western World: A New Economic History*, Cambridge: Cambridge University Press.

Osborne, M. J. and Rubinstein, A. (1994), *A Course in Game Theory*, Cambridge, MA: MIT Press.

Popper, K. R. (1944), *The Open Society and Its Enemies*, two vols., London: Routledge.

Prager, T. (1962), *Wirtschaftswunder oder keines?* Wien.

Praszkier, R. (1996), 'Mental and Cognitive Factors in the Transformation Process'. Lecture at the 3rd AGENDA Workshop on 'Lessons from Transformation. Austrian Academy of Sciences, Research Unit for Socio-Economics, Vienna, 12–14 April 1996.

Putnam, R. D. (1995), 'Tuning In, Tuning Out: The Strange Disappearance of Social Capital' *Political Science & Politics*, December 1995.

Robbins, L. C. (1978), *The Theory of Economic Policy in English Classical Political Economy*, London: Macmillan.

Scharpf, F. W. (1996), 'The Impact of Globalization on Democracy and the Welfare State'. Founder's Prize Award Lecture to the 8th International Conference on Socio-Economics. Geneva University, 12–14 July 1996.

Sen, A. K. (1973), *On Economic Inequality*, Oxford: The Clarendon Press.

Sinn, H.-W. (1995), 'Theory of the Welfare State', *Scandinavian Journal of Economics*, No. 4, Stockholm.

Steindl, J. (1982), 'The Role of Household Savings in the Modern Economy', *Banca Nazionale del Lavoro Quarterly Review* No. 140, March, reprinted in J. Steindl, *Economic Papers 1941–1988*, Basingstoke: Macmillan, 1990.

Streek, L. (1996), 'Public Power Beyond the Nation State?' In: Boyer, R. and Drache, D. (eds), *States against Markets. The Limits of Globalization*, London: Routledge.

Tobin, J. (1982), 'Adjustment Responsibilities of Surplus and Deficit Countries'. In: Tobin, J. (ed.), *Essays in Economics, Theory and Policy*, Cambridge, MA: MIT Press.

Part II

Aspects of the
New Capitalism

5 'Big Business'

(Almost) twenty-five years on

Malcolm Sawyer

Introduction

I had the good fortune to work with Sam Aaronovitch over more than a decade, but would regard our book on *Big Business* (Aaronovitch and Sawyer 1975a) as the most wide-ranging and significant of our publications. In this chapter, I return to some of the issues which we raised in *Big Business* a quarter of a century after it was written.

As we said in the introduction to *Big Business*, it grew out of discussions while we were both at University College London and our realization of the complementarity of work which we had initially conducted quite independently. Sam had been working on issues of concentration, mergers and competition for many years (as reflected in Aaronovitch 1955, 1961) and then more formally for his Oxford PhD thesis starting in 1968 (Aaronovitch 1972). I had started teaching and research in the Autumn of 1968 and had developed some similar research interests. We were, though, coming to these subjects from different directions: Sam from an intellectual background in Marxism and a record of intense political activity, and I from an orthodox training at the London School of Economics with little exposure to heterodox economics (though those were the days of student protest) or even to industrial economics. Yet while we come from apparently diverse backgrounds, we converged on our general view of the workings of capitalism. Some would see this as a variant of Monopoly Capitalism (Sam had written a book with that phrase as part of the subtitle; Aaronovitch 1955). We would both argue that capitalism involves monopoly and competition, which are not the polar opposites presented by the structure–conduct performance paradigm (which we critically examined in Chapter 1 of *Big Business*), but rather are intimately linked through the tendency of competition to produce winners and losers. As a sub-heading in Aaronovitch (1955, p. 25) put it, 'Monopolies do not abolish all competition but give rise to fiercer rivalries'.

We were fortunate that we possessed complementary skills. Sam appreciated my technical skills from a mathematics degree and my knowledge of economic orthodoxy, and I valued his wide and insightful knowledge of Marxian theory. But perhaps most importantly, we liked each other and could work together in a non-dogmatic environment in which we could explore ideas. While *Big Business* focused on issues of concentration, competition and mergers, our later work was in some respects more narrowly focused on pricing behaviour, though with the effects of industrial structure very much in mind, and with the implications for inflation and its control also to the fore (Aaronovitch and Sawyer 1982, and Sawyer with Aaronovitch and Samson 1983).[1]

Writing a book in 1973 and 1974 with publication in 1975 on broad issues of capitalist development could be seen in retrospect as a foolhardy exercise for the trends of the previous quarter-of-a-century which most had confidently observed were about to be sharply changed. In *Big Business* we could write, for example, that economic slow downs now meant a reduction in the rate of growth but no fall in output. Of central importance for our analysis was the growth of concentration which had been observed in the UK in the 1950s and 1960s, and we analysed the reasons for this growth with emphasis on the role of mergers. It is still something of a mystery as to why the merger booms of the early 1970s and the second half of the 1980s appear not to have produced similar increases. The sectoral balance may be relevant since concentration data typically relates only to manufacturing, which is of declining importance (especially in terms of employment).

Big Business covered a range of issues from the rather dry and technical (e.g. factor analysis of different measures of concentration) through to the nature of managerial capitalism. Perhaps the central one was, 'What is the nature and consequences of competition?' (a topic to which I have returned increasingly in recent years, e.g. Sawyer (1992, 1994), and which has made appearances in writing on the causes of unemployment, e.g. Sawyer (1995)). For this chapter, though, I will focus on three other issues (though they are still closely related to that question of the nature of competition). In the next section, I address the question of what has happened to industrial concentration, and in particular why the trend towards increased concentration which we found for the 1950s and 1960s failed to continue after circa 1970. The subsequent section considers our concept of the costs of rivalry. As the term suggests, this incorporates the idea that competition has costs and benefits, but further that some of those costs fall on business itself, which will take steps to reduce those costs. The final main section discusses what we termed 'insiders' and 'outsiders' among shareholders, which arose from an attempt to take a more sophisticated view of the relationship between shareholders and managers than that portrayed in much of the 'divorce between ownership and control' literature.

Whatever happened to concentration?

In *Big Business*, and perhaps more clearly in some related papers (Aaronovitch and Sawyer 1974, 1975b), we found that there had been a rising trend of concentration in the UK through the 1950s and the 1960s (so that, for example, the share of the largest 100 firms in manufacturing industry had been increasing at 1 per cent point per annum for 20 years). Further, mergers were a major contributory factor and our own estimates for the period 1958 to 1967 were given in Aaronovitch and Sawyer (1975b) where we reported that at least half of the increase in concentration could be ascribed to acquisitions.[2] These findings were not unique to us, and authors such as Hannah and Kay (1977) and Prais (1976) presented similar empirical conclusions even if they worked from a different theoretical framework and drew different policy conclusions. While we did not fully accept some of the more dramatic projections on concentration, we thought that the forces pushing concentration upwards would continue, and we saw the merger boom of the early 1970s as some confirmation of that view (writing in 1974, the most recent Census of Production data from which we could calculate concentration figures related to 1968).[3]

The recent course of trends in industrial concentration can be conveniently summarized by the course of aggregate concentration. The share of the largest 100 firms in manufacturing net output was estimated to be 16 per cent in the first decade of this century, around 22–24 per cent in the inter-war period, and then rose steadily from a level of 22 per cent in 1949 to 41 per cent in 1968. Since then, the share of the largest 100 firms has been rather steady, and was 36 per cent in 1991 (with the share of employment at 29 per cent). The average level of concentration in manufacturing fell during the 1980s: the precise figures depend on what weights are applied in calculating the average. Using the relative size of industries in 1980 as weights, the average five-firm concentration ratio declined from 45.3 per cent in 1980 to 42.4 per cent in 1987. Allowing for international trade slightly sharpens the trend, with the trade-adjusted concentration ratio falling from an average of 34.5 per cent in 1980 to 29.8 per cent in 1987 (Henley 1994).[4] While only a relatively small part of the decline could be explained, the predominant factor in the decline of concentration was estimated to be a decline in the extent of economies of scale. Attaran and Saghaf (1988) for the United States[5] and Cortes (1998) for Japan indicate some upward movement in concentration, but at a relatively slow pace.

The figures on mergers and acquisitions indicate that the pace of merger activity has, if anything, been faster in the past 15 years or so than it was during the 1960s (which was itself higher than during the 1950s; cf. Table 7.1 in Aaronovitch and Sawyer 1975a). In the case of the UK, a real index of expenditure on acquiring subsidiaries (deflated by the FT 500 index of share prices) peaked at nearly 700 in the late 1980s compared with a figure of 357 at the height of the merger boom of the early 1970s (with index takes a value of 100 in 1963).[6] Since the immediate impact of an acquisition is to increase concentration, it would seem to be clearly the case that in the absence of take-overs concentration would have declined significantly. Two related questions arise from these figures: why did the trend change so sharply around 1970? and why do high levels of merger activity no longer raise concentration? (Although this may suggest that forces other than mergers are now tending to reduce concentration whereas prior to 1970 they would have left concentration broadly unchanged.)

It can first be noted that domestic concentration figures have lost some of their meaning as indicators of market dominance since international trade has grown. Of particular importance is the increased import penetration in manufactures. Cowling (1982) has pointed out that much of international trade involves multi-nationals. It is estimated that around 30 per cent of international trade involves goods and services being moved between branches of the same multi-national located in different countries. Therefore the interpretation of concentration figures may have to change over time. But it is a different matter to say that the trend in concentration would be different.

There are no doubt many reasons why recorded concentration is essentially flat (at least for the UK) after circa 1970, but here I review four aspects. The first is not a reason but rather an observation, namely that most of the statistics refer to manufacturing which has declined quite dramatically in importance. Its share of employment, for example, has fallen from 26.5 per cent in 1981 to 18 per cent in 1995, even though the drop in its share of output is less dramatic. Casual impressions suggest that concentration in some areas of distribution and services (e.g. food distribution, electrical goods) has increased, but there is a notable lack of information on concentration in the service sector.[7] The focus on the manu-facturing sector, which is enforced by the availability of statistics, may lead us to overlook what is happening in other sectors, and we have to leave open the possibility that concentration outside manufacturing has increased.

The second aspect is the general trend towards globalization which clearly means that concentration figures calculated at the national level have much less relevance for issues of market power and competition. Adjustments are often made (e.g. Henley 1994) for the role of international trade, though as Cowling (1982) points out, these adjustments make the implicit assumption that there are no links between the foreign suppliers of imports and the domestic producers, whereas often multi-national enterprises are both. It is also widely considered that one-third or more of international trade now takes the form of the movement of goods and services from one branch of a multi-national enterprise to another branch. Outward investment by companies has no immediate impact on the level of concentration, and may indirectly diminish domestic concentration if the outward investment is a substitute for domestic investment. As Stephen Hymer suggested, a domestic oligopolistic impasse may stimulate enterprises to expand overseas if domestic expansion requires expensive competitive wars against their rivals to increase their market share. Inward investment would only raise concentration if it were made by multi-nationals who already have a well-established domestic base. The initial investment by a 'newcomer' could tend to lower domestic concentration (depending on the size of that investment) when it involves construction of productive capacity or no change when it involves the acquisition of an established domestic producer. In the limiting case, international competition (or shifts in the composition of demand) can wipe out a domestic industry. If, as may often be the case, the domestic industry which dies was previously highly concentrated, then clearly average concentration declines.

In an era of transnational investment, the expansion of large companies will often occur in a range of countries. Hence, if company A which is a dominant producer in country X, expands into country Y, then concentration in X does not rise, and it may or may not rise in Y (depending on the scale and form of the inward investment). This may change the scope of the market in which A operates, and that would depend on whether it had previously been exporting to Y. The trends towards increased concentration are then exhibited at the international, rather than the national, level. There are many indicators on the increasing role of multi-national enterprises, but one which is particularly apposite here is that the number of foreign-owned firms among the largest (by net output) 100 manufacturing enterprises has risen from 18 in 1979 to 29 in 1992. In 1992, foreign-owned enterprises accounted for nearly 18 per cent of employment, and produced 24 per cent of net output, up from 19 per cent in 1983.[8] The growth of Japanese-owned enterprises has been quite rapid: growing in number from 24 in 1983 to 117 in 1992, with the share of employment rising from 0.5 per cent to 7.5 per cent (the figures for the Japanese share of net output are almost identical).

The third aspect arises from the changing structure of firms, and the mechanisms of control over employees and suppliers which they employ. In particular, the general trend over the past 20 years would appear to be more towards vertical disintegration (e.g. through contracting out), whereas in earlier times the trend appeared to be towards vertical integration.

Most of the discussion on measures of concentration has focused on the relative merits of various statistical measures (these, and the empirical relationship between them, are discussed in Aaronovitch and Sawyer 1975a, Chapter 3) and on the definition of industry and the appropriate level of aggregation. However, another aspect to which we drew some limited attention, is the definition of a firm. While this appeared to be an arcane issue (and anyway we had to accept the legal definition of a firm), it has become relevant in the era of downsizing and outsourcing.

Downsizing and outsourcing have been widely discussed over the past two decades or so. Whatever the pressures behind those changes, they often have the effect of reducing measured concentration. But the 'reality' of these recorded changes may be questioned. For the purpose of the measurement of concentration, the firm is defined in legal rather than economic terms: for example, employment is the number of people employed by a named legal entity rather than the number of people whose livelihood depends on that entity. A self-employed bricklayer is not included as part of the employees of a construction company even if the bulk of her/his work is for that company. Cowling and Sugden (1996) argue that a firm should be viewed as a centre of strategic decision making. From that it follows that a firm should be more identified with its 'sphere of influence' than with those it directly employs (though often the two will coincide). The growth of franchising and of own-brand products are two clear examples where the 'central' firm is much smaller in legal terms than its 'sphere of influence'. There has also been some well-known splitting of some large companies such as ICI and Hanson which would have the effect of reducing measured concentration.

Finally, there is the effect of possible shifts in government policy towards competition, size and the role of small businesses. In *Big Business*, we argued that 'at the risk of much over-simplification we see this thrust [of government policies] as rarely hindering the process of concentration (therefore allowing it to continue) and often actively fostering it' (p. 306) and could report government statements such as 'British industry faces the problem of the small size of many of its production units compared with those in the United States and some other competing countries' (*National Plan* 1965). The explicit encouragement of large scale has clearly diminished in the past 25 years, and been replaced by the general encouragement of small businesses and the cult of the entrepreneur. Nevertheless, as indicated above, mergers have continued apace, and any limit on them has been very muted.

There is some element of paradox here: in an era when the phenomenon of globalization is much in evidence and countries compete to have foreign direct investment on their soil, there is a policy emphasis on small businesses. Transnational corporations are almost by definition large companies: while it is conceivable that a company with less than 200 employees (the oft used definition of a small business) operates as a multi-national business, it would be rather unusual. Globalization itself is the result of the long process of capitalism expanding into new territory and of concentration and centralization.

In *Big Business*, we argued that 'advanced capitalist economies are typically oligopolistic' (p. 157) and that 'capitalism has certain characteristics which make the trend towards increased concentration inevitable in the sense that one cannot conceive any choice of policy which would have averted this without causing a basic change in the economic system' (p. 158). It is clear that economies have remained oligopolistic, even if concentration has not increased (at the national level) significantly. We can also mention, as an aside, that whatever has happened to the level of concentration, profitability has risen over the past 15 years or so, and the rise of globalization has not led to an intensification of competition at the expenses of profits (cf. Glyn 1997).

The costs of rivalry

In *Big Business*, we introduced the idea that there are costs associated with rivalry and competition. These costs are incurred by individual firms in the belief that by doing so their own profits are enhanced in the short run, over what they would be otherwise. (Hence those costs may be incurred to prevent profits falling, and given that other firms are bearing similar costs.) We then argued that those costs of rivalry would build up, undermining the collective profitability of the firms involved, leading to firms seeking measures to reduce the rivalry and the costs. Mergers and acquisitions were seen as one route of 'taking out' rivals and reducing those costs.

We defined 'the costs of competition as those costs of production and distribution which are generated within a system in which rivalry between independent units is a major way of co-ordinating production and distribution' (p. 218). We also viewed unemployment from a lack of co-ordination of consumption and investment plans as a cost of competition. Further, we argued that 'the costs of competition and rivalry are essentially costs imposed on society and on firms by other firms during the process of competition' (p. 223). We distinguished among the costs of rivalry 'those costs generated by the process of rivalry which fall on the firms themselves and which consequently could be reduced by firms if the latter could reduce rivalry' (p. 219).

The general theme of the 'costs of rivalry' is that there are costs associated with the process of competition, and that whatever the merits of the competitive process in the employment of resources through investment and research and development, it also involves costs. The formal 'demonstration' of the benefits of competition comes from the static model of perfect competition and the use of the Pareto criteria. But atomistic competition has shown a general unstable tendency and the processes of concentration and centralization generally continue apace (cf. *Big Business*, Chapter 1).[9]

There are some common features of this general view of competition with that which is presented in Frank and Cook (1995) for situations where 'winner-takes-all' (to use part of the title of Frank and Cook's book). Frank and Cook particularly apply their ideas to explaining the widening disparities of individual incomes and to sectors such as entertainment and the media, sport and education. The three key (and related) aspects in our view of this approach are:

1   As the expression indicates, there is no reward for being second and 'winner takes all'. The key element here is that there is a sharp discontinuity between first place (whether that means being the first to do something or being the largest) and second place. The example which Frank and Cook cite is that winning an Olympic gold medal in a high-profile event leads to fame and glory (and endorsements), whereas finishing second rates 'a footnote in the history books'.

2   The gains from competition (in some spheres) are mainly relative rather than absolute. Standing up at a sports event when others are sitting brings a gain in terms of the view. But all standing up yields no gain in view over all sitting down, and indeed may involve some loss of comfort. As Frank and Cook argue, extensive training and performance-enhancing drugs can raise an individual's absolute performance to some degree, but the effect on relative performance is more important to the individual.

3   The competition to be first generates wasteful investment. This general idea has applied to, for example, patent races where any firm entering the race incurs costs, but only the first one receives the patent and the profits which arise therefrom. The social gains arise from the patent, but the social costs arise from the number of firms and the costs which each incurs.

One other issue which Frank and Cook raise is the use of custom and norms to limit competition to be first. Norms (whether backed by some legal or social sanctions) are built up among people who interact with one another, and are likely to be effective at the regional or national level. The spread of capitalism carries with it the spread of capitalist norms. But a feature of the past 30 years or so has been the expansion of different capitalisms, notably the spread of multi-nationals not only from the United States and United Kingdom but from

Germany and Japan (and many others). The norms of one group of multi-nationals clashes with the norms of others, although there is the common 'norm' of the desire for profits. The clash of norms appears as an intensification of competition, but may be a preliminary to the establishment of a new set of norms which again will limit the intensity of competition.

In retrospect, I would see the significance of the notion of costs of competition and rivalry arising from two different elements. The first is that rivalry imposes costs on firms which they can seek to reduce through the elimination of that rivalry, hence mergers and acquisitions. The second is that competition does not lead to optimal outcomes, and that there is a wide variety of costs imposed on society by competition. These may range from the costs of unemployment and excess capacity through to inefficiencies of production.

Insiders and outsiders

In *Big Business* we presented a view of the large corporation in which separation between ownership and control ran counter to the then-prevailing orthodoxy as represented by the managerial theories of the firm (e.g. Berle and Means 1932, Baumol 1959, Marris 1964 and popularized by Galbraith 1969). In this section, I want to argue that many of the features of the large corporation presented in our view of the large corporation have become increasingly relevant in the intervening years, and the picture presented by the managerial theorists has faded.

We acknowledged that there was some separation between ownership and control in that many shareholders were not involved in decision-making and management of the large corporation. But we went on to argue that 'the separation of ownership from control has been made too "absolute", its extent exaggerated and its significance misinterpreted' (p. 160).

Our approach to the large corporation was in terms of three sets of 'players', namely the directors and top executives, those shareholders whom we labelled as 'insiders', and those labelled as 'outsiders'. 'Insiders' were 'those who have both a substantial stake in a firm and play some kind of executive and controlling role' (p. 162), while the 'outsiders' were those 'who hold equity in companies which they do not seek to control'. It was the separation between the directors and the 'insiders' which we saw as being too 'absolute', and in effect saw an alliance between the directors and the 'insiders' at the expense of the 'outsiders'. In any event, we argued that directors and top executives were substantial owners of shares.

The 'outsiders', though, could exercise some influence, notably at the time of take-over bids, in the sense that their ownership rights enabled them to decide the future ownership of the firms. But outside those situations, individual shareholders can exercise little influence. The rising importance of institutional shareholders (and the corresponding decline of individual shareholders) can change the balance between 'insiders' and 'outsiders' in that institutional shareholders have at least the potential to intervene in the management of the companies which they own.[10]

We pointed to evidence that managerial income was increasingly linked with profits (rather than with size and sales, as postulated by the managerial theorists). There can be little doubt that notions of performance-related pay have been used to justify a closer linkage between the income of directors and top executives and profitability, and in turn that these linkages have led to large increases in their incomes. Although there may be doubts over the degree to which these linkages provide incentives for the executives, and whether the size of the linkage is sufficient for this purpose, there can be little doubt about the increasing scale of their use. The use of share options and the like mean that the executives become owners in the company, and this is a significant route through which the effects of the separation between ownership and management are muted. The increasing use of profit-related pay has also been a significant source of increasing inequality as larger incomes accrue to the top executives.

We also introduced the notion of 'profits of control': the 'power to control a firm includes power of allocating some portion of the profit in a variety of forms (including some which are treated as costs, open or concealed), and therefore reducing the possible profit that could otherwise have been declared' (p. 166). The control lies with the executives and the 'insiders', enabling them to cream off these 'profits of control'. One of the mechanisms through which that creaming off takes place is executive pay, which, as just mentioned, has been increasing rapidly.

Conclusion

It is a salutary experience to review what one wrote (or helped to write) nearly a quarter of a century ago, especially when the work was a mixture of theory, evidence, policy and prediction. One is tempted to look for aspects of the theorising which could be seen as the forerunner of ideas which others developed. In this short paper, I have attempted to answer the question of why concentration has been broadly constant since the early 1970s. I have also pointed to two ideas in *Big Business*, the concept of the 'costs of rivalry', and the distinction between 'insiders' and 'outsiders' among company shareholders. These ideas have stood the test of time and are worthy of further development.

Notes

1 I am also particularly grateful to Sam in his role as editor of a series on Radical Economics, as the idea for me to write a book on Michal Kalecki (Sawyer 1985) arose from our discussions and he enthusiastically promoted the idea.
2 We calculated that acquisitions raised the 25 firm concentration ratio by 4.32 per cent (against an actual increase of 3.91 per cent) but the 100 firm ratio by 5.64 per cent compared with the actual increase of 10.38 per cent.
3 'If the rate of increase of concentration from 1958–68 has continued up to 1974 then the average level of five-firm concentration would now stand out 76 per cent, compared with an estimated 52 per cent in 1935. One rather circumstantial piece of evidence of the accuracy of this 1974 estimate comes from figures of acquisitions, and suggests that 76 per cent may be about the right order of magnitude' (Aaronovitch

and Sawyer 1974, p. 16). These five-firm concentration ratios were measured at the 4-digit level and are not comparable with those cited in the text.

4 See also Davies and Geroski (1997).

5 They report that 'all these changes, though small, pointed towards more concentration within the largest 500 manufacturing companies' (p. 1502).

6 For a graphical representation of the trend in merger activity, see Sawyer (1996).

7 In *Big Business*, we devoted a chapter to concentration outside of the manufacturing sector (Chapter 5). A major source of information was the *Census of Distribution*, which has been discontinued. I am unaware of any systematic study of recent trends in concentration outside the manufacturing sector.

8 The source of the data in this and the next paragraph is Business Statistics Office, *Census of Production*, 1992, London: HMSO, 1995

9 This is not contradicted by the view that concentration has levelled off in many countries (though what has happened world-wide). We noted in *Big Business* that there are few, if any, examples of industries moving from an oligopolistic structure to an atomistically competitive one (though there are clearly cases where an initial monopoly becomes an oligopoly). The experiences of the de-regulated industries in the USA and UK are instructive in this regard.

10 Ownership by financial institutions (mainly banks, unit trusts, pension funds and insurance companies) has risen almost continuously, and the proportion of shares held by individuals declined, for example from 30.4 per cent at the end of 1981 to 20.3 per cent in 1993 (figures taken from CSO, *Share Register Survey Report*, London: HMSO 1991 and 'The 1993 share register survey', *Economic Trends*, October 1993).

References

Aaronovitch, S. (1955), *Monopoly: A Study of British Monopoly Capitalism*, London: Lawrence and Wishart.

Aaronovitch, S. (1961), *The Ruling Class*, London: Lawrence and Wishart.

Aaronovitch, S. (1972), 'Determinants of merger activity in U.K. manufacturing industry, 1955–1968', D.Phil. Thesis, University of Oxford.

Aaronovitch, S. and Sawyer, M. (1974), 'The concentration of British manufacturing', *Lloyds Bank Review*, no. 114.

Aaronovitch, S. and Sawyer, M. (1975a), *Big Business*, London: Macmillan.

Aaronovitch, S. and Sawyer, M. (1975b), 'Mergers, growth and concentration', *Oxford Economic Papers*, Vol. 27, no. 1, pp. 136–55.

Aaronovitch, S. and Sawyer, M. (1982), 'Price Change and Oligopoly', *Journal of Industrial Economics*, Vol. 30, pp. 137–48.

Attaran, M. and Saghaf, M. (1988), 'Concentration trends and profitability in the US manufacturing sector: 1970–84', *Applied Economics*, Vol. 209, pp. 1497–510.

Baumol, W. (1959), *Business Behaviour, Value and Growth*, London: Macmillan.

Berle, A. and Means, G. C. (1932), *The Modern Corporation and Private Property*, New York: Commerce Clearing House.

Cortes, B. S. (1998), 'Trends in industrial concentration in Japan, 1983–92', *International Review of Applied Economics*, Vol. 12, No. 2, pp. 271–82.

Cowling, K. (1982), *Monopoly Capitalism*, London: Macmillan.

Cowling, K. and Sugden, R. (1996), 'The essence of the modern corporation: markets, strategic decision-making and the theory of the firm', mimeo.

Davies, S. W. and Geroski, P. A. (1997), 'Changes in concentration, turbulence, and the dynamics of market shares', *Review of Economics and Statistics*, Vol. 79(3), pp. 383–91.

Frank, R. and Cook, P. (1995), *The Winner-Take-All Society*, New York: The Free Press.

Galbraith, J. K. (1969), *The New Industrial State*, Harmondsworth: Penguin.

Glyn, A. (1997), 'Does aggregate profitability really matter?', *Cambridge Journal of Economics*, Vol. 21(5), pp. 593–620.

Hannah, L. and Kay, J. (1977), *Concentration in Modern Industry*, London: Macmillan.

Henley, A. (1994), 'Industrial deconcentration in U.K. manufacturing', *Manchester School of Economic and Social Studies*, Vol. 62, pp. 40–59.

Marris, R. (1964), *The Economic Theory of 'Managerial' Capitalism*, London: Macmillan.

National Plan (1965), London: HMSO.

Prais, S. J. (1976), *The Evolution of Giant Firms in Britain*, Cambridge: Cambridge University Press.

Sawyer, M. (with S. Aaronovitch and P. Samson) (1983), *Business Pricing and Inflation*, London: Macmillan.

Sawyer, M. (1985), *The Economics of Michal Kalecki*, London: Macmillan.

Sawyer, M. (1992), 'On the nature of markets', *Social Concept*, Vol. 6.

Sawyer, M. (1994) 'Post Keynesian and Marxist notions of competition: towards a synthesis', in Glick, M. (ed.), *Competition, Technology and Money: Classical and Post-Keynesian Perspectives*, Aldershot: Edward Elgar.

Sawyer, M. (1995), *Unemployment, Imperfect Competition and Macro-economics*, Aldershot: Edward Elgar.

Sawyer, M. (1996) 'Industry: Its Structure and Policies Towards It', in Artis, M. (ed.), *The U.K. Economy*, Oxford: Oxford University Press.

6 Military expenditure and globalization[1]

Ron Smith

The end of the Cold War and the extension of capitalist globalization to much more of the world have implications for conflict and military expenditures. This essay reviews the changed strategic situation, the extended process of globalization, how this process impacts on different types of states and the military decision-making process within them. Globalization will influence military expenditures through its effects on internal conflicts, military technology and organization, and the organization of the system as a whole. However, these influences will be complex and contradictory.

Introduction

When Jan Toporowski asked me to write a chapter for Sam's Festschrift, my immediate response was to use the opportunity to reconsider the book Sam and I created with Jean Gardiner and Roger Moore: *The Political Economy of British Capitalism* (Aaronovitch *et al.* 1981). After a moment's thought about the magnitude of the task, I decided to reconsider just one bit of one chapter: the treatment of military spending. This was largely based on my papers on military expenditure and capitalism (Smith 1977, 1978). The basic argument was that military expenditure is best explained in terms of its strategic functions for capitalism, and that while military expenditure is rational for capitalism – necessary to defend the system against a variety of threats – it is also contradictory: undermining the economic base through its negative effects on accumulation and growth.[2] This argument was contrasted with other explanations common on the left which emphasized either the domestic political power of a Military Industrial Complex or the domestic economic functions of military expenditure. The domestic politics, while important, are better seen as a transmission mechanism for the strategic requirements and there is little evidence for economic functionalist explanations of military expenditure.[3]

   While I would still emphasize the priority of strategic explanations of military expenditure, the end of the Cold War and the removal of antagonism between capitalist and communist systems has completely changed the strategic environment. The demise of central planning and the extension of 'market friendly' policies to most of the world has left capitalism as the only system, and a system that can now internationalize over much larger portions of the globe. Later, I discuss the changing strategic environment that followed the move from two competing systems to a single system, and the main characteristic of the single system, the process of globalization. Military expenditures are determined by governments. Therefore, the way that globalization influences different types of states is central to the explanation of military expenditure. This point, along with the transmission mechanisms within states by which perceptions of threat, conflict and system dynamics are transformed into military expenditures and forces are discussed later. Finally, the linkages between globalization, conflict and military expenditure are reviewed. I have chosen a very narrow focus, and there is a range of other issues such as the economic effects of military expenditure, which I have ignored. Hartley and Sandler (1995) is a good introduction to these wider issues.

The changing strategic environment

In earlier papers, I suggested that there were three dimensions to the strategic requirement. 'The capitalist states as a group must defend the system, the "free world" from the threat of communism as represented by the Warsaw Pact, China and national liberation movements in the third world. Secondly, among the capitalist states, inter-imperialist influence and the ability of a hegemonic power to organise the system depend on relative military power. Finally, within each state, military expenditure provides an insurance against internal threats to the existing order, by virtue of both the integrative functions of militarism and the potential for domestic coercion provided by military power'. (Smith 1977, p. 74). The first dimension, the inter-systemic conflict, has disappeared; the second dimension, the intra-systemic dynamics, has become much more problematical; though the third dimension, the domestic role, remains important in many countries.

The dissolution of the Soviet Union, the transformation of the Chinese economy, and the changing ideology of revolutionary movements in the Third World have completely altered the strategic landscape. Western states may perceive potential Russian and Chinese threats; however, they are not communist threats or ideological challenges to the economic organization of the system. Along with the demise of the 'Second World' of Central Planning, has been a transformation in what, for lack of a better term, I will continue to call the Third World. A number of countries that were both poor and slow growing, including China, have taken off rapidly and some are even approaching the per-capita incomes of the traditional industrialized countries. However, much of the world's population remain incredibly poor and, particularly in sub-Saharan Africa, are getting poorer. Insurrections remain common, but they are mainly driven by programmes that bear little ideological relation to those of the national liberation movements of an earlier generation. When traditional national liberation movements come to power, they are likely to be economically conservative, as in South Africa; keen to establish their credentials with the World Bank and foreign investors.

The lack of systemic enemies is reflected in military expenditure. Total NATO spending in constant 1990 dollars fell over the period 1987 to 1996 by 25 per cent: from $530 billion to $395 billion (SIPRI 1997, Appendix 6B). As a share of GDP, over the same period, military expenditure fell from 6.3 per cent to 3.8 per cent in the US and from 4.6 per cent to 3.0 per cent in the UK. The burden of military expenditure was reduced in all the other NATO countries except Turkey. For most NATO countries, the downward trend in military expenditure seems likely to continue. Most countries have been conducting continuous defence reviews for the last few years, trying to adjust force structures to lower budgets and new realities. In the UK, there were the Conservative reviews: 'Options for Change' and 'Front Line First' and then the Labour Strategic Defence Review. There have been similar patterns of reviews in the US: the Bottom Up Review and the Quadrennial Review. France was slow to review but has now done so, abolishing conscription and reconsidering its interventionist strategy in Africa.

Lack of data makes it difficult to judge what has happened in the former communist countries. In Russia, military expenditures have almost certainly fallen, primarily as a result of economic constraints. In China, the share of GDP devoted to the military has probably remained stable, but the economy has been growing so rapidly that this finances quite large increases in military spending. Other rapidly growing East Asian countries have also been increasing their real military spending, though not their share of GDP. The end of the Cold War also saw a reduction in the arms trade, with exports of major weapons systems falling from $44 billion in 1987 to $23 billion in 1996 (SIPRI 1997, Appendix 9A). The main exception to this trend was again East Asia: China, South Korea and Taiwan accounted for over 30 per cent of the total arms imports. The economic troubles of the Asian tigers will undoubtedly affect the growth of their military expenditures and arms imports.

Military force plays a central role in insurance against the internal threats which many governments face; most conflict is within and not between states. Since the end of the Cold War, the number of major armed conflicts has declined from 37 in 1990 to 27 in 1996 (SIPRI 1997, Table 1.2).[4] In 1995, all the conflicts were internal, while in 1996, all but one – the India–Pakistan confrontation over Kashmir – were internal. Dan Smith (1997) provides a list of 93 wars between 1990 and 1995, which involved 70 states and killed about 5.5 million people. Of these one was a large inter-state war (the Gulf War) while three were small interstate wars (Peru–Ecuador, India–Pakistan and Senegal–Mauritania). Three wars were associated with the dissolution of states, former Yugoslavia, Armenia–Azerbaijan and Ethiopia–Eritrea; the rest were internal.

While inter-state wars are rare, inter-state antagonism is common. There are a large number of bi-polar hostilities which have prompted arms races, such as Greece–Turkey, India–Pakistan, Iran–Iraq, North–South Korea, Taiwan–China and Syria–Israel. In the Middle East and East Asia there are a range of disputed issues, over territory, sea-space and access to water, and these disputes encourage countries to acquire the military capability to protect what they see as their rights. However, for much of the globe, such as Europe outside the Balkans, and Latin America, there are few specific antagonisms or disputes. Yet the countries continue to spend on the military. This is justified partly by the argument that armed forces provide an insurance against unspecified threats which may arise in the future, and partly by the argument that countries need the capability to project force. This may be at a relatively low level, serving on UN peace-keeping missions, or it may be at a higher level, such as the UK use of force to recover the Falklands–Malvinas from Argentina. In terms of force-projection capability, the US is unique.

The specific security issues – internal conflicts, regional antagonisms, the US role as a global sheriff – appear in a quite different light in the context of a single economic system than they did in the context of two competing economic systems. The main characteristic of that single system is globalization and I will briefly discuss that process.

Globalization

The concept of globalization has been the subject of substantial dispute. I use it partly as a description of certain pervasive processes which interact, and partly as a synonym for the internationalization of capitalism, since this has been the driving force behind globalization. The underlying processes involved in globalization include:

1 Technological: particularly changes in the costs and capabilities of methods of transport and communications.
2 Economic: increased cross-border flows of goods, money and factors of production, labour and capital.
3 Political: the increased importance of international institutions, from the IMF to the EU, relative to national governments.
4 Social: the creation of an international Civil Society, which links individuals into international communities defined by characteristics other than nationality, such as profession, religion or interests, and which shares an international culture which may displace traditional national cultures.

While globalization is characteristic of capitalism, it is not inexorable. The heyday of globalization was the late nineteenth century, but it was reversed by the First World War. In the nineteenth century, changes in transport and communications technology, particularly the steamship and telegraph, led to very rapid growth in trade and international finance. The transport cost reductions which opened the European market to American grain had political and economic consequences which were as profound as any produced by the new international division of labour today. Measures of openness (e.g. ratios of exports or foreign investment to GDP) have only recently achieved their pre-First World War levels and the nineteenth century flows of labour dwarf those we see today. The economic driving mechanisms of most current concern: the power and productivity of markets and free trade, their destructive effect on traditional social patterns, their globalization and the consequent growing international inequality, were all described by Marx and Engels in the Communist Manifesto. This historical perspective is useful in giving us another era to judge the political and security impacts of globalization.[5]

There are two general visions of the impact of globalization on conflict; both dating back to at least the eighteenth century. The liberal vision was that the close economic links and extensive trade associated with the expansion of capital make the costs of war much higher and thus reduce the probability of war. Of course, the extent to which economic integration inhibits war depends on the priority given to economic interests relative to other goals and the degree to which non-violence is a norm. The Manchester Liberals, with their belief that trade would stop war were only partly right. The First World War followed a period when there was a very high level of economic integration and apparently strong international norms of non-violence through, for instance, the Socialist International.

The alternative mercantilist vision sees globalization as a process by which national capitals, represented by their respective states, compete against each other with weapons such as competitiveness and protection. The mercantilist explanation emphasizes that when fundamental interests are threatened, this economic antagonism can easily turn into military antagonism. The Leninist explanation of the First World War – war as the pursuit of economic interests by other means – has its echoes among the more apocalyptic US mercantilists today. However, the internationalization of capitalism has substantially reduced the importance of these state-firm links and the extent to which American multinationals are fundamentally American, rather than global profit maximizers is a matter of dispute.

Although they differ in their degree of integration into the international system, states are more likely to see themselves as victims of international market forces rather than as representatives of them. National states have lost autonomy over monetary, fiscal and exchange rate policy to international market forces, mediated by flows of finance, multi-national firms and international organizations. The Malaysian prime minister's complaints about George Soros and other international speculators after the 1997 financial crisis or the Kenyan and South Korean resistance to the demands of the IMF are examples. US domestic political discussion of trade issues dwells on the vulnerability of the US to international market forces and the new international division of labor.

Globalization and states

Military expenditure decisions are made by governments of nation states within an international system. Thus, the impact of globalization on military expenditures will be mediated by the way particular types of states fit into the international economic and political systems. It is useful to distinguish three types: pre-modern states driven by personal interests; modern states driven by national interests; and post-modern states driven by systemic interests.

Pre-modern states are largely predatory, dominated by acquisitive individuals or groups who see power as an opportunity for personal gain. They are not integrated into the globalizing sytem, but are subject to occasional intervention by that system. They have little in the way of impersonal national bureacratic and legal structures; they have difficulty in establishing either legitimacy or stability and are prone to succession crises, since much of the power is personal and easily challenged. The kingdoms of feudal Europe and the 'kleptocracies' of the current Third World are pre-modern in this sense. Conflict is endemic, and although primarily internal can easily spill over borders; the papers in Volden and Smith (1997) discuss these conflicts. For the international system, and for international capital, the problem is seen as 'state failure': the inability of governments in countries such as Somalia, Zaire or Liberia to meet the minimal functions of a state, maintenance of order and security of property.

To the extent that globalization makes countries more interdependent, the spillovers of domestic conflict from these states are greater and there is more incentive for neigbours or the international community to intervene to try to resolve them. However, most of these countries are so poorly integrated into the international system that the incentives to intervene are rather small. Under imperialism, the Third World was worth exploiting as a source of cheap labour, natural resources and captive markets. Under the new international division of labour, many parts of the Third World lack even the minimum social, human and physical infrastructure capital to make them worth exploiting. When international firms operate in these countries (primarily in extractive industries, for there are few other profitable opportunities), they are likely to provide their own order through heavily armed private security forces.

Modern states, which arose in Europe from the seventeenth century, are based on a permanent state apparatus and a notion of loyalty to a national identity often – though not always – attached to membership of an ethnic group. They rested on a notion of sovereignty as the state being the ultimate power within an area, and subject to no power above it. One of the main characteristics of modern states in Europe was their tendency to fight each other to establish their claims over territories and resources and their relative power relationships. In Europe, the process of state formation was a very brutal business, the product of centuries of war. Whether new states in the rest of the world need a series of protracted wars to establish themselves as modern states has been extensively debated.

Post-modern states are highly integrated, both economically and socially, into the international system. They are typically rich and they perceive the cost of military conflict as being very high and dispute resolution by other means more effective. The cost of military conflict is high because it disrupts economic interdependence, provokes non-violent international retaliation (runs on the currency, withdrawal of foreign investment etc.), and because it is now very expensive to project force at long distances to protect one's interests. Even Britain and France, both very reluctant post-modernizers, are starting to recognize this. This interest in peace is reinforced by norms, established over long periods of time, which legitimate that interest, these norms being most developed in traditionally neutral countries such as Sweden and Switzerland. Of course, the links between post-modernism and military expenditure may be complex. Neutral countries have tended to spend more on defence than similar allied powers.

For post-modern states multilateral organizations can act as an alternative to the use of force, either through insurance, arbitration, international pressure or conflict resolution. Spain tries to recover Gibraltar through the EU and NATO rather than by force. Small countries which cannot afford the option of large forces, sign up with organizations like NATO, to provide an insurance for their security. This was clearly an element in the desire to join by many of the former Warsaw Pact countries. Many in France and Germany saw the European Community as insurance against another war between them. Perhaps one of NATO's greatest achievements has been to stop Greece and Turkey actually going to war (so far, although without the Soviet threat in the background, US and NATO leverage on them may be less effective).

While the United States is post-modern in being constrained by systemic interests, these interests constrain it quite differently from the way in which smaller states are thereby constrained. The United States is less dependent or interdependent than other states; it is unique in its global capability to project military power; and, because of its importance in international capitalism, it has both more incentive and more capability to use force to protect systemic interests. Thus, it has a hegemonic role in organizing the system.

The classification above, based on how the states fitted into the international system, is correlated with the more common classification in terms of type of government: from autocratic to democratic; pre-modern states tend to be auto-cratic; and post-modern states tend to be democratic. Empirically, democracies are as prone as other forms of state to go to war, but they rarely do so with other democracies. Internal conflict also tends to be lower in democracies (where there are alternative routes to obtain change) and autocracies (where it is repressed), and higher in between. There is a vast literature on this apparent pattern of 'democratic peace' and its implications for future conflict levels. Gleditsch and Hegre (1997) and Hegre *et al.* (1997) are recent quantitative contributions.

Transmission mechanisms

Perceptions of threats and interests, national or systemic, are converted into military expenditures through a domestic transmission mechanism, the military and industrial experts who decide, or try and persuade the civil society, which weapons and forces are needed. One could argue that the falls in military expenditure have been smaller and the reviews less radical than the changed situation warranted, because the transmission mechanism – the military industrial specialists – have not adjusted to the new realities. Industrial countries have continued to invest in the type of equipment optimized to fight the Cold War. This inertia is partly the product of the influence of the powerful military and industrial coalitions that have formed around traditional weapons systems, and partly the product of lack of imagination: it is difficult to imagine what military equipment will be required in the new international situation. Given a generalized desire for insurance against unknown threats but not knowing what to buy, the temptation is to continue to buy what was useful in the past: prepare to fight the last war.

The Cold War, while dangerous and threatening was rather predictable: each side knew who, where and how they were supposed to fight and could plan accordingly. The world is now less dangerous, but is also less stable and predictable. Military planners do not know who, where and in particular how they are supposed to fight. The most direct link between capitalism and military expenditure is the way the structure of the economy influences the structure of military forces; how the forces of production determine the forces of destruction. The transformation in technology and production methods within capitalism as a whole has implications for the nature of future conflict and armaments. After the Second World War, military and civilian technologies tended to diverge but are now reconverging. In many areas military technology is behind commercial technology, and the focus is on technological spin-in to the military rather than spin-off from it. The products of commercially driven information and communications technologies, nanotechnology and biotechnology have the potential to revolutionize military affairs.

These new technologies may be more useful to non-state agents than to traditional military organizations. Cheap and accurate remotely piloted vehicles, using global positioning systems are now becoming widely used for crop spraying. With suitable chemical or biological weapons, they provide a reliable strategic delivery system for weapons of mass destruction at low cost. The Sarin attack on the Tokyo underground is an indication that non-state agents can use these technologies. Military organizations, locked into traditional weapons systems, and spending vast amounts of money trying to make marginal advances at the frontiers of mature technologies, are at a serious disadvantage.[6] The transformation of combat and military organization by technology is not a new phenomenon; Engels in *Anti Duhring* made the same point about battleships and their vulnerability to torpedoes (Engels 1975, p. 199). To further complicate matters there is often little scope for a military response to what many states see as the most pressing security concerns: terrorism, drugs, environmental and demographic threats as well as more speculative threats like information warfare.

In many explanations of military expenditure the defence industry plays a crucial role in the transmission mechanism. Defence industries are crucial attributes of modern states, pre-modern states do not have them, and it is difficult to imagine what a post-modern defence industry would look like since the impact of globalization has been relatively muted in the defence industry. For the firms in that industry the state was their dominant customer, and for the state the firms were a strategic resource, providing the security of self-sufficiency in arms. But now no state can be self-sufficient in modern weapons. Even the US, which is closest to self-sufficiency, is dependent on components and sub-systems bought on the world market. Missiles which are American on the outside are Japanese on the inside. While the US can afford to attempt to produce the full range of state-of-the-art weapons, no other country can even afford to try and has to depend on trade and international collaboration to meet their needs. Thus, transnational defence links are growing.

The end of the Cold War has seen rapid consolidation in the US industry, with the formation of a handful of dominant companies: Boeing–McDonnell Douglas, Lockheed–Martin and Raytheon. This concentration was aided by Pentagon subsidies and the perception by many firms that their defence divisions were worth more to the budding monopolists than to themselves. Defence specialists like General Dynamics downsized, and Civilian firms like Ford, IBM and General Motors reduced their defence dependence by selling their military units to competitors. The consolidation allowed restructuring and the US industry cut both employment and costs substantially. In Europe, where excess capacity was larger and costs higher, market forces have not produced a comparable restructuring, primarily because the links between the large defence firms and national states has proved a major obstacle to transnational mergers. There are a range of collaborative and joint ventures between European arms manufacturers, but they have not allowed the restructuring and cost saving that the US mergers and acquisitions produced. The symbiosis of defence industry and state is complex. There are many examples of defence firms shaping state policies, particularly with respect to arms exports in the UK and France; but European defence firms also suffer from their dependence on small national states and markets. There is a drive to internationalization by the European defence firms which need to establish the scale to compete with the US giants, but that drive is being constrained by the nationalism of their states. That same nationalism inhibits the formation of European defence forces.

Conclusion

This brief and very selective review suggests a number of ways that globalization might influence military expenditures, but it does not suggest that the links are direct or simple. The end of the Cold War and extended globalization influence military technology and organization, the prevalence of conflicts, and the international organization of the system, but the influences are complex.

For example, there is a variety of causal links between the end of the Cold War and the decline in the number of conflicts. There is less incentive for the super-powers to support local proxies in domestic conflict, and less scope for dissaffected local groups to gain resources and support by involving the super-powers. Peace-making is also relatively easier when the UN is united. However, the dissolution of some of the former communist countries, the Soviet Union and Yugoslavia in particular, has added new conflicts to the older ones. In some cases the Cold War may have inhibited conflict, where the super-powers restrained their clients, fearing that a local conflict could escalate into a global confrontation.

The evolution of the structure of the system as a whole will influence the prevalence of conflict. For instance, Mansfield (1994) conducts a statistical analysis of the association in the period 1880–1980 between the frequency of war, the concentration of power (measured by the dispersion of economic, military and demographic variables) and trade (the export–GDP ratio), which could be interpreted as a globalization measure. His main conclusion is that the influence of the concentration of power on war is non-monotonic: wars are less common when power is relatively dispersed or highly concentrated, and more common in between. Similarly, trade is higher when power is dispersed or concentrated, and lower in between. Even after allowing for the concentration of power, increased trade tends to reduce the probability of war. This is a similar pattern to that noted by Olson (1982) within countries. Distributional conflict is lower (and growth higher) when there is either a dominant agent, for instance an encompassing coalition of labour and capital, or when there are a large number of small competitive actors. Distributional conflict is higher in the intermediate case when there is a relatively small number of competing groups.

With the possible exception of the defence industry, international capitalism as a whole has little to gain from war; the losses through the destruction of assets and the removal of opportunities for profitable trade tend to exceed the gains from war profiteering. This does not necessarily make capitalism a force for peace. Globalization may bring benefits in terms of increased growth and prosperity for some, but others lose out: both traditional ruling class interests displaced by international market forces and those who suffer the inequality and unemployment produced by the new international division of labour. To those who suffer, conflict can seem an effective way of reversing their loss of status and possessions. The costs of war also seem smaller to those not well integrated into the international system; to those who fear the loss of basic resources such as land and water; and to those who feel excluded from basic rights within their country, such as Tamils and Kurds. The spread of democracy, by providing alternative means of conflict resolution, may inhibit the military expression of these grievances.

Currently, power in the international system is highly concentrated, the US faces no rivals, and this reduces the probability of major conflict. The close economic links and extensive trade associated with the expansion of capital make the costs of war much higher and thus reduce the probability of war. But the high costs of war to tightly integrated societies make its threat more effective, and war – should it come – tends to be much more destructive. Civil wars – conflicts within a highly integrated area – tend to be very destructive, and the First World War followed a period of high integration and relative peace.

Notes

1   I am grateful for comments from Dan Smith, Kristian Gleditsch, Nils Petter Gleditsch and participants in an Institute of Behavioural Science seminar in Boulder.
2   Kennedy (1988) provides a historical analysis of the contradictory role of military expenditure in the rise and fall of the great powers. Of course, military expenditure was also contradictory for communism, undermining the economic base of the Soviet Union.

3   Economic functionalist explanations of military expenditure, as a way to maintain full employment, are still occasionally advanced [see for instance Pivetti's (1992) defence of underconsumptionist theories and the response by Dunne and Smith (1994)], but they are much less prevalent now than they were in the 1970s.

4   The Uppsala data, which SIPRI publishes, define a major armed conflict as prolonged combat between the military forces of two or more governments, or of one government and at least one organized armed group, and incurring battle-related deaths of at least 1,000 people for the duration of the conflict.

5   Gowa (1994) and Mansfield (1994) are examples of the use of nineteenth century data to investigate the relationship between economic interdependence and conflict.

6   Gansler (1995, p. 10) gives the average cycle time from concept to production of US weapons systems in the early 1990s as 16.5 years. Such procurement lags mean not only that the electronics in these systems is obsolete before they are produced, but also that the military cannot match opponents such as the Colombian drug cartels who are said to replace their whole communication systems every two years from commercial sources.

References

Aaronovitch, S. *et al.* (1981), *The Political Economy of British Capitalism*, Maidenhead: McGraw-Hill.

Dunne, J. P. and Smith, R. P. (1994), 'Is military spending a burden? A "Marxo-marginalist" response to Pivetti', *Cambridge Journal of Economics*, Vol. 18, no. 4, pp. 515–21.

Engels, F. (1975), *Anti-Dühring: Herr Engen Dühring's Revolution in Science*, Moscow: Progress Publishers.

Gansler, J. S. (1995), *Defense Conversion*, Cambridge, MA: MIT Press for the Twentieth Century Fund.

Gleditsch N. P. and Hegre H. (1997), 'Peace and Democracy, three levels of analysis', *Journal of Conflict Resolution*, Vol. 41, no. 2, pp. 283–310.

Gowa, J. (1994), *Allies Adversaries and International Trade*, Princeton NJ, Princeton University Press.

Hartley, K. and Sandler, T. (1995), *Handbook of Defense Economics*, Amsterdam: North Holland.

Hegre, H., Ellingsen T., Gleditsch N. P., and Gates S. (1997), *Towards a Democratric Civil Peace*, mimeo, International Peace Research Institute Oslo (PRIO).

Kennedy, P. (1988), *The Rise and Fall of the Great Powers, Economic Change and Military Conflict 1500–2000*, London: Unwin Hyman.

Mansfield, E.D. (1994), *Power Trade and War*, Princeton, NJ: Princeton University Press.

Olson, M. (1982), *The Rise and Decline of Nations*, New Haven: Yale University Press.

Pivetti, M. (1992), 'Military spending as a burden on growth: an underconsumptionist critique', *Cambridge Journal of Economics*, Vol. 16, no. 4, pp. 373–84.

SIPRI (1997), *Armaments, Disarmament and International Security, SIPRI Yearbook*, Oxford: Oxford University Press for Stockholm International Peace Research Institute.

Smith, D. (1997), *The State of War and Peace Atlas*, Harmondsworth: Penguin Books.

Smith, R. P. (1977), 'Military expenditure and capitalism', *Cambridge Journal of Economics*, Vol. 1, no. 1, pp. 61–76.

Smith, R. P. (1978), 'Military expenditure and capitalism: a reply', *Cambridge Journal of Economics*, Vol. 2, no. 3, pp. 299–304.

Volden, K. and Smith, D. (eds) (1997), *Causes of conflict in the Third World*, International Peace Research Institute Oslo (PRIO).

7 Co-operation, coercion and autonomy in the contest for European unity

Jörg Huffschmid

Introduction: the question of a 'European Economic Government'

The starting point for the following considerations is my perception of a strong contradiction in the behaviour of the French government shortly after it came to office. In Amsterdam, on 16 June 1997, the French Prime Minister Lionel Jospin signed the 'stability pact' which locks fiscal policies of the member countries in the future Monetary Union (MU) still more tightly into a corset of austerity than the provisions of the Treaty of Maastricht (TM) had done, e.g. by obliging member countries to pursue the objective of balanced budgets.[1] This signature obviously further reduced the room for manoeuvre for an expansionary fiscal policy as a basic macroeconomic requirement for more employment. Two days later, on 19 June, the same Lionel Jospin addressed the French national assembly and explained his government's programme, focusing unequivocally on the fight against unemployment, announcing, among other measures a rise in the minimum wage, costly publicly financed jobs for young unemployed persons and a law reducing the legal working time to 35 hours per week without wage losses, and promising subsidies for rapidly complying firms. Although these measures will be partly financed through higher taxes on capital gains it seems clear that, for a transitory period, they would increase the public deficit. It follows that Jospin, although announcing his intention to keep the deficit under control, was also making it clear that this was not his main concern.

In order to reconcile the apparent contradiction the French government had already previously claimed that, as a counterpart to the European Central Bank (ECB), a central *'economic government'* of the EU is to be established, where economic policy in general should be discussed with binding co-ordination.[2] This claim was rather brusquely rejected by the German government which evoked the principle of subsidiarity in order to declare economic policy in general – and employment policy in particular – a matter of national competence.

In the meantime the arguments have calmed down. At the December 1997 summit in Luxembourg, where the question of a tighter coordination of economic policies among member countries was on the agenda, nothing like a European economic government with binding powers was envisaged, and nobody complained about this.[3] It is remarkable that in the two or three months in late 1997, French formulations about economic policy coordination had become much more modest and the term economic government ceased to appear in them. Does this reflect a retreat by the French side in the face of strong German resistance to such a body, or does it reflect a change in the attitude of the French government itself?

The answer to this question would require a detailed analysis of the complex structure of the positions within the government and the no less complicated relationships between the government and the president – a task which I cannot accomplish. But the question also gives rise to more general deliberations about the benefits and the limits of tight and binding co-operation, i.e. a kind of European economic government within the framework of European integration. In the light of such deliberations it may well be that the French claim for a European economic government was not so well designed to protect the new orientation in French economic policy, let alone to change the course of European economic policy altogether. Conversely, the German rejection of this institution may have been premature with regard to enforcing and continuing the prevailing neo-liberal policy and preventing a French exit from this line.

European integration has always been and remains a contested area, as Sam Aaronovitch has repeatedly pointed out in his work (cf. Aaronovitch and Grahl 1996, pp. 1–3). In this contest, some parties fight against European unity as such and prefer to go the national way instead. I will not deal with this – as I see it dangerous – line of argument which, if successful, could in the long run lead into another European catastrophe. Instead, I will take as a basis of my argument that European unity is the common objective of the contesting parties, but that the ways and means towards this goal are highly controversial. However, in the heated debate one assumption is usually uncontroversial: the high road to unity has to be co-operation and co-ordination in order to reach an 'ever closer union', as the TM phrases it. Co-operation has reached the status of a procedural rule of the game of European unification: it is imperative for any European objective – just like price stability has been transformed from an economic goal among others to not only the most important of all economic goals but also a rule of the game which must be respected in the pursuit of all other objectives. On the theoretical level, the chief witness for the essential role of co-operation is the famous prisoners' dilemma: co-operation pays out, non-co-operation is a risky business. Therefore we must, above all, co-operate.

This view can be contested itself on good grounds. The argument of the prisoners' dilemma assumes two roughly equally strong and shrewd prisoners, each of whom needs the other one and has no separate influence over the other. This is probably not the case in prison, and in European integration it is certainly not the case. A critical discussion of the general and ubiquitous claim for co-operation in the process of European integration will of course not reject the concept in general, because European unity is highly desirable and by definition requires some sort of co-operation. But it will analyse the kind and goals of co-operation, the positions and relative strengths of the co-operating partners, as well as ways to achieve a co-operative environment conducive to the welfare of people. Under certain circumstances it seems that not unconditional co-operation as such, but a particular hybrid of co-operation and autonomous non-co-operation is a more appropriate pattern to promote sustainable European integration.

In the following sections I will very briefly muster some stages and events in the history of the EEC/EU under the perspective of co-operation and non-cooperation (p. 89), before analysing the gradual transition of co-operation among equals to an imposed co-operation in the monetary field, a co-operation which has much more the character of coercion within a formally co-operative framework (p. 92). This situation of imposed co-operation raises the problem of possible ways out when the political situation in one country changes considerably, as it did in France with the elections of 1997 (p. 94). In the final section of the chapter, some cautious conclusions will be drawn with regard to the relationship between co-operation and autonomy in the present stage of European integration.

Co-operation and non-co-operation: stages, cases and the change of climate

The treaty establishing the European Economic Community (EEC) puts forward only few areas of direct and genuine competence of the Community as a supra-national institution: agricultural and commercial policies, and parts of competition and transport policies. In some of these areas decisions can only be taken unanimously – which requires a very high degree of co-operative spirit and preparedness to engage in compromise if progress in integration is not to be blocked. In most areas of European policy the treaty provides for intense inter-governmental co-operation to precede the passing of binding European directives and regulations. The rationale for this is that co-operation is based on the perception of common interests and the opportunity for particular countries to follow specific interests is preserved.

The dynamics embodied in such a structural dependency on co-operation and compromise between member countries have generated in various cases a dense interconnection of co-operative relationships leading to new political initiatives and new political institutions.

A prominent example for this is the development of a European regional policy based on the combination of already existing (social and agricultural) funds and the creation of new (European Fund for Regional Development and Cohesion Fund) budgets. The structural funds and (more or less) coherent regional policies were for the most part responses to perceived problems emerging from the various rounds of enlargements of the EEC: the entry of Ireland, Greece, Spain and Portugal into the EEC greatly extended the heterogeneity of economic structures and the disparities of income distribution throughout the EEC and required off-setting measures and institutions.

A high degree of co-operation was initially also presupposed in the Community measures accompanying the creation of the single European market. The technical and other standards relevant for market access in the member countries needed to be harmonized and this 'approximation of laws' has to be accomplished by unanimous vote. This gave every member country the opportunity to block any harmonization which went against that country's specific interests.

With hindsight, this treaty provision seems only comprehensible if seen as one step on a relatively short transitory road to much closer union – as for instance envisaged in the *Memorandum of the Commission about the action plan for the second stage of the Community* of 1962 (Europäische Kommission 1962). It proposed a comprehensive integration of economic policies of the member states leading to a policy merger in most areas, to common macro-economic (fiscal and monetary) and structural policies, including a much larger Community budget, etc. In a similar way the Werner Report of 1970 (Europäische Kommission 1970) proposed the transition within ten years (by 1980!) to a comprehensive European Economic and Monetary Union with a European Central Bank (ECB) and a European economic policy institution with supra-national powers and competence – a European economic government.[4] This plan, welcomed and accepted by the council in 1971, was however buried under the impact of inflation and crisis in the first half of the 1970s.

Even after the failure of the Werner plan, the aspirations for intra-Community co-operation remained high. A prominent example of this is the establishment of the European funds for monetary cooperation (EFMC) in 1972 and of the European Monetary System (EMS) in 1979. Both were responses to the collapse of the Bretton Woods system of fixed exchange rates and tried to replace it on a more limited scope by a zone of European stability, based on the obligation to mutual assistance for currencies which had come under pressure. Unfortunately, the EMS was subsequently instrumentalized in a quite different way, namely used as an instrument to enforce the fundamentalist position of the Bundesbank upon the rest of the EEC. But this is already a story of non-co-operation. . . .

It is not the first case of non-co-operation and autonomous action against the rest of the member countries. From the beginning of the EC there had existed not only strong resistance against the relinquishment of national sovereignty in exchange for a European state, but also strong reservations against tight co-operation with majority voting.

A glaring example of this reservation is the policy of the 'empty chair', practised by France in 1965 when de Gaulle saw French agricultural interests threatened by Community decisions. This very explicit and physically visible act of non-co-operation led to the Luxembourg compromise which changed the rules of the game: it was then agreed that, even if majority voting was provided for in the treaty, it would not been applied if a member country declared that vital interests would be affected. On the one hand this agreement strengthened the ability of particular countries to enforce particular national interests; on the other hand it provided a strong obstacle to further integration, if there was no sufficient convergence of interests behind it. Third, it supported the practice of 'package deals' binding together decisions on unconnected matters satisfying the differing interests of different countries.

Since the mid 1980s, something has deeply changed with regard to co-operation and non-co-operation in the EEC and subsequently the EU. On the one hand, the cases of true co-operation and compromise have become rarer and the cases of non-co-operation more frequent. On the other hand, where policy convergence was achieved it was not so much the result of co-operation and compromise but of unilateral imposition and coercion from the side of the German Bundesbank and government, the other member countries being pressurized into a common co-operation framework.

That the co-operative approximation of economic policies in general is no longer a primary goal among the member countries of the Community can be concluded from several changes and events in the course of European integration policy since the mid 1980s: In the pursuit of the single market, the objective of harmonization has been widely abandoned and replaced by the principle of mutual recognition, which surrenders the playing field to the strongest forces of the market and undermines political co-operation. Second, the Maastricht Treaty introduced the principle of subsidiarity which restricts the possibilities for Europe-wide economic policy and requires that policy be left to national authorities wherever possible. This principle has been endlessly invoked in the debate about a European employment policy and led to the clause in the already rather weak chapter on employment that the EU has to respect national competences.

Third, the perspective for a genuine Community budget has been continuously cut back: Whereas the MacDougall Report of 1977 (cf. European Commission 1977, p. 14) had recommended a size of 5–7 per cent of Community GDP as necessary for the EU budget to fulfil basic functions of the Community, a paper around the the Delors report of 1989 spoke of 3 per cent of Community GDP as being appropriate for the common budget (cf. Lamfalussy 1989, p. 95). The Delors I package of 1993 envisaged only 1.2 per cent for 1993 which should be modestly raised to 1.27 per cent in 1999. In spite of growing tasks accompanying the next enlargement round it has been made clear that, apart from prior enlargements, the community budget will not be extended (cf. Europäische Kommission 1997, p. 95). This will create further problems and conflicts.

Fourth, even the most prominent example of intra-Community co-operation, the EMS, has been poisoned from the beginning by the initially more tacit, then more outspoken and recently very practical obstruction from the side of the German Bundesbank and of the conservative German government which came into office in 1982. The former president of the Bundesbank, Otmar Emminger, proudly revealed in his memoirs of 1986, that the unconditional obligation of the central banks of those countries, whose currencies came under pressure to intervene in the currency markets – the basic cornerstone of the co-operative arrangement of the EMS – was not so unconditional for the German Bundesbank after all. In response to a letter of the Bundesbank to the minister for economic affairs expressing reservations about this obligation, the minister assured the Bundesbank, that it did not have to intervene, if it felt constrained by monetary and other considerations (Emminger 1986, p. 362). In subsequent years the Bundesbank succeeded in transforming the EMS from an institution which aimed at intra-European exchange rate stability, through a co-operative arrangement of burden-sharing in necessary adjustment processes, into an institution imposing strict austerity in economic policy upon all other member countries, via an uncontestable monetary priority, thus contributing to the slowdown of economic growth and rise in unemployment throughout Europe.

From co-operation to coercion: the French experience 1981–1983 and the exogenous German coercion

That co-operation and compromise were no longer the basic imperatives of the European Community became clear when, at the beginning of the 1980s, the French government tried to introduce a more expansionary economic policy in order to overcome recession and unemployment (cf. Hoang-Ngoc 1996, pp. 68ff, Halimi *et al.* 1994, pp. 97–115). The reduction in interest rates and the expansion of public demand led to massive capital flight (mainly to Germany) and to an increase in the trade deficit. German exporters and banks profited most from both. At the same time, the German government and Bundesbank strictly refused to soften their austerity prone and exclusively anti-inflationary policy stance.

The consequences of this non-co-operation are well known: it marked the end of the 'French experiment' and the abrupt policy reversal towards the German economic doctrine. This experience is since then usually presented as proof for the assertion that there is no possibility of conducting an autonomous economic policy in a highly internationalized environment. However, this assertion is not so self-evident as it may appear at the first glance. In any case the French experience cannot be generalized.

First, Germany was obviously capable of conducting an autonomous economic policy at that time, more or less against the rest of continental Europe. Great Britain, a couple of years earlier, had already changed towards a monetarist policy line against the whole of continental Europe. The new policy pattern of the US was also 'autonomously' introduced in a big policy turnaround by the Federal Reserve Bank at the beginning of the 1980s. The question of policy autonomy is not so much a question of international environment but of size, weight, power and determination to follow and enforce one's own interests, co-operatively or not.

Second, it is debatable whether France would have been able to continue with a different economic policy at the beginning of the 1980s. France has a big and powerful economy, and can exert considerable influence upon the international environment. But a continuation of expansionary fiscal and softer monetary policies against the hostile neighbours Germany and Great Britain would have required more determined action to prevent capital flight and protect trade to secure a balanced trade position. Some measures were taken, but they were not sufficient to protect the French upswing, which had started in 1980. Further going measures would have required a decision to reduce, at least temporarily, co-operation based on terms imposed by a dominant power and harmful to the

French interests. But the French government was not prepared to take this step of non-co-operation. Of course it would have been a risky step, without a guarantee of success, but one cannot be sure that it would necessarily have failed and made things worse. With hindsight, and with regard to the real economic deterioration in the 1980s, one can safely assume that things would probably not have got worse if France had taken the risk of non-co-operation with Germany.

In the 15 years since the first French experience, the process of European integration has become much more asymmetrical, non-cooperative and biased towards a pattern which was basically imposed by the German Bundesbank and government. This was accomplished essentially in two steps:

1   The strictly and exclusively disinflationary policy of the Bundesbank led to a lower inflation rate in Germany than in other countries, inducing large and growing trade surpluses with consequent large flows of money and capital into Germany. Both tendencies exerted an upward pressure upon the DM parity, within the EMS, and outside against the US dollar and the Japanese yen.

2   The Bundesbank acted to prevent the off-setting mechanisms of such tendencies from becoming effective: trade surpluses would normally lead to price increases, thus lowering the inflation differentials *vis-à-vis* the trade partners, even under conditions of fixed exchange rates. Nominal realignments (11 appreciations of the DM between 1979 and 1987) would have worked in a similar direction, reducing price differentials between domestic and imported goods for the importers. However, these mechanisms can only become effective if the central bank of the surplus country does not take measures against them. This is precisely what the Bundesbank did: in re-enforcing the disinflationary policy it sterilized the export surplus-induced money by restricting the money supply even more strongly, and thus made largely ineffective the nominal re-valuation. Maintaining inflation differentials resulted in sustained competitive advantages for German exporters (cf. Herr 1991).

This economic strategy was as beneficial for German exporters as it was harmful for neighbouring economies. It raised the German trade and current account balance to ever higher surpluses, reaching unprecedented levels in 1989. On the other side, these surpluses were reflected in growing deficits of most of the European trade partners (cf. Huffschmid 1994, pp. 98–106). Continuous 'autonomous' beggar-my-neighbour policy under the umbrella of an allegedly tight co-operative arrangement of monetary policy has made Germany the creditor of Europe and turned most European countries into debtors of Germany.

The German surplus disappeared temporarily as a consequence of German unity. But the German non-co-operative policy position did not disappear. In 1992, as a consequence of the German high interest policy and its Europe-wide diffusion through liberalized capital markets, the pressure on the Italian and the British currencies became extreme and the Bundesbank foresaw that it would not be able to sterilize the money which would flow into Germany. As a result of regular intervention it forced Italy and the UK out of the ERM by threatening not to meet its obligation to unlimited intervention. A year later the EMS was effectively terminated when the width of the permitted fluctuation band was extended from 2.25 percent to 15 per cent above and below the central rate. This extension of permitted volatility appears to be a strange preparation for the final and irreversible fixing and locking of the exchange rates in the envisaged monetary union.

But perhaps it is not so strange. By following a non-co-operative, autonomous, policy Germany at last forced the other members of the EU to adopt the same policy orientation in order to avoid further deficits. Of course there were also forces and interests within these countries favourable to such changes, but the main pressure came from outside. Thus, in the 1990s a new co-operative pattern had been established, enforced by clear non-co-operation, coercion and domi-nance from the side of the leading economy and the policy of its government and central bank.

Co-operation and autonomy to change the terms of integration

Within the last two years it has become evident that neo-liberal policies generate protest, opposition and some resistance among the people, as living conditions are severely affected by cuts of wages and social benefits, by dismissals and unemployment. In some countries opposition has reached the strength of social movements, and in France and the United Kingdom it has led to changes in government. In other countries, like Germany, the perspective is less clear for the government but quite clear for the Bundesbank: it will continue or even re-inforce its strictly monetarist policy, having firmly incorporated this policy orientation into the terms of the monetary union which is to begin on 1 January 1999. If not altered, this policy will be the binding monetary framework for all, possibly 11, joining members. This neo-liberal frame of co-operation poses severe problems for countries determined to alter their domestic economic policy course toward a more socially sustainable orientation. The problem of the relationship between co-operation and autonomy is particularly acute for the French government. Leaving aside the extremes of complete abandonment of co-operation and of complete sub-ordination to the monetarist rule, there seem to exist three possible ways in which this relationship could be shaped.

First, the French government could, without abandoning co-operation alto-gether, withdraw from the already-reached and agreed level of co-operation, because it regards the neo-liberal terms of this level as imposed, unfair and harmful for economic and social development. The most important step in such a direction would be to demand a postponement of the start of the monetary union, thereby causing a deceleration of the integration process giving time and political room for manoeuvre, which could be used for a re-definition of the purposes and instruments of integration. The monetary framework so re-defined could be a truly co-operative European Monetary System without loopholes (and with possible extensions to the candidates for enlargement in Eastern Europe).

This seemingly reasonable variant, has obviously never been seriously taken into consideration by the French government. It would have been a risky option because it would have been met with stiff opposition and adamant resistance by the German government and Bundesbank. The result would have been a high level of conflict, the outcome of which could not be predicted. It is highly possible that the notorious 'markets' would have determined the outcome by massive capital flight from France to Germany, which would have been equally embarrassing for both countries and to resist which they would probably have had to join forces. In any case, after the end of 1997 it was too late to postpone the Monetary Union without changing the Treaty of Amsterdam. If the Union did not begin in 1999, this would not be the result of an orderly postponement but of turmoil and chaos in the first half of 1998.

Second, the French government can go forward and extend and intensify the intra-EU co-operation. This is the line of the socialist argument during the election campaign in early 1997: to complement the central institution of the European Central Bank by an equally centralized and equally competent economic policy institution, the 'European economic government' more or less along the lines which had been proposed in the Werner Report of 1970. The expectation behind this conception is that, through this centralized body, a change of the orientation in economic policy could be initiated and gradually enforced throughout the EU. This proposal was emphatically rejected by the German government and is not raised any more as a definite proposal by the French either. The European economic government has in the meantime boiled down to regular meetings of the ministers for economics and finance, the formulation and passing of regular reports about the economic situation, the adoption of regular recommendations about the 'broad guidelines of the economic policies of the Member States and the Community' and regular 'multilateral surveillance' of the extent to which such guidelines are followed. All of this had already been incorporated in article 103 of the Maastricht Treaty, and none of its recommendations is binding. At the summit of December 1997 nothing substantial was added to these provisions. The newly created Euro-council for the members of the future monetary union is an 'informal club' without any competence. The *Financial Times* is quite right when it called the 'summit deal a setback to French ambitions to to sell the euro-club as a political counterweight to the future European central bank . . .' (Barber 1997, p. 2).

There is also a question as to whether such a competent European economic policy authority, if really installed, could be used to change overall line of economic policy. Under the prevailing circumstances it seems more probable that the substance of such 'government' would be a compromise which would not alter the general line: a compromise about the 'culture of flexibility', employability, adaptability, etc. A macro-economic turnaround or even initial steps for such a turnaround cannot be expected. But the opposite could happen: the European economic government could hinder the French government from conducting an effective macro-economic turnaround. The situation is obviously different following the election of a Social Democrat government in Germany.

Third, the French government can choose to maintain the present level and pace of European integration and co-operation and at the same time pursue an autonomous domestic policy which deviates from the neo-liberal pattern and follows a more employment-oriented path. This option comes close to the Mitterand case of the early 1980s. It will in all probability come up, rather early on, against the problem of protecting such a course from capital flight and currency turmoil. While the latter will disappear as a French problem and be extended to all participating members in the monetary union, the former remains as long as conditions for capital are better in Germany or the Netherlands than in France. Whether this is the case depends not so much on the wage level as on tax legislation and interest rates. The latter will be fixed by the future European Central Bank and they will, according to the ECB's policy stance, remain rather high, thus obstructing the French efforts to stimulate growth. The scope for further tax re-distribution to the benefit of lower-income groups is limited as long as there is heavy tax competition. Therefore, the option to stimulate employment by compulsory reduction of working time seems to be the most promising autonomous option, although this will also require government subsidies for small firms, and thereby lead to more government expenditure with ensuing higher deficits. But perhaps it is not unreasonable to risk the conflict with the EU – or rather with the dominating German position in the EU – over this level of the public deficit. For the provisions of the stability pact of Amsterdam are not really practicable, and therefore the sanction mechanism is more a theoretical than a real threat. The main importance of the stability pact is its ideological character, emphasizing once more the neo-liberal doctrine. If this doctrine is challenged by the practical policy of a member state, which could very well happen, then it will not be enforceable.

Summary and conclusion

The purpose of the foregoing sections was to formulate some cautious reservations against unconditional support for unconditional adherence to intra-European co-operation in the formulation and conduct of economic policy. Co-operation is only beneficial to all if there is, first, a solid basis of common interests and, second, if it leads to true compromises between different interests, borne by either symmetric power relations or by an asymmetric inclination of stronger partners to accept compromises in the interest of the weaker ones. It has been briefly argued that throughout the process of European integration there have been cases of enhanced co-operation leading to progressive new institutional arrangements, but there have also been cases of non-co-operation which altered the pace and direction of integration. In the past 15 years the balance changed towards non-co-operative events. This has been particularly evident in the area of monetary policy: co-operation in the framework of the EMS has been gradually undermined by the German Bundesbank and replaced by a monetary regime which was and is harmful for most European countries and beneficial for German exporters and money holders. Co-operation among equals with compromises amongst equals was transformed into co-operation under coercion imposed without compromise by Germany. The internal tensions and contradictions of such a policy have led to a change of government in France. Unconditional co-operation under neo-liberal hegemony does not appear to be a promising way of loosening the neo-liberal grip on Europe. Instead, the pursuit and the political and economic protection of an autonomous employment-oriented policy outside the framework of a European economic government, not outside the European Union, could lead to a position of strength which would then manoeuvre Germany into a situation in which negotiations with true compromises are possible.

The foregoing considerations cannot of course exhaustively answer the question raised in the introduction of why the French government has dropped the demand for a European economic government with far-reaching powers. But one conclusion can be drawn: if it did so not for reasons of resignation but deliberately because it saw, under the present circumstances and power relations, more dangers than chances in such a government, it was well advised.

Notes

1 This obligation is referred to in Council Regulations nr. 1466/97 and 1467/97 both of 7 July 1997, cf. Official Journal nr. L/209 of 2 August 1997.

2 Whereas the term 'economic government' is frequently used in French publications, in official declarations and interviews the government speaks more often of a 'Stability Council' or an 'economic pole' which should serve as counterpart and partner of the ECB as the 'monetary pole' (cf. Barber 1997a, Strauss-Kahn 1997).

3 The discussions of this summit were mainly about who would have access to a newly created Euro Council, not about its competences in matters of economic policy: it was common agreement that it would not have any competence (cf. Barber 1997b).

4 'ein wirtschaftspolitisches Entscheidungsgremium und ein gemeinschaftliches Zentralbanksystem' (an economic policy decision authority and a common system of central banks – author's translation). For the economic policy institution the Werner Report proposed: 'Das wirtschaftspolitische Entscheidungsgremium wird unabhängig und in gemeinsamem Interesse die Gesamtwirtschaftspolitik der Gemeinschaft mitbestimmen. Da der Gemeinschaftshaushalt als konjunkturpolitisches Instrument nicht ausreichend sein wird, muß das wirtschaftspolitische Entscheidungsgremium in der Lage sein, die nationalen Haushalte, namentlich hinsichtlich der Höhe und Entwicklung der Haushaltssalden sowie der Art der Finanzierung der Defizite oder der Verwendung der Überschüsse zu beeinflussen. . . . wird es schließlih auch für die anderen vergemeinschafteten Bereiche der Wirtschafts- und Sozialpolitik verantwortlich sein.' (The economic policy decision authority will independently and in the common interest co-determine the general economic policy of the Community. Because the common budget will not be sufficient to serve as a business cycle instrument, the economic policy decision authority must be able to influence national budgets particularly with respect to the volume and the development of budgetary balances as well as the way of financing deficits or the use of surpluses – author's translation) *Europäische Kommission* 1970, p. 5.

References

Aaronovitch, S. and Grahl, J. (1996), Building on Maastricht, Contribution to the workshop: Alternative Economic policy in Europe, Brussels, manuscript.

Amtsblatt der Europäische Gemeinschaften, (1970) C 135, vom 11.11.1970, 'Bericht an Rat und Kommission über die stufenweise Verwirklichung der Wirtschafts- und Währungsunion in der Gemeinschaft'.

Barber, L. (1997a), Close to the boiling point, *The Financial Times*, 16 June 1997, p. 17.

Barber, L. (1997b), Germany wins the day at EU summit, *The Financial Times*, 15 December 1997, p. 2.

Emminger, O. (1986), *D-Mark, Dollar, Währungskrisen. Erinnerungen eines ehemaligen Bundesbankpräsidenten*, Stuttgart, Deutsche Verlags-Anstalt.

Europäische Kommission (1962), Memorandum der Kommission über das Aktionsprogramm der Gemeinschaft für die zweite Stufe, Brussels.

Europäische Kommission (1970), Bericht an Rat und Kommission über die stufenweise Verwirklichung der Wirtschafts- und Währungsunion in der Gemeinschaft, in: Amtsblatt der Europäischen Gemeinschaften Nr. C136 of 11 November 1970, pp. 1–38 (Werner Report).

European Commission (1977), Report of the study group on the role of public finance in European integration, chaired by Sir Donald MacDougall, Economic and Financial Series, No A13, Brussels.

Europäische Kommission (1997), Agenda 2000. Eine stärkere und erweiterte Union. Kom(97) 2000 endg. of 15 June 1997, Brussels.

Halimi, S., Michie, J. and Milne, S. (1994), 'The Mitterand Experience', in Michie, J. and Smith, J. G. (eds), *Unemployment in Europe*, London: Academic Press, pp. 97–115.

Herr, H. (1991), 'Der Merkantilismus der Bundesrepublik in der Weltwirtschaft', in Voy, K., Polster, W. and Thomasberger, C. (eds), *Marktwirtschaft und politische Regulierung*, Marburg: Metropolis, pp. 227–61.

Hoang-Ngoc, L. (1996), Salaires et emploi. Une critique de la pensée unique. Paris: Syros.

Huffschmid, J. (1994), Wem gehört Europa? Wirtschaftspolitik und Kapitalstrategien, Vol. 1: Wirtschaftspolitik in der EG. Heilbronn: Distel-Verlag.

Lamfalussy, A. (1989), Macro-coordination of fiscal policies in an economic and monetary union in Europe, in 'Committee for the Study of Economic and Monetary Union' (ed.), *Report on Economic and Monetary Union in the European Community*, Office for Official Publications of the European Communities, Brussels.

Strauss-Kahn, D. (1997), Je eher der Euro kommt, desto besser, *Die Zeit*, 25 July 1997, p. 11.

8   Unequal exchange re-visited

Paul Levine

Introduction

During the 1950s and 1960s an important literature emerged that seriously challenged the mainstream economists' orthodoxy that free trade would benefit the less-developed countries. The title of this essay refers to the contribution by the Marxist economist Arghiri Emmanuel with the spectacular title: *Unequal Exchange: A study of the Imperialism of Trade* (Emmanuel, 1972, but first appearing in 1968). Unequal exchange existed in the sense that this exchange represented a very unequal exchange of labour time or value, e.g. ten hours of the labour of an Indian tea plantation worker exchanged for one hour of the labour of a Western car worker. He argued that the developed countries (the 'North') exploited the less-developed countries (the 'South'), primarily through trade rather than through investment and the re-patriation of profits, as traditionally argued by Marxists, and as a consequence free trade would hold back the progress of the South.

The conclusion that laissez-faire trade would damage the South also has roots in more orthodox economics. A notable example is the work of Bhagwati (1958), who argued that growth in the South could be immiserizing because the favourable effect on welfare of growth at constant prices could be outweighed by a deterioration of the terms of trade. Bhagwati's immiserizing effect comes about if world demand for the South's primary products are sufficiently price inelastic. But in a celebrated paper, Lewis (1954) showed that the terms of trade could deteriorate quite independently of any assumptions about demand.

The background for the contributions of Bhagwati, Emmanuel and Lewis was the early post-war period when the South was locked into a colonial division of labour in which they largely exported primary goods in exchange for imported manufactures. A secular deterioration of their terms of trade coupled with relatively low output growth in the non-traded sector resulted in the relative impoverishment of the South up to the end of the 1960s. But since then the world economy has experienced a significant transformation involving at least part of what were formerly the less-developed countries.

A new pattern of trade has emerged between the South and the North. As Vernon (1966) and others have observed, new innovative goods are being developed and produced in the North and exported to other countries, North or

South. Eventually, the South develops the ability to imitate many of these activities and production shifts, with or without the intermediation of transnational companies, to this region where they enjoy a low-wage competitive advantage.

How have these trade patterns affected growth and development in the South? Led by the 'tiger economies' – Hong Kong, Singapore, Taiwan and South Korea – rapid economic growth has spread to China and to Thailand, Malaysia and Indonesia in the past three decades. More recently, India has been showing signs of joining Asia's rapidly growing economies. Taking Asia as a whole and excluding Japan, which is excluded from 'Asia' for the purposes of this essay, this region of the world has been growing at three times the rate of the mature economies of the West. The financial crisis affecting Asia (including Japan) that started in 1997 is a strong indication that these high growth rates are not sustainable. I return to this issue of long-term-sustainable growth later in the chapter. Nonetheless, given that these countries are home to over half the world's population, the significance of these trends for the future structure of the World economy can hardly be exaggerated.

Figure 8.1 shows the changing share of world GDP for five blocs of the world: the EU12 (i.e. first 12 members), the US, Japan, 'Asia' and Latin America. In 1970, Asia contained 40 per cent of the world's population, but enjoyed only a 7 per cent share of world GDP. In 1997, it contained 50–55 per cent of the world's population and its GDP share is around 20 per cent. Forecasters predict lower growth in the future but still a continuation of a much higher rate than the North, especially when a 'contagion affect' on Northern growth is taken into account.

% of total, at 1990 prices and exchange rates (average of market and PPP)

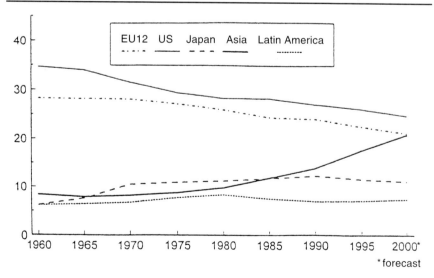

Figure 8.1 Changing shares of World GDP

The trend in world shares indicated in Figure 8.1 should therefore continue, though possibly at a lower rate.

These trends have been accompanied by a spectacular growth in Asian trade with the other regions of the world and between themselves. A prominent feature of these economies has been their openness. One of the most robust empirical findings in the growth literature is that openness increases growth. Among these is a study by Sachs and Warner (1995). In an examination of 78 countries outside the former Soviet bloc, they divide countries between those having open and those having closed trade policies according to the absence or presence of significant tariff rates, non-tariff barriers, a black-market premium on the currency, a socialist economic system and a state monopoly on major exports. A country with at least one of these features is deemed to be 'closed', otherwise it is 'open'. According to this classification, Hong Kong and Thailand have been open throughout the post-war period, Malaysia and Singapore have been open since independence (in 1963 and 1965 respectively), Taiwan opened in 1963, South Korea in 1968, Indonesia in 1970 and India in 1994. China is classified as closed owing to its inconvertible currency, high black-market premiums on the yuan and a large state sector. Nevertheless, Sachs and Warner point out that non-state enterprises, which account for most of the output growth, import inputs almost duty-free and export goods to world markets without state involvement.

Using this classification, Sachs and Warner find a strong association between openness and growth, both within the group of developing countries and the group of developed countries. Within the former group the open economies grew at 4.5 per cent per year on average over 1966–90 compared with 0.7 per cent for the closed economies. Within the group of developed countries the corresponding figures are 2.3 per cent and 0.7 per cent. A number of more sophisticated cross-country growth regressions are also undertaken, but the main conclusion that openness increases growth emerges as extremely robust.

It would seem then that the free-trade pessimism of Emmanuel and others was clearly wrong, at least for Asia. Some of the poorest countries are escaping from their former poverty and this should be a cause for celebration. But rather than taking satisfaction from this phenomenon and stressing its positive side, many influential bodies and individuals are taking a rather different tack. Despite their economic progress Asian income per head and wages still remain far below that of the North. Unequal exchange, although becoming less unequal, is now emerging as a problem not for the poor, but rather for the affluent countries. For instance, the European Commission's 1993 White Paper, 'Growth, Competitiveness and Employment' raised concern over the rise of nations that 'are competing with us – even in our own markets – at cost levels that we simply cannot match'. This spectre of low-wage competition from the developing countries, which is threatening jobs in the North, was also the concern of the late Sir James Goldsmith who endorsed the EC position, and went on to develop a general critique of free trade between unequal economies. His argument – that developing countries are also suffering from free trade – actually contains some parallels with Emmanuel.

Perhaps closest to the position of Emmanuel is that of Christian Aid in their 'Supermarkets Third World Charter'. Christian Aid quotes the example of a coffee plantation worker in Brazil earning 56p an hour. This represents an unequal exchange of about six hours of his or her time for one hour of a low-paid United Kingdom worker. Their answer is the campaign for supermarkets to insist on 'fair pay, prices and conditions all the way down the production chain' and to enlist the support of the shopper to exercise pressure on their own supermarkets. Of course Brazilian coffee plantation workers are not competing with producers in the West, so the problem here is not one of low-wage competition; but in principle the campaign for fair wages and conditions can be applied to supermarkets or other importers selling goods which are also produced in the West. Concern over low wages and poor conditions would then be combined with a concern for threatened jobs in the West. Both these problems can be alleviated, it seems, by the achievement of 'fair pay and conditions'. What could be simpler?

Low-wage competition: so what's the problem?

The idea that low-wage competition from the South threatens both jobs and wages in the North is intuitive and certainly rings true for workers involved in the relevant industries. It seems obvious that if someone in the world can do my job, perhaps not as efficiently but for a fifth of my wage, or less, then either I must expect a fall in my wage, or I become unemployed. On the other hand, as a consumer there are obvious benefits if the goods I buy are produced by people earning very low wages. Suppose that wage differentials are 6:1 between the developed and underdeveloped world. Suppose in addition productivity differences are only 2:1. Then wage costs per worker will differ by a proportion 3:1. Under competitive conditions the drop in the price when production, in its entirety, moves to the low-wage economies will be by the same proportion; i.e. running shoes costing £60 when produced in the UK will cost only £20 when imported from low-wage economies.

But before we become over-excited at the prospect of cheap consumer goods, or over-concerned at the prospect of low-wage competition, one point needs to be made clear. The fact is: the shift in production from the South to the North has been very limited, and an indication of this is to be seen from the following trade figures.

The figures in Table 8.1 reveal trade between the West and Asia to be a very small proportion of Western GDP. It is difficult to believe such a small amount of trade could have a significant impact on the West and be responsible for a significant part of unemployment rates of 10–15 per cent that we observe in the EU. Nevertheless, in a careful study Wood (1994) argues that properly conducted factor content calculations reveal a substantial reduction in demand for unskilled workers as a result of changes in North–South trade. Furthermore, the growth trends indicate that there is every reason to believe that trade will increase substantially. As more firms in Asia produce for Western markets, the price

Table 8.1 Western and Japanese trade with Asia

	Exports to Asia (% of GDP)	Imports from Asia (% of GDP)
US	1.4	2.5
Japan	3.5	2.1
Germany	1.6	1.7
France	1.1	1.1
UK	1.8	2.3
EU total	1.4	1.5

changes that accompany a transfer of production from high- to low-wage cost economies will reflect these cost differentials. Consumers in the West will enjoy large benefits in terms of cheaper imports; but what about employment?

In order to assess what might happen it is helpful to look for analogous changes in the past and to see how advanced industrialized countries have coped. Do we have such an analogy? In fact we do. The fears of society, and of workers in particular, regarding the availability of a much cheaper source of goods than those produced by the existing workforce is by no means new. Technical progress throughout the industrial revolution, and indeed throughout history, has constituted precisely the same threat to individual workers, but has also brought huge benefits to people as consumers.

When people talk about workers being displaced, whether it be workers being displaced by machines, indigenous workers by immigrants, men by women (women by men) or in the case under consideration, indigenous workers by overseas workers, they often commit the same fallacy. The fallacy consists in believing that somehow there is a fixed amount of work to be shared out between workers, machines, men, women and overseas workers. Regarding technical progress, when the level of productivity rises is there a tendency for unemployment to increase? Over the long term, history provides a very emphatic answer to this question. Consider the level of productivity in the US and the UK (measured as real GDP per head of population at fixed 1985 prices). Over the past 120 years, this increased by about eight-fold in the US and by about five-fold in the UK. By contrast, the unemployment rate (per cent of workforce who are unemployed) reveals no trend over the very long term (Layard *et al.* 1991). This is a very significant point. It suggests that in market economies there are powerful equilibrating mechanisms at work that have ensured that the number of jobs available responds to huge changes in the numbers of people wanting to work, despite continuous productivity change and profound changes in the structure of employment. For example, over this 120-year period employment in the UK in agriculture dropped from 30 per cent to only 2 per cent of the workforce.

If there is a threat from low wage–cost competition from the South it takes the form of temporary periods of adjustment when the flow of workers from declining industries into unemployment exceeds the flow of additional workers into expanding industries. But here the issues involved are essentially the same as those of unemployment induced by technical change: both phenomena displace workers from some sectors, shift demand domestically and globally to new sectors and raise differentials between those workers for whom demand is rising and those for whom demand is falling. Since the progressive, expanding, sectors generally require more skilled workers, there is an increase in the skilled/ unskilled wage differential and therefore a general increase in income inequality. Dealing with these structural changes requires a well-trained, highly educated and therefore flexible workforce. The important point is to address the 'competitiveness' problem in the global economy not as one requiring a new approach to trade, but rather as it really is. First, it is a labour market problem requiring policies to improve training, education and help to unemployed, especially the long-term unemployed. Second, it is a distribution problem requiring changes in the tax and social security regimes to prevent the emergence of a new underclass of low-paid and frequently unemployed workers. In short, these are policies aimed at making everyone stakeholders in our society.

Up to now I have identified the benefits of trade with low-cost producers as a static terms of trade effect affecting the level of Northern consumption. But there is a quite separate set of issues concerning the growth of Asian economies and the effect of growth in one part of the world on growth in another.

Understanding growth

A vast theoretical and empirical literature has emerged since the 1980s which has transformed the way economists think about growth. It contrasts with the earlier neo-classical theory which invoked *exogenous* technical change to explain sustained growth. By contrast, the focus of *endogenous* growth (EG) is on how the consumption/savings decisions of households, the investment decisions of firms, and public policy in various forms, determine growth. While the classical model could be described as a model *with* long-run growth, the new literature offers a number of possible models *of* long-run growth.

Perhaps ironically for a school of thought to emerge from the University of Chicago with Paul Romer, positive externalities from R&D expenditure and investment in physical or human capital (education and training) figure prominently in this theory and indeed can provide the engine for sustained growth. It follows that there is a potential role for government to raise growth by intervening in the areas of investment, R&D, training and education.

The EG literature can usefully be divided into two broad strands: the first builds on Romer (1986), and is closest to the classical tradition and emphasizes capital accumulation as the engine of growth with capital broadly defined to include human and physical components. In the second broad strand of the literature, following Romer (1990), the discovery of new goods and of new processes provides the engine of growth. R&D activity provides blueprints for these innovations and a feature of this literature is the attempt to understand the economic forces that drive R&D.

In the 'old growth' Solow model, because there are diminishing returns to capital accumulation holding labour fixed, the only source of sustained growth is exogenous technical change. A rise in society's rate of saving will then increase the level of income but have no permanent effect on growth. In Romer (1986) each individual firm faces diminishing returns from its own investment but enjoys the benefits of knowledge externalities from aggregate investment. If this spillover effect is sufficiently strong, then diminishing returns to investment no longer occur and the more people save the higher the growth rate.

Can this genre of EG models explain the exceptional growth of the Asian economies? It is certainly true that these countries have displayed exceptionally high rates of saving and of investment in both physical and human capital. However, in a carefully argued paper, Young (1995) contests that the East Asian phenomenon is perfectly consistent with the old-growth model with diminishing returns to capital. Drawing on earlier work by Mankiw *et al.* (1992), Young uses growth accounting to decompose growth into components due to higher inputs (physical and human capital, raw labour) and a residual assumed to be attributable to higher productivity growth of all inputs. The latter is referred to as total factor productivity (TFP). His results reveal that higher rates of growth in factor inputs rather than extraordinary TFP growth can explain most of East Asia's growth experience. Compared with the G7 economies, the TFP growth has been relatively, but not exceptionally, high in Hong Kong, South Korea and Taiwan, but not in Singapore. These findings suggest that the high growth rates observed in the past two to three decades must eventually peter out and that diminishing returns to capital investment provides a possible fundamental explanation for the current financial crisis.

It would seem then that the empirical evidence does not support the view that sustained growth is possible by capital deepening alone. In order to understand long-term growth we therefore need to turn to the second wave of EG models in which growth is driven by R&D investment. From our international perspective, the theory of R&D-driven EG consists of three building blocks: (i) an economic theory of technical knowledge; (ii) the endogenous determination of the level of R&D activity; and (iii) globalization. Let me consider these in turn.

Two types of technical knowledge result from commercial R&D. The first is specific technical information which allows a particular product to be produced. This may be excludable to others to a certain extent by patent protection and industrial secrecy. The second is a more general form of knowledge which provides a technological spillover between firms and between generations of workers. This spillover is crucial for growth. Over time, flows of such information build up into a growing stock that the literature refers to as 'knowledge capital' – a body of scientific knowledge and techniques not specific to any one production process.

Knowledge capital has two important characteristics that drive growth. First, it is a public good: it is non-rival (i.e. one firm's 'consumption' of knowledge does not reduce the amount available to others) and it is non-excludable. Second, it increases with the cumulative R&D experience and therefore with the total variety of goods and industrial processes in the economy. It seems reasonable to assert that there is no limit to the growth of this stock of knowledge capital; there are no diminishing returns in its production and there is no reason to expect humans will exhaust the potential for increasing knowledge.

The second element of the theory asks the question: what drives R&D investment? Joseph Schumpeter's classic book, *Capitalism, Socialism and Democracy* (Schumpeter 1942), continues to influence the way modern growth theorists approach this question. Drawing on Schumpeter, their answer is that it is the expected profitability of the new product which results from the investment. This profitability will reflect the expected monopoly in the new product and conditions in the relevant factor and product markets, and will take into account the possibility of losing the monopoly position through an erosion of patent rights. Monopoly profits from the sale of new goods plays a central role in Schumpeter's analysis.

The picture that emerges is of an economy whose growth depends on the interaction between firms producing distinctive goods and earning monopoly profits, with similar or different firms engaging in R&D activity to invent new blueprints, and consumers making savings and consumption decisions and supplying labour. These decentralized activities are co-ordinated through financial, product and labour markets, and through activities of the state.

Globalization of economies adds a third dimension to the theory of growth. Trade, borrowing and lending in world financial markets and the international mobility of factors of production (especially people) can all contribute to growth on a world scale. *Knowledge capital now becomes a public good on an international scale.* Every country can benefit from the emergence of new scientific knowledge and techniques in any single country. However, countries that are best equipped to both absorb these spillovers, and to generate new ideas themselves, will out-perform others.

Up to this point we have referred to two products of R&D: first, a private new innovative good protected, albeit imperfectly, by patent laws and consisting of a blueprint for a new good or industrial process; and second, a public good we have described as 'knowledge capital'. A third product of R&D relates to global-ization and to a new pattern of international trade now observed in the world economy. I have observed that a new trade pattern has emerged in recent decades. New innovative goods are being developed and produced in the North and exported to other countries, North or South. Eventually the South develops the ability to imitate many of these activities and production shifts to this region. In this stage of development, R&D in the South must be devoted to the achievement of the ability to imitate rather than to the production of new goods.

But trade between nations engaged in producing innovative goods in the North and trade between the innovative North and the imitating South clearly do not exhaust all the possible trading patterns. Table 8.2 compares shares of R&D expenditure in GDP, growth of R&D expenditure and patents granted for South Korea and Taiwan with two typical Northern countries. The figures indicates that Korea and Taiwan have becomes centres for innovation in their own right.

Table 8.2 Innovation performance

Country	R&D 1993 (% of GDP)	Ranking	Growth in R&D[a] 1989–93	Ranking	Patents granted[b] 1989–93	Ranking
Korea	2.1	11	9.7	10	9.3	10
Taiwan	1.8	13	16.7	4	66.5	1
UK	2.1	10	−1.9	29	7.9	12
US	2.8	4	−1.1	28	20.5	6

a   Annual real compound percentage growth in total expenditure on R&D.
b   Average annual number of patents granted to residents per 100,000 inhabitants.

Source: Currie *et al.* 1999.

This suggests a third intermediate phase of development: innovation in the North and innovation co-existing alongside imitation in the South.

A number of questions arise. What factors determine which phase of development a country or bloc finds itself? In whatever stage of development we find ourselves, will the 'invisible hand of the market work?', i.e. will the market left to itself achieve a socially efficient level of R&D activity, given that there are knowledge externalities within and between countries, and given that monopoly power in product markets is essential to drive R&D and, with it, economic growth. Can any sub-optimality be redressed by government support for R&D? Finally, should we distinguish between support to the three forms of R&D activity discussed, R&D for innovation in the North, innovation in the South and imitation in the South?

A North–South model of trade and endogenous growth

My account of the growth process up to this point amounts to an informal, descriptive model. The great strength of descriptive theory, such as that of Schumpeter, is that, it first allows for the integration of economic, sociological, political and historical factors and, second, it permits new ideas to flourish unfettered by the need to formalize and to demonstrate data compatibility. However, in order to address the questions we have posed we need to go beyond the descriptive approach and proceed to a formal model.

The details of the model, which builds on the work of Grossman and Helpman (1992) and the general ideas discussed up to this point, are set out fully in Currie *et al.* (1999), and here I provide a brief sketch. The key features of the model are:

1   Growth is driven by the production of new varieties of goods and by the accumulation of knowledge capital in the North and South. Growth can persist indefinitely because there is no limit to the potential for increasing knowledge. The expanding variety of goods can consist of consumption goods or inputs into production.

2   R&D in the North is devoted to the development of new innovative goods which are then produced in that region. Over time, each Northern good is eventually copied by the South and production is shifted to that region.

3   Southern producers invest in two forms of R&D: imitation and innovation. Research into imitation enables the South eventually to copy Northern goods, and is a mechanism for transferring technology from the advanced region. Research into innovation enables the South to add new varieties to the world's stock of goods. Both copied and innovative goods are then produced in the South. Innovation is harder and therefore more costly than imitation, but it is also more profitable – which is the reason both these activities can co-exist.

4   R&D, as well as producing blueprints for new goods, generates knowledge capital which is a public good within and between the two regions. Spillovers between regions take longer than within regions. The time taken for a unit of knowledge capital to spread from the North to the South is crucial for the outcome.

5   What distinguishes the North from the South is, first, that it provides a more conducive environment for innovation. Second, the superior ability of the North to absorb knowledge capital from the South. This ensures that the knowledge capital per worker and the real wage is higher in the North at every point in time.

6   The final feature of our model is that unemployment effects are ignored by assuming that labour markets clear. This may seem surprising in view of my comment that the 'competitiveness' problem for the North is a labour market problem. This modelling approach of the profession reflects the traditional separation of long-term growth and labour market issues among macro-economists. In the standard neo-classical growth models of the 1970s, long-term productivity growth would simply be determined by exogenous technical change. The equilibrium rate of unemployment, either under the guise of a natural rate or NAIRU, would be determined by the institutional structure of the labour markets. This dichotomy has been carried over to the endogenous growth era.

Given this set-up, the two key features that determine the trading patterns between North and South are: (i) the speed with which the South absorbs knowledge capital from the North; and (ii) the relative cost of imitating compared with innovating in the South. Figure 8.2 shows how these two features determine which of the three 'phases of development' occurs in the South: imitation, imitation and innovation, and innovation only. Along the vertical axis κ is the speed at which the South learns from the North. κ^{-1} is average time taken for an idea implemented in the North to be transferred to the South. Along the horizontal axis is the relative cost of copying relative to innovating in the South (α_c/α).

Progression from a phase with imitation only in the South to higher phases can take place if, first, the cost of copying relative to innovation increases and, second, the rate of assimilation of knowledge capital by the South increases. In

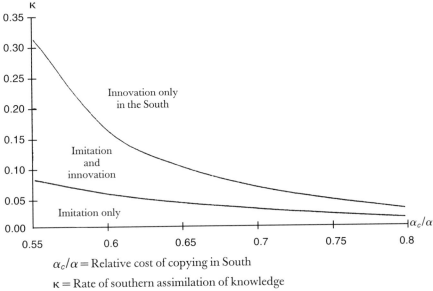

$\alpha_c/\alpha =$ Relative cost of copying in South

$\kappa =$ Rate of southern assimilation of knowledge

Figure 8.2 Phases of development

our model, imitation never occurs in the North. One can think of this as reflecting a high degree of international property rights (IPR) protection within advanced countries in the North. But no IPR protection is perfect and one must also consider what happens if it can be eroded. There is a further reason why imitation is more difficult in the North, unless we allow collusion between firms. The reason is that to capture the market, an imitating firm must charge a price – the 'limit price' – that drives its rival out of the market. In doing so, a Northern firm will drive its own profits to zero. Investment in an imitating blueprint can never be worthwhile for a Northern firm. By contrast, a Southern firm can limit price by setting the price at the Northern average wage cost. With Southern wages much lower, this still leaves the Southern firm earning substantial profits from imitation.

One clear policy implication emerges from our analysis. Consider what happens as the rate of knowledge assimilation by the South from the North rises, i.e. the parameter κ increases. Measures that would bring this about would include investment in education and training that will increase the stock of human capital in the South.

Figure 8.3 shows the effect on world growth as we carry out this experiment. These figures refer to a long-run, steady-state in which the growth rates in the North and South are equal. The important point to notice is that the North can benefit from economic development in the South, in that its own growth rate rises. In this case the North is benefiting from increasing knowledge transfers to the South, possibly by financing part of the costs itself in the form of aid.

Apart from policies that influence the two aspects – knowledge assimilation

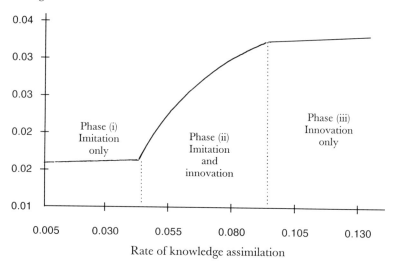

Figure 8.3 World growth and development

and the relative cost of copying in the South – do market forces provide sufficient incentives for innovation and growth? Our model indicates otherwise. Each investment into a new good generates knowledge capital whose public good aspect is of course ignored by the firm evaluating the viability of the project for a new blueprint. This means that the market outcome is inefficient, with a growth rate below that attainable by a mythical social planner. Government support for R&D in the form of the payment of a fraction of R&D expenses can ameliorate this situation, but these must be designed carefully.

Suppose that the South has just entered the middle phase of development where it has a small innovative sector but is mainly imitating. In this situation, subsidies (possibly in the form of aid) that find their way into Southern imitation will be counter-productive, since imitation is a relatively wasteful activity from a global perspective. It fails to create new goods. It also provides a disincentive to the innovators in the North who face the increased possibility of being forced out of the market.

Suppose subsidies are provided to Northern innovators. This will increase the growth of innovations in the North, but will also make imitation in the South more profitable because Northern wages rise and the Southern limit price is then higher. We find that for a range of plausible parameter values the overall result is a drop in the global growth rate.

Our third policy experiment for raising world growth, subsidising Southern innovation, gives by far the best outcome. This adds to the stock of the world's new goods and poses a lesser threat to Northern producers than copying.

Now let us consider the welfare implications of higher growth from increased Southern innovation. One needs to be cautious about implying that welfare automatically increases with growth, even from a narrow view of welfare that ignores distribution, unemployment and the environmental impact. An increase in growth does not necessarily increase welfare measured in terms of consumption of the average citizen over a long period of time. To measure welfare from consumption at different times, present and future, we discount the expected flow over a life-time. Growth could be very costly in terms of the investment necessary to sustain that growth. The Soviet example springs to mind; high growth matched by very high forced savings (or investment ratios) is not necessarily synonymous with economic welfare. In the international context, high growth could be accompanied by a deterioration in a country's terms of trade, i.e. import costs relative to export prices rise. This actually happens to the North in our middle phase of Southern development.

When Southern innovation is subsidised, this increases growth; but as South shifts production from copied goods to innovative goods then the price of their exports to the North rises. However, in our simulations the benefits of higher growth for the North dominate, even when the North pays for the subsidies.

In Figure 8.4, Northern welfare is plotted on the vertical axis and Southern welfare on the horizontal axis. *O* marks the point where there are no subsidies; the shaded region is where both North and South benefit compared with no

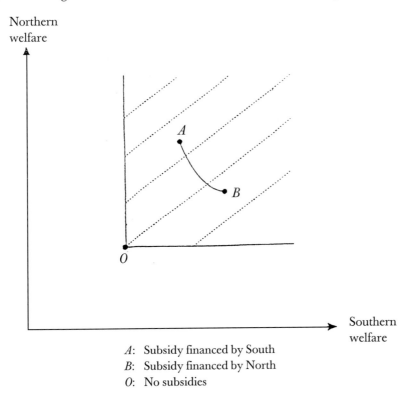

A: Subsidy financed by South
B: Subsidy financed by North
O: No subsidies

Figure 8.4 Aid which benefits everyone

subsidies. At B, the North is still in this region: i.e. the rich countries themselves actually benefit from helping the poor countries. This is important because history is littered with grand global designs that were never implemented because they were not based on mutual interest.

Conclusions

Let me conclude by emphasizing three points. The first concerns the question of low wage-cost competitiveness and the benefits to the North in the Southern copying phase of development. I have stressed the analogy with technical progress. As with technical progress, importing low-cost goods brings about considerable economic benefits for the rich countries of the world and releases labour for other activities. The problems of adjusting to these structural changes should be approached with policies directed at the labour market and distribution, and not the trade regime.

The Luddites in the nineteenth century regarded technical change itself as the problem. Their modern counterparts are those who regard low-cost imports as requiring a new trade policy. Luddism has become a pejorative term. One must hope that the same will happen to the modern advocates of regulated trade. We should resist the temptation to impose conditions for 'fair trade'. This could start as a voluntary contribution to low-paid workers in a 'supermarkets' charter', and personally I would support these initiatives. But this approach could also degenerate into support for import controls, a real threat now facing the world. One thing that history tells us is that the world has grown richer in periods of trade liberalization and that those who have benefited the most, like the countries of Asia, are those who have participated in this growth of world trade. The experience of the twentieth century is that autarky, such as that followed in Eastern Europe, the Soviet Union and China until the 1980s, and India until more recently, has simply not worked.

My second point concerns unequal exchange: We in the rich countries cannot expect this to continue for ever. We cannot expect the rest of the world to provide us with cheap goods indefinitely. Development brings about higher average wages, incomes and conditions of work. This has happened in Japan, in the Asian tigers and is beginning to happen in the rest of Asia. But then the terms of trade benefits for the North will disappear, the second real 'threat' to our living standards. However, this is a scenario we must accept morally and realistically.

Finally, there are compensating dynamic benefits to the North from Southern development. This has been shown by our research drawing on recent advances in growth theory. Basically, economic growth is about productivity growth and productivity growth is about innovation. It is about harnessing human potential for creative activity in the production of new and/or better quality goods and more efficient production processes. Endogenous growth theory indicates that laissez-faire policies will not enable this potential to be realized. But it also suggests that the regulation of trade is not the appropriate focus for intervention.

The financial crisis in Asia has inspired attacks on the recent trends towards more open economic policies. Although short-run pragmatism is inevitable, this essay has argued that a permanent reversal of these trends would be a great mistake. Openness presents the prospect of the whole world, rather than a small part of it, participating in the growth process. The primary beneficiaries of this process will be the people living in the poor countries of the world. Far from constituting a threat to us in the affluent North, their progress will bring material benefits from the resulting increase in world-wide growth.

Acknowledgement

Financial support from the Leverhulme Trust Grant Number No. F/124/N 'Growth, innovation and competitiveness: the challenge of Asia for the West' is gratefully acknowledged.

References

Bhagwati, J. (1958), 'Immiserizing growth: a geometrical note', *Review of Economic Studies*, Vol. 25, June, pp. 201–5.

Currie, D. A., Levine, P., Pearlman, J. and Chui, M. (1999), 'Phases of Imitation and Innovation in a North–South Endogenous Growth Model', *Oxford Economic Papers*, Vol. 51, pp. 60–88.

Emmanuel, A. (1972), *Unequal Exchange: A Study of the Imperialism of Trade*, New York: Monthly Review Press.

European Commission (1993), *Growth, Competitiveness and Employment*, White Paper, Brussels.

Grossman, G. M. and Helpman, E. (1992), *Innovation and Growth in the Global Economy*, Cambridge, MA: MIT Press.

Layard, R., Nickell, S. and Jackman, R. (1991), *Unemployment: Macroeconomic Performance and the Labour Market*, Oxford: Oxford University Press.

Lewis, W. A. (1954), 'Economic development with unlimited supplies of labour', *Manchester School*, Vol. 22, no. 2, pp. 139–91.

Mankiw, N. G., Romer, P. M. and Weil, D. N. (1992), 'A contribution to the empirics of economic growth', *Quarterly Journal of Economics*, Vol. 107, May, pp. 407–37.

Romer, P. M. (1986), 'Increasing returns and long-run growth', *Journal of Political Economy*, Vol. 94, October, pp. 1002–37.

Romer, P. M. (1990), 'Endogenous technical change', *Journal of Political Economy*, Vol. 98, October, S71–S102.

Schumpeter, J. (1942), *Capitalism, Socialism and Democracy*, New York: Harper.

Sachs, J. D. and Warner A. (1995), 'Economic reform and the process of global integration', *Brooking Papers on Economic Activity*, Vol. 1, pp. 1–117.

Vernon, R. (1966), 'International Investment and International Trade in the Product Cycle', *Quarterly Journal of Economics*, Vol. 80, May, pp. 190–207.

Wood, A. (1994), *North–South Trade, Employment and Inequality*, Oxford: The Clarendon Press.

Young, A. (1995), 'The tyranny of numbers: confronting the statistical realities of the East Asian growth experience', *Quarterly Journal of Economics*, Vol. 110, August, pp. 641–80.

9 The agrarian question in an age of 'New Capitalism'

A. Haroon Akram-Lodhi[1]

'The most dramatic and far-reaching social change of the second half of this century, and the one which cuts us off for ever from the world of the past, is the death of the peasantry'.

(Hobsbawm 1995, p. 289)

Introduction

In 1899, two remarkable books were published, one in Stuttgart and one in Moscow: *The Agrarian Question* by Karl Kautsky and *The Development of Capitalism in Russia* by V. I. Lenin. Although written without the knowledge of the other, both books shared a similar concern. Kautsky expressed this concern thus: 'is capital, and in what ways is capital, taking hold of agriculture, revolutionizing it, smashing the old forms of production and of poverty and establishing the new forms which must succeed?' (Kautsky 1980, p. 46). In examining the central processes underpinning the development of capitalist relations of production in agriculture, and thus the development of agriculture in capitalist societies, Kautsky and Lenin together defined an issue known as the 'agrarian question'. This issue has been a major concern within political economy for a century.

With the exception of his early work on Kenya, the major focus of the work of Sam Aaronovitch has involved understanding the concentration and central-ization of capital, their implications for accumulation, and the pivotal role of the state in structuring accumulation. These issues may appear to be far removed from the agrarian question. However, they are of relevance to the study of the agrarian question at the end of the twentieth century. In the 1990s it appears that national economies are becoming increasingly integrated into global circuits of production, trade and finance. Global integration has been accompanied by a strengthening of processes of concentration and centralization, by a globalization of accumulation, and by a seeming weakening of the role of the state. These developments have had an affect upon the role of agriculture in the evolution of the capitalist mode of production. Some have argued that tectonic shifts are underway in what has become a truly global agro-food system (Friedmann 1993, Bonanno *et al.* 1994, Goodman and Watts 1997). Indeed for some of these observers, the evolution of a seemingly 'new' global capitalism marks a decisive theoretical and practical break: old issues have disappeared into history, and new paradigms are required.

This essay rests upon two propositions. The first is that in an era of global-ization the agrarian question continues to illuminate areas of vital importance when understanding the development of capitalism. The second is that the impact of globalization upon the agrarian question can be better conceptualized and understood through the use of some of the propositions central to the work of Sam Aaronovitch. The following section discusses the nature of the agrarian question as it is posed within political economy. A later section (p. 117) examines whether the agrarian question still exists in an era of 'new' capitalism, while another (p. 119) details the extent of structural transformation in an age of globalization and suggests that the agrarian question is still relevant. Finally, some tentative comments are made on the deepening complexity of the agrarian question in an era of globalization.

The agrarian question

One of the most important contemporary writers on the agrarian question (and an old comrade of Sam Aaronovitch) has defined it as 'the continuing existence in the countryside . . . of substantive obstacles to an unleashing of the forces capable of generating economic development, both inside and outside agri-culture' (Byres 1991a, p. 9). With such a definition the agrarian question assumes both historical interest and contemporary relevance. Historical interest comes from understanding the manner in which developed market economies resolved the agrarian question and overcame rural obstacles to the structural transfor-mation which is at the heart of economic development. Structural transformation implies changes in the pattern of production, with a shift from an economy dominated by agriculture to an economy driven by manufacturing; produced inputs; more capital-intensive production techniques and technologies in both the agricultural and the non-agricultural sectors; a shift in employment from agricultural to non-agricultural occupations; and the formation of a home market capable of sustaining accumulation. These historical processes have contem-porary relevance: in a host of developing and transitional economies obstacles within agriculture continue to constrain the structural transformation of the economy by inhibiting accumulation. These constraints limit the livelihood of millions of people.

As Bernstein (1996) notes in his assessment of the work of Byres, analysis of the agrarian question proceeds by breaking the concept down into three problematics. The first problematic is termed by Bernstein 'accumulation'. Derived from an understanding rooted in the work of Preobrazhensky [1924] (1965), this problematic is based upon the recognition that agriculture has the potential capacity to create sustainably productive resources surplus to its reproductive requirements, and that these surplus resources could be used to support the heavy resource costs of structural transformation and thus capital accumulation. This problematic therefore seeks to understand the extent to which agriculture can supply a sustainable surplus and meet these resource costs, the ways by which such a surplus can be appropriated to fund accumulation, and the ease with which such an appropriation may occur (Byres 1991b, p. 11).

The second problematic is termed by Bernstein 'production'. Rooted in an analysis drawn directly from Lenin [1899] (1964) and Kautsky [1899] (1988), this problematic explores 'the extent to which capitalism has developed in the countryside, the forms that it takes, and the barriers which may impede its development' (Byres 1991b, p. 9). In exploring developments surrounding the possible emergence of agrarian capital and agrarian wage labour, this problematic focuses upon issues affecting the structural transformation of petty commodity producing peasant labour into a commodified form, labour power, through the restructuring of labour processes and processes of class formation and differentiation.

The third problematic is termed by Bernstein 'politics'. In countries which have or which have had large peasant populations, emancipatory political formations have had to seek explicitly to create and sustain alliances with substantive elements of the peasant population when emancipatory political practices have been successful in fomenting social, political and economic change. Drawing directly from the original theorization by Engels [1894] (1950), the politics problematic focuses upon examining the impact of political forces and forms on the evolution of rural change that is explicit in both the accumulation and production problematics.

Thus, in terms of accumulation, production and politics, agriculture has had (in developed market economies) and continues to have (in contemporary developing and transitional economies) the capacity to facilitate or constrain structural transformation and economic development. In order to remove agricultural obstacles to accumulation, the agrarian question must, in a sense, be 'resolved', through some form of successful 'agrarian transition'. Paraphrasing Byres (1996, p. 3), an agrarian transition happens when changes occur in the countryside that are necessary to the overall development of a mode of production and to the ultimate dominance of that mode of production within a particular economy. Many context-specific 'paths' of agrarian transition have been attempted (Byres 1991b), within the context of both capitalist and post-capitalist modes of production. However, the only seemingly successful and sustainable examples of agrarian transition appear to follow a capitalist path, and for this reason analysis of the agrarian question tends to focus upon circumstances contributing to or inhibiting a capitalist agrarian transition.

Current efforts at facilitating a successful capitalist agrarian transition in contemporary poor and transitional economies are dominated by the initiatives of the World Bank and supported by the International Monetary Fund (IMF), the World Trade Organization (WTO) and the major capitalist economies. In particular, the structural adjustment programmes initiated at the behest of the World Bank in many economies are predicated upon an implicit theoretical conceptualization of the factors which impede the development of capitalism and thus prevent the resolution of the agrarian question. At its most basic, for the

World Bank, capitalism in agriculture is impeded by state intervention in rural economies. Therefore structural adjustment programmes promulgate a series of supply side reforms which seek to withdraw the state in order to both enhance the capacity of agriculture to generate resources capable of funding accumulation and to ensure that these resources are allocated through market processes. Deregulating reforms seek to homogenize the form of capitalist development across economies, to assist in the full fruition of capitalist relations of production in rural areas, and in so doing to overcome barriers to capitalist development. It should be stressed that despite the fact that many alternative paths of transition have been completed, and that the character of such paths depends upon the specific characteristics of rural class relations, forms of production, patterns of investment and intersectoral links (Byres 1991a, Bernstein 1994), structural adjustment programmes are essentially seeking to replicate the outcome of a single path (the path traversed by the North and West of the United States in the eighteenth and nineteenth centuries) on the diverse range of developing and transitional economies.

Thus, the World Bank and other orthodox analysts have not critically evaluated successful capitalist agrarian transitions. If they had, they would have witnessed a conundrum: it would appear possible, in many historical cases, to remove the obstacles to economic development located within the countryside and unleash the structural transformation of an economy in a capitalist direction without 'the full development of capitalism in the countryside', in the sense of the dominance of capitalist social relations of production in agriculture (agrarian capital and wage labour) (Bernstein 1996, pp. 24–5, Byres 1991a, 1996). This conundrum has been and continues to be the subject of extensive debate within political economy.

The end of the agrarian question

Policies designed to resolve the agrarian question through encouraging the development of rural capitalism and thus facilitating a capitalist path of agrarian transition are a critical factor affecting the rural livelihoods of millions of people, many of whom who are among the world's poorest. Yet it is becoming increasingly clear that many activists and academics are starting to question the continued relevance of the issues located within the agrarian question. The reason is an, at times unstated, belief that the globalization of economic activity has ushered in an era of capitalism which is distinctly different from that which has gone before it.

At the heart of the new global capitalism lies transnational capital, which is restructuring the world economy. Between 1980 and 1996, foreign trade grew twice as fast as the value of output (*The Economist* 18 October 1997), indicating a deepening global division of labour. Over the same period, foreign direct investment by transnational capital grew three times as fast as world output, indicating the development of global circuits of production within which these divisions of labour should be located. Indeed, sales by the foreign affiliates of transnationals have been growing more than 20 per cent faster than the growth of exports, and in 1995 such sales exceeded the value of world exports. Moreover, some 70 per cent of international royalties on technology occur between foreign affiliates and their 'parent' transnational. Part of the explanation for the growth in international economic activity lies in the actions of international financial and trading institutions such as the IMF and the General Agreement on Tariffs and Trade and its successor, the WTO, which have facilitated a sharp reduction in barriers to trade since the 1950s and the creation of a more liberal international trade and investment environment.

More important however has been technological progress. Efficient and inexpensive communications and information management systems have reduced the barriers of time and space which had restricted production and sales to national economies. Information technology has permitted transnational capital to re-engineer divisions of labour and organize the labour process on a global scale, so as to be able to allocate more flexibly increasingly multi-specialized capital and labour. Flexible specialization has not been restricted to manufactures. The information technology upon which flexible specialization rests has also expanded the range of tradeable services. Developments in organizational structures have facilitated an increased capacity to manage complex networks and thus capture economies of scope. Improvements in transportation systems have, particularly in combination with flexible specialization, enhanced the possibilities of both cross-border production and meeting cross-border demand. Cumulatively, these changes have facilitated the re-structuring of the capitalist labour process by transnational capital. As a consequence, foreign direct investment flows by transnational capital increased at three times the average annual rate of domestic investment between 1986 and 1996 (UNCTAD 1997). There can be little doubt that, at the heart of the new capitalism, lies transnational capital and its control of the flexible specialization labour process.

However, it is not the increasing power of transnational capital in the global economy which warrants re-examination of the agrarian question. Rather, the issue is that large parts of the world which have not been significant parts of the global economy are being increasingly drawn into international economic processes prior to undergoing an agrarian transition. This is quite a different conjuncture than that obtaining when the developed market economies became integrated into the global economy. For the most part, developed market economies were either undergoing or had successfully completed an agrarian transition prior to integration. This difference has important implications for the very possibility of successfully completing an agrarian transition. As classically formulated, the agrarian question is about the limits to accumulation within an economy. Implicit in the approach is the possibility that limits to accumulation may be capable of being transcended. In those developed market economies which have undergone an agrarian transition and thus transcended the limits to accumulation, a pivotal agent in that process has been the state. Yet the institutions and actors that are seeking to promote a capitalist path of agrarian transition within developing and transitional economies through the implementation of structural adjustment programmes seek to squeeze the state and thus reduce its power to intervene (Wuyts 1996). The implication is that 'the dynamics of agrarian issues are significantly displaced from the national context, in which the state is the main actor' (Kearney 1996, p. 128). In such circumstances the capacity to construct a path of agrarian transition may be open to doubt.

Other writers are more nuanced in their questions. In particular, in an important essay Bernstein (1996) argues that international dynamics have affected the possible role of agriculture in the development process by changing the conditions of industrialization. Bernstein argues that the problematics of accumulation and of production are inexorably changing as developing and transitional economies become integrated into the global agro-food system, and comes to a dramatic conclusion: the breakdown of boundaries which has occurred in the era of globalization may signal the 'death' of the agrarian question except in the third problematic, that of politics. Once again, the capacity to construct a path of agrarian transition may be questionable. Thus, for a range of analysts and activists the agrarian question, as classically formulated, may no longer be useful because the world to which it alludes no longer exists; the question has become redundant.

Globalization and structural transformation

In order to evaluate whether the agrarian question has in fact become redundant it is necessary to assess the extent to which transnational capital has integrated the global agro-food system and in so doing has irreversibly altered the processes of accumulation and production which serve as the foundation upon which structural transformation occurs. A starting point for such an assessment is an understanding of the quantitative importance of transnational capital in the global agro-food system. Here the answer is clear: there can be little doubt that empirically transnational capital is increasingly dominating the global agro-food system. Using foreign assets is a common indicator of 'transnationality' (Ietto-Gillies 1992). Table 9.1 ranks the ten largest agro-food transnationals by the size of their foreign assets in 1995. Table 9.1 also provides data on aggregate market capitalization and turnover. A first point to note about Table 9.1 is that the size of agro-food transnational capital is quite striking. Thus, Coca-Cola and Philip Morris both have a market capitalization in excess of US$ 100 billion. Moreover, the size of agro-food transnational capital in relation to countries is notable. If data on transnational turnover are compared with its closest macro-economic equivalent, data on national production, the comparative size of Nestlé is dramatic: with a turnover of US$ 41.1 billion, Nestlé is larger than many lower-middle income countries. Indeed, even Danone, the smallest transnational by total market capitalization listed in the top ten, had a turnover in 1997 worth more than the total GDP of Zambia and Zimbabwe combined. A third point to note about Table 9.1 is the country of origin of these transnationals. They all originate in the developed market economies. It is of interest that the largest agro-food transnational from a developing country in 1995 was Panamerican

Table 9.1 The top 10 agro-food transnationals, ranked by foreign assets

Company	Country	Total assets, 1995 (bn $)	Foreign assets, 1995 (bn $)	Rank in top 100	Rank in UNCTAD TNC index	Market capital-ization, 1997 (bn $)	Rank in top 500	Turn-over, 1997 (bn $)
Nestlé	Switzerland	38.2	33.2	9	1	54.3	41	41.1
Unilever	UK/Netherlands	30.1	25.8	17	8	57.5	33	53.7
Philip Morris	USA	53.8	19.5	26	62	100.7	12	54.6
Seagram	Canada	21.4	17.5	30	4	12.7	311	9.7*
BAT Industries	UK	55.1	17.5	31	23	27.0	118	11.6
Grand Metropolitan	UK	17.5	9.5	65	19	20.0	182	14.4
McDonald's	US	15.4	8.2	71	42	32.8	86	10.7
PepsiCo	US	25.4	7.7	79	84	61.5	30	31.6
Coca-Cola	US	15.0	7.5	80	31	151.3	5	18.5
Danone	France	19.0	6.7	89	63	11.3	354	14.0

Note: * is for 1995

Source: UNCTAD 1997, *Financial Times* 22 January 1998

Beverages, from Mexico. With total assets in 1995 of US$ 1.4 billion, Pan-american Beverages was less than 8 per cent of the size of Danone.

However, the agro-food sector within which these transnationals operate is a less significant one in international economic relationships. Table 9.2 gives data on the growth of global agricultural trade between 1990 and 1994. The table demonstrates that the growth in both the volume and the value of world agricultural trade dramatically exceeds the growth in the volume of world agricultural production and, indeed, world output as a whole. Divisions of labour are indeed deepening. Moreover, the value of the largest component of world agricultural trade, food trade, is growing faster than the growth in the value of world agricultural trade, indicating that food trade is to some extent driving the expansion of world agricultural trade. Be that as it may, Table 9.2 also demonstrates that between 1984 and 1994 the share of world trade accounted for by agro-food commodities declined by some 1.5 per cent, indicating that while agro-food trade is growing, the sector is not as dynamic as other components of world trade. Its declining significance is a long-run structural feature of world trade, and is consistent with Engels' Law.

At the same time, there is sharp bifurcation in the global food trade. Table 9.3 gives information on global food exports and imports by regions of the world for 1994. The global food trade is dominated by the developed market economies of Western Europe and North America. Indeed, almost half of world food trade is accounted for by Western Europe, and this trade is dominated by that which occurs within the European Union under the Common Agricultural Policy. Thus, while transnationals may be important in the global agro-food system, for such transnationals the developed market economies are much more important than the developing and transitional economies. Africa, the Middle East and

Table 9.2 Global agricultural trade

	1990–4 (% per annum)
Growth of world GDP	1.0
Growth in volume of world agricultural production	1.0
Growth in volume of world agricultural trade	4.5
Growth in value of world agricultural trade	4.0
Growth in value of world food trade	5.0
Share of agricultural trade in world merchandise exports, 1994	12.0
Change in share of agricultural trade in world merchandise exports, 1984–94	–1.5
Share of food trade in world merchandise exports, 1994	9.3

Source: World Trade Organization 1995

Table 9.3 Global food trade (%) by region, 1994

Exports		Imports	
Western Europe	47.0	Western Europe	48.5
Asia	19.0	Asia	22.5
North America	16.5	North America	11.0
Latin America	11.0	Latin America	5.5
Africa	3.5	Africa	4.0
Middle East	1.0	Middle East	4.0

Source: World Trade Organization 1995

Latin America are comparatively small and relatively less important in overall global food trade. While the table does not demonstrate it, so too are China and India, the two largest countries within the Asia region.

The implication that can be drawn from Tables 9.1–9.3 is that while trans-national capital dominates the global agro-food system, that dominance is in absolute terms most significant in the developed market economies where the transnationals have in fact originated. Such a finding is not surprising. Although the issues raised by the impact of globalization on economic relationships may appear new, they do so, in part, because of an inadequate attention to previous work on corporate rivalry and re-structuring. Here, some of the classic and early work of Sam Aaronovitch can be of assistance in understanding whether globalization is 'new'.

Aaronovitch did not see globalization as some kind of 'new' capitalism. Rather, globalization and the increasing dominance of transnational capital would be seen as a logical outcome of capitalism. Within the capitalist mode of production, an individual capital must control the labour process in order to foster accumulation. However 'each capital's drive for accumulation impinges on other blocks of capital' (Aaronovitch 1981, p. 261; see also Aaronovitch 1977). The rivalry implied in the drive for accumulation 'gives rise to the tendency for concentration to increase. . . . To accumulate and compete success-fully, size and market power are both sought' (Aaronovitch 1981, p. 263–4). A by-product of size and market power is control over the finance and credit needed to further concentrate the production of commodities. At the same time, the control over finance and credit which comes with size and market power facilitates the centralization of capital, in which 'existing blocks of capital are amalgamated into larger agglomerations' (Aaronovitch 1981, p. 262). As firms grow and face the emergence of spatial limits to accumulation, 'the pursuit of the advantages of size is carried on at an international level' (Aaronovitch 1981, p. 264). Thus, driven by accumulation under conditions of rivalry the emergence of agro-food transnational capital may be viewed as the outcome of the 'continuous and dynamic restructuring' which is central to the capitalist mode of production (Aaronovitch 1981, p. 259). It is not surprising that such restructuring has gone furthest in those areas where the capitalist mode of production is most advanced, namely the developed market economies, because the coercive constraint of competition is sharpest in those economies. Thus, it is not surprising that in absolute terms the dominance of transnational capital within the agro-food system is greatest in the developed market economies.

In this light, recent doubts about the historic originality of current global-ization processes appear appropriate (Weiss 1997). Stocks of outward foreign direct investment as a share of GDP for The Netherlands, the UK, France, Germany and the US were less in 1996 than they were in 1914 (*The Economist* 18 October 1997). Merchandise trade as a share of GDP for the UK and France was only slightly more in 1996 than it was in 1913. Current evidence of globalization may in fact represent a sustained cyclical upswing consistent with the re-structuring of capital in an effort to renew conditions favourable to accumulation. If such is the case, this does not mean that transnational capital and the globalization of the agro-food system should be ignored. Rather, the circumstances which gave rise to this conjuncture must be carefully and critically evaluated before concepts such as the agrarian question are deemed to be obsolete. After all, few would deny the relevance of the agrarian question during the last sustained cyclical upswing in globalization, prior to the First World War.

The current phase of global agro-food restructuring can be traced back to the collapse of the second international food regime of 1945 to 1973 (Friedmann 1987). Transnationals controlled a capital-intensive productivity revolution in many developed market economies' agriculture (Hobsbawm 1995). Agricultural output per capita increased at an historically unparalleled rate. Indeed, since 1961 world food production has grown some 20 per cent faster than world population. This productivity revolution led to growing grain surpluses in both the USA and the European Community, and intensifying rivalry in the world grain trade. With rivalry came instability. Growing disorder in world food markets led to deepening attempts by agro-food transnational capital to regulate the operation of global food markets in their own interest in the spheres of production, trade, processing and consumption, through the integration of agro-food commodity chains (Friedmann 1993). However, while similar processes may be observed in manufacturing industry, these processes have not occurred in agriculture on anything like the scale witnessed in manufacturing. Global agriculture 'is not characterised by vertically integrated transnational production systems. Neither do key firms centrally coordinate global intra-firm divisions of labour involving global outsourcing' (Watts and Goodman 1997, p. 14). The process of agro-food restructuring in the developed market economies remains incomplete; and as such, its final shape remains contingent.

At the same time, the productivity revolution was much more intermittent in the developing and transitional economies. The diffusion of technological capabilities was less widespread. Moreover, the organization of agricultural production in developing and transitional economies commonly generated a structure of agrarian relations which fostered three sub-optimal outcomes when technology was diffused. The first sub-optimal outcome was that technical change was often restricted in its availability (Smits and Tims 1998). The second sub-optimal outcome was that not all of those productivity improvements which did occur were the consequence of technical change. In many instances, 'the factors *driving* poor peasants to intensify labour effort are more important than the factors *permitting* them to do so' (Dyer 1996, p. 123). The third sub-optimal outcome was that, despite the diffusion of technology, the structure of agrarian relations served to restrict severely the employment-generating and income-augmenting possibilities of international trade. For some in developing and transitional economies, the restructuring of agricultural production so that food output could be supplied to segmented markets in the developed market economies meant that the international agro-food trade became a mechanism of economic retrogression, in that essential domestic productive capacity was undermined (Patnaik 1996, Little and Watts 1994).

Table 9.4 gives evidence of the intermittent character of the productivity revolution in global agriculture by providing data on cereal yields in kilograms per hectare for 1980 and 1995. The table demonstrates the consistently superior agrarian productivity record of the high-income countries. Moreover, Table 9.4 also shows that in 1995 only the high-income countries and East Asia and the Pacific had agrarian productivity levels in excess of the world average. Thus, much of the developing world was underperforming in terms of agrarian productivity. What is more noticeable about Table 9.4 however is the inter-temporal evidence. In 1995, the Middle East and North Africa, South Asia and sub-Saharan Africa all had agrarian productivity levels which were less than the world average for 1980. Indeed, for sub-Saharan Africa, agrarian productivity declined between 1980 and 1995. Some regions of the world consistently underperform in terms of agrarian productivity.

Given this it is not surprising that, despite the growing integration of the global agro-food system, there has been a marked lack of structural transformation in much of the world's agriculture. Table 9.5 gives some details on the extent of structural transformation by providing evidence of global agricultural production and structure. The table demonstrates that the rate of growth of global agricultural production slowed in the period 1990–5 when compared with the

Table 9.4 Agricultural productivity

Region	Cereal yields (kg/ha)	
	1980	1995
High-income	3350	4183
East Asia/The Pacific	2711	4069
Latin America/The Caribbean	1798	2517
Middle East/North Africa	1254	1827
South Asia	1438	2130
Sub-Saharan Africa	1050	988
World	2309	2730

Source: World Bank 1997

Table 9.5 Global agricultural production and structure

Region	Growth of GDP (%)		Growth of agriculture (%)		Agriculture in GDP (%)		Agricultural labour force (%)	
	1980–90	1990–5	1980–90	1990–5	1980	1995	1980	1990
High income	3.2	2.0	2.3	0.6	3	2	9	6
East Asia/The Pacific	7.6	10.3	4.8	3.9	27	18	73	70
Latin America/ The Caribbean	1.7	3.2	2.0	2.3	10	10	34	25
Middle East/ North Africa	0.2	2.3	4.5	3.3	9	..	48	36
South Asia	5.7	4.6	3.2	3.0	39	30	70	64
Sub-Saharan Africa	1.7	1.4	1.9	1.5	24	20	72	68
World	3.1	2.0	2.8	1.3	7	5	53	49

Source: World Bank 1997

decade of the 1980s. This slowdown occurred in all regions of the world except Latin America and the Caribbean. Table 9.5 also demonstrates that an important indicator of structural transformation, a shift in the importance of agriculture in the overall pattern of economic activity, appears to be evident world-wide. World-wide, agriculture accounts for only 5 per cent of value added. In no region does agriculture comprise more than one-third of all value added. However, another indicator of structural transformation, a shift in the pattern of employment from agriculture to non-agriculture, is not evident. In the world as a whole, agriculture employs half of all the labour force. In East Asia, the Pacific, South Asia and sub-Saharan Africa, two-thirds of the labour force are employed in agriculture.

Table 9.6 gives evidence of a third indicator of structural transformation, the shift in the pattern of agricultural inputs towards those of a greater capital-intensity, by detailing global agricultural inputs. Three points stand out from Table 9.6. The first point is that there is an increase in irrigated arable land in all

Table 9.6 Global agricultural inputs

Region	Arable land (per capita)		Irrigated land (% of arable)		Fertilizer consumption ('00g/ha)		Tractors ('000)	
	1980	1994	1980	1994	1980–1	1994–5	1980	1990
High-income	0.49	0.43	9.5	10.5	1285	1169	14180	15374
East Asia/The Pacific	0.14	0.11	32.2	34.8	1027	1976	888	1049
Latin America/ The Caribbean	0.38	0.30	9.8	12.3	541	647	1101	1517
Middle East/ North Africa	0.31	0.24	23.2	28.6	400	565	302	532
South Asia	0.23	0.18	27.8	34.1	346	803	512	1585
Sub-Saharan Africa	0.40	0.28	3.7	4.1	145	135	277	258
World	0.32	0.26	15.0	17.3	817	852	21245	25945

Source: World Bank 1997

regions of the world. However, in sub-Saharan Africa the increase is from a very low base, and therefore water remains a key production constraint. The second point is that in 1994–5 only the high-income countries and East Asia and the Pacific were able to achieve levels of fertilizer consumption greater than the world average in 1980–1. The third point is that, although all regions bar sub-Saharan Africa have witnessed an increase in farm mechanization, this increase is disproportionately attributable to the high income countries. Developing and transitional economies have a far lesser degree of farm mechanization. In aggregate, Table 9.6 does not give consistent evidence of a structural transformation in the use of agricultural inputs. The picture is far more mixed, with productivity-enhancing technologies being used world-wide, but to a far lesser extent in developing and transitional economies than in the most productive area of the world agro-food economy, the high-income economies. Moreover, the picture for sub-Saharan Africa is dismal, with declines in agrarian productivity being matched by declines in the use of fertilizer and farm machinery.

Several conclusions follow from the preceding three tables. First, as one would expect the agrarian question as such does not exist in the developed market economies. The structural transformation of agriculture has occurred, and thus agriculture is not an obstacle to economic development. Second, the terrain of the agrarian question in developing and transitional economies has altered. Third, however, it would appear that in many developing and transitional economies structural changes in agriculture have been limited: it would not be appropriate to describe these changes as being indicative of wholesale structural transformation. Fourth, in many instances the lack of structural transformation can be ascribed to a lack of technological dynamism in agriculture. This is especially the case if comparison is made with the high-income economies, where fewer people than ever before feed more.

Indeed, in many ways it is the lack of technological dynamism which has led some to argue that 'the category *peasant*, whatever validity it may once have had, has been outdistanced by contemporary history' (Kearney 1996, p. 1). Limited productivity gains in developing and transitional economies, in the context of re-structuring within global agro-food commodity chains, led many peasant farmers into a position where they could not compete with the import of food surpluses dumped from the developed market economies. In a sense absolute advantage overwhelmed any possibility of using comparative advantage. In such a situation, it appeared to many outside observers that farmers in developing and transitional economies seemed to face one of two possibilities. The first possibility was to leave agriculture and move to the cities. This occurred in many places: particularly in Latin America, but also in the Maghreb and the Middle East. The second possibility was to adapt and diversify livelihood strategies in ways which appeared to eradicate 'conventional distinctions between "peasant-traditional-subsistence" and "farmer-modern-commercial"' agriculture (Kearney 1996, p. 129). This possibility was however misleading. It was not so much that peasants began to diversify livelihoods. Remittances and informal activities have been significant sources of livelihood security among peasants in a range of developing and transitional economies since the last century, and in some instances for much longer. Thus, it was more the case that livelihood security strategies which had always been both complex and predicated on a core engagement in agricultural activities began to be better understood by outsiders.

The restructuring of the global agro-food system has been dominated by transnational capital. Its effects however have been profoundly uneven. Increasing integration in the developed market economies has been accompanied by real, yet circumscribed, integration in the developing and transitional economies. Alongside circumscribed integration there has been limited productivity gains and at best partial structural transformation. Caught within re-structuring global agro-food commodity chains dominated by transnational capital, many peasant farmers migrated. For those who did not, livelihood security strategies, despite having a core role assigned to agricultural activities, became even more complex than they previously had been. It is not so much that the peasantry has died, as rather parts of its body have been amputated. In this context, contrary to those who believe that the agrarian question has become redundant, the lack of structural transformation in Africa, South Asia and parts of Latin America and East Asia implies that issues of accumulation, production and politics remain of central importance in developing and transitional economies. It is not that the agrarian question has ended; rather, it has become more complex.

Globalization, paths of transition and the agrarian question

The concept of the agrarian question contains with it three problematics: accumulation, production, and politics. If indeed the era of globalization has rendered the agrarian question more complex, the issue that remains to be examined is the implication of globalization for these three problematics. This examination can be facilitated through an analysis of the impact of globalization on possible paths of agrarian transition.

The impact of globalization on possible paths of agrarian transition can be divided into three broad categories. The first category concerns those small developing and transitional economies which remain largely excluded from integration into the global economy. Simply put, for these economies the agrarian question remains. The issue of generating resources for structural transformation through a re-structuring of rural production systems remains an urgent one, along with the question of political agency in facilitating processes of re-structuring. Constructing a path of agrarian transition remains a possibility, even if it is limited, since the idea that the state is powerless in an era of globalization can be, in many instances, fallacious (Weiss 1997). However, these economies do now face an additional complication in constructing a path of agrarian transition. In addition to seeking to construct a relatively autonomous, nationally based path of agrarian transition, the possibility also exists of negotiating a process of integration into the global economy in a path of agrarian transition which utilizes the potential of globalization without succumbing to it (Thomas 1974, Fitzgerald 1986). Granted, the amount of state competence required for such a strategy is high. But the examples of South Korea and Taiwan indicate that such a strategy is possible. Moreover, as the East Asian examples demonstrate, the potential benefits to an economy and to the people who live and work within that economy from constructing such a path of agrarian transition are high.

The second category concerns large developing and transitional economies such as China, India, Brazil and Indonesia. Most of these economies have already commenced a process of integration into the global economy. Nonetheless, these economies still have an agrarian question. In larger developing and transitional economies, macro-economic processes do not work as they do in developed market economies (Patnaik 1995). Agriculture acts as a fundamental constraint upon economic development, in that agricultural production and productivity affects real wages, inflation, investment and accumulation in countries where a high proportion of additional income is spent on locally produced food, the supply of which is price inelastic (Sen 1981). The agrarian constraint to economic development in these larger developing and transitional economies can only be removed by re-structuring agrarian relations. This in turn implies re-constructing accumulation strategies and production systems while at the same time working with rural political forms and forces which seek agrarian reform. For these economies, the agrarian question is not redundant: while it must be negotiated within the context of globalization, the construction of a path of agrarian transition remains a pressing development issue.

The third category concerns those smaller developing and transitional economies which have begun a process of integration into the global economy. For this category of economies, economic decision-making has increasingly been abdicated at the national level, as structural adjustment programmes largely formulated outside the countries concerned seek to insert these countries in the global economy. However, this does not mean that these economies' agrarian question has ceased. Bernstein (1996) is certainly correct to argue that the capacity of agriculture to act as a source of resources for industrialization in these economies has changed as they have become integrated into the global economy. Nonetheless, such an emphasis on the conditions governing accumulation implicitly prioritizes accumulation over production and politics. In developing and transitional economies, in all three categories, rural political practices, forms and forces are rooted in issues based upon the prevailing parameters of the accumulation process and the production systems which facilitate such a process. Despite globalization, many in rural politics seek to re-fashion development by constructing a new social structure of accumulation in order to unleash forces capable of generating economic development for the betterment of the majority. Indeed, the late 1990s has witnessed a remarkable revival in peasant movements and a restatement of the case for agrarian reform (Brass 1995, Borras 1997, Petras 1997, Spoor 1997, Kay 1998). Rural politics is thus both shaped by and shapes accumulation and production as it seeks to construct a path of transition in an era of deepening globalization. Indeed, in an era of deepening globalization politics, production and accumulation are becoming if anything even more dynamically inter-related. The agrarian question therefore remains.

This is not to say that globalization is irrelevant to the agrarian question. Rather, as is implied within each of the three categories, the impact of globalization upon the agrarian question has been to add a new and deeper layer of complexity to it. Nonetheless, the construction of a context-specific path of agrarian transition remains central in developing and transitional economies.

At the same time, superimposed on the construction of a context-specific path of agrarian transition there is now, in a sense, a global agrarian question. Within the global economy, social differentiation is increasing. At the same time, agro-food transnational capital produces for the one billion members of the planetary population who are comparatively affluent. The global segmentation of agro-food markets by transnational capital thus parallels differentiation among the global population. However, the fundamentals of the capitalist mode of production have not changed. As the work of Aaronovitch makes clear, the sustainability of transnational agro-food-based accumulation depends upon a continual re-structuring of capital, production systems and the accumulation process itself if crisis is to be avoided. If such re-structuring does not occur, limits to further agro-food-based accumulation will emerge. The capacity to transcend limits to agro-food-based accumulation and re-structure agro-food production systems may be driven by global agro-food politics. Clearly this is an agrarian question, albeit a global one: is it possible for transnational capital to build a sustainable global agro-food system when its existing accumulation strategy is based upon eroding the livelihood security of the majority and thus socially excluding four billion people? The answer to the question can be framed by turning the question on its head: it will become necessary to restructure production systems and accumulation processes and reach the excluded four billion if the global agrarian question is not to generate substantive obstacles to global economic development, both inside and outside agriculture.

Conclusion

In the wake of the emergence of a 'new', global, capitalism, some have suggested that the agrarian question as it was classically formulated within political economy has become redundant. This chapter has sought to demonstrate that such is not the case. Globalization is not as new as some suppose, nor is it as sweeping. Rather, as Sam Aaronovitch would recognize, it is a logical development within the capitalist mode of production. In terms of its impact upon accumulation, production and politics, globalization has added a new layer to the possible ways in which the problematics of the agrarian question might be resolved. There is now a wider, more complex, range of possible, context-specific, paths of agrarian transition capable of being constructed. As a consequence, the strategy of the World Bank to resolve specific agrarian questions looks especially vapid: the attempt to replicate the end results of a path that has only happened once when new possibilities are emerging seems extremely inappropriate. Indeed, it is highly unlikely that a successful path of agrarian transition will resemble that sought by the World Bank. After all, 'capitalist agrarian transition is protean in its manifest diversity' (Byres 1996, quoted in Watts and Goodman 1997, p. 1).

At the same time, the emergence of a global agrarian question could have profound implications. If indeed there is now a global agrarian question, it follows that the resolution of this question requires a global path of agrarian transition which will re-structure accumulation, production and politics. If such is the case it is worth noting that a capitalist agrarian transition represents only one possible means of resolving the global agrarian question. In a world where more food per capita is produced than at any other time in human history, and yet where more people are hungry than at any other time in human history, it is worth remembering that other, post-capitalist, paths of agrarian transition may be possible.

Notes

1   My thanks to Susan Johnson, Ardeshir Sepehri, Jan Toporowski and to the cast and crew of 125 Bromley Road, Catford, who provided me with a place to work.

References

Aaronovitch, S. (1977), 'The firm and concentration', in Green, F. and Nore, P. (eds), *Economics: An Anti-Text*, London: Macmillan, pp. 76–88.
Aaronovitch, S. (1981), 'The reorganizing of capital: concentration and centralization', in Aaronovitch, S. and Smith, R. with Gardiner, J. and Moore, R., *The Political Economy of British Capitalism: A Marxist Analysis*, London: McGraw-Hill Book Company Ltd, pp. 259–74.
Bernstein, H. (1994), 'Agrarian classes in capitalist development', in Sklair, L. (ed.), *Capitalism and Development*, London, Routledge, pp. 40–71.

Bernstein, H. (1996), 'Agrarian questions then and now', in Bernstein, H. and Brass, T. (eds), *Agrarian Questions: Essays in Appreciation of T.J. Byres*, London: Frank Cass, pp. 22–59.

Bonanno, A., Busch, L., Friedland, W., Gouveia, L. and Mingione, E. (eds) (1994), *From Columbus to Conagra: The Globalization of Agriculture and Food*, Lawrence, KS: University of Kansas Press.

Borras, S. (1997), 'The bibingka strategy to land reform implementation: autonomous peasant mobilizations and state reformists in the Philippines', Unpublished M.A. Dissertation, Institute of Social Studies, The Hague.

Brass, T. (ed.) (1995), *New Farmers' Movements in India*, London: Frank Cass.

Byres, T. J. (1991a), 'Agrarian question' in Bottomore, T., Harris, L., Kiernan, V. G. and Miliband, R. (eds), *A Dictionary of Marxist Thought*, Second edition, Oxford: Blackwell Publishers, pp. 9–11.

Byres, T. J. (1991b), 'The agrarian question and differing forms of capitalist agrarian transition: an essay with reference to Asia' in Breman, J. and Mundle, S. (eds), *Rural Transformation in Asia*, Delhi: Oxford University Press, pp. 3–76.

Byres, T.J. (1996), *Capitalism From Above and Capitalism From Below: An Essay in Comparative Political Economy*, London: Macmillan.

Dyer, G. (1996), 'The logic of peasant agriculture under semi-feudalism' in Bernstein, H. and Brass, T. (eds), *Agrarian Questions: Essays in Appreciation of T.J. Byres*, London: Frank Cass, pp. 103–52.

The Economist, various issues.

Engels, F. (1894) (1950), 'The peasant question in France and Germany' in Marx, K. and Engels, F., *Selected Works Volume II*, London: Lawrence and Wishart, pp. 381–99.

Financial Times, various issues.

Fitzgerald, E. V. K. (1986), 'Notes on the analysis of the small underdeveloped economy in transition', in Fagen, R. R., Diana Deere, C. and Coraggio, J. L. (eds), *Transition and Development: Problems of Third World Socialism*, New York: Monthly Review Press, pp. 28–53.

Friedmann, H. (1987), 'The family farm and the international food regimes', in Shanin, T. (ed.), *Peasants and Peasant Societies*, Second edition, Harmondsworth: Penguin Books, pp. 247–58.

Friedmann, H. (1993), 'The political economy of food: a global crisis', in *New Left Review* Vol. 197, pp. 29–57.

Goodman, D. and Watts, M. (eds) (1997), *Globalising Food: Agrarian Questions and Global Restructuring*, London: Routledge.

Hobsbawm, E. (1995), *Age of Extremes: The Short Twentieth Century 1914–1991*, London: Abacus.

Ietto-Gillies, G. (1992), *International Production: Trends, Theories, Effects*, Cambridge: Polity Press.

Kautsky, K. (1899) (1988), *The Agrarian Question*, London: Zwan.

Kautsky, K. (1899) (1980), 'Summary of selected parts of Kautsky's The Agrarian Question', translated by J. Banaji, in Wolpe, H. (ed.), *The Articulation of Modes of Production*, London: Routledge Kegan Paul Ltd, pp. 45–92.

Kay, C. (1998), 'Latin America's agrarian reform: lights and shadows', paper presented to the Rural Development Research Seminar, Institute of Social Studies, The Hague, February.

Kearney, M. (1996), *Reconceptualizing the Peasantry: Anthropology in Global Perspective*, Boulder: Westview Press.

Lenin, V. I. (1899) (1964), *The Development of Capitalism in Russia*, Moscow: Progress Publishers.

Little, P. and Watts, M. (1994), *Living Under Contract: Contract Farming and Agrarian Transformation in Sub-Saharan Africa*, Madison: University of Wisconsin Press.

Patnaik, P. (1995), 'Introduction: Some Indian Themes in Macroeconomics', in Patnaik, P. (ed.), *Macroeconomics*, Delhi: Oxford University Press, pp. 1–27.

Patnaik, P. (1996), 'Trade as a mechanism of economic retrogression' in Bernstein, H. and Brass, T. (eds), *Agrarian Questions: Essays in Appreciation of T.J. Byres*, London: Frank Cass, pp. 211–25.

Petras, J. (1997), 'Latin America: the resurgence of the left' in *New Left Review* No. 223, pp. 17–47.

Preobrazhensky, E. O. (1924) (1965), *The New Economics*, London: Clarendon Press.

Sen, A. (1981), 'The agrarian constraint to economic development: the case of India', unpublished Ph.D. Thesis, University of Cambridge, Cambridge, UK.

Smits, M. J. and Tims, W. (1998), 'The Distribution of New Wheat Varieties in the Pakistan Punjab: The Role and Functioning of Institutions', paper presented to the Development Economics Seminar, Institute of Social Studies, The Hague, January.

Spoor, M. (ed.) (1997), *The 'Market Panacea': Agrarian Transformation in Developing Countries and Former Socialist Economies*, London: Intermediate Technology Publications.

Thomas, C. (1974), *Dependence and Transformation*, New York: Monthly Review Press.

UNCTAD (1997), *World Investment Report 1997*, New York: United Nations.

Watts, M. and Goodman, D. (1997), 'Agrarian Questions: Global Appetite, Local Metabolism: Nature, Culture, and Industry, in *fin-de-siecle* Agro food Systems' in Goodman, D. and Watts, M. (eds), *Globalising Food: Agrarian Questions and Global Restructuring*, London: Routledge, pp. 1–32.

Weiss, L. (1997), 'Globalization and the myth of the powerless state', in *New Left Review*, No. 225, pp. 3–27.

World Bank (1997), *World Development Indicators 1997*, Baltimore: Johns Hopkins Press.

World Trade Organization (1995), *International Trade 1995*, Geneva: World Trade Organization.

Wuyts, M. (1996), 'Foreign Aid, Structural Adjustment and Public Management: the Mozambican Experience', in *Development and Change*, Vol. 27(4), pp. 717–50.

Part III
Finance and the New Capitalism

10 Two views of the City

Alan Budd[1]

This paper considers two ways of analysing the financial sector or, more specifically, that part of it which is popularly known as the 'City'. The first is derived from Marxist analysis and has been particularly applied by Sam Aaronovitch. The second can be variously known as bourgeois, neo-classical or orthodox economics. The two approaches appear to offer conflicting accounts. However it is suggested that the second approach, if extended in a fairly familiar way, can also be used to analyse the features emphasized by the first.

I shall use neo-classical (NC) as a broad rather than a narrow term. A more accurate term might be non-Marxist but that would be too wide and would provide very few limitations on the kind of analysis that could be included. I intend NC to cover the current broad consensus of Anglo-Saxon economics. In terms of macro-economic analysis, it would include most of those who use Keynesian analysis for the short term and something closer to neo-classical analysis for the long term.

Marxist analysis can be characterized both by a particular means of analysing production and accumulation and by a more general approach to economic relationships with a particular emphasis on class. It also produces a different approach to dynamics which emphasizes contradiction and instability rather than a tendency to equilibrium.

Aaronovitch and Smith (1981) describe the limitations of NC economics as follows: '. . . any treatment of economics that merely regards it as a set of technical relationships must be inadequate, because economic processes are rooted in a set of social and political relationships from which they cannot be separated' (Aaronovitch and Smith 1981, p. 1).

Marxist analysis, they claim, provides the most coherent and comprehensive account of economic processes available. This is because it recognizes the way in which the structure of class relations in Britain has influenced the pattern of its development. NC analysis, by contrast, cannot recognize the laws of motion of the system: 'Neo-classical economics is primarily concerned with the process by which the self-interest of individual economic agents – firms maximising profits and consumers maximising utility – leads, through the operations of supply, demand and exchange in a free market, to an equilibrium'. (Aaronovitch and Smith 1981, p. 16).

NC economics, in their view, cannot provide an adequate account of economic behaviour because of the limited scope of the questions it asks, and the method of inquiry that it uses to answer them. In particular it pays inadequate attention to the social processes involved in economic activity: 'To provide a complete economic analysis requires the integration of ideology and politics into the theory, and explicit treatment of the feedbacks between them and the economy' (Aaronovitch and Smith 1981, p. 19).

The resolution of long-running disputes between Marxist and neo-classical economists is far beyond the scope of this paper or the talents of its author. The aim is to cast some light on the issue by studying a narrow topic. The following sections provide first a Marxist and then a neo-classical account of the City.

Finance capital and financial capital: a Marxist interpretation

In *The Ruling Class*, Aaronovitch was seeking to analyse the British economy in ways which applied equally well to the UK as to other economies. He thus examined 'the Marxist conception of finance capital, formed by the fusion of banking and cognate capital with industrial capital'. He was at some pains to demonstrate the links between City institutions, such as the merchant banks, and major UK enterprises. He could thus apply standard Marxist analysis to the UK as another example of an international phenomenon and emphasize the class conflict embodied in the capitalist system: 'those who collectively constitute the owners have a different class interest from those who collectively must sell their ability to work to these owners' (Aaronovitch 1961, p. 69).

This class interest dominated conflicts between capitalists: 'The fact that the capitalist class is composed of groupings very often competing both on a national and international scale does not abolish their common class interest. They may differ on what mixture of concession or repression they are to pursue in relation to the working-class movement; they may differ on the best means of containing world communism or the national liberation movements – but they experience a common need to preserve their class positions' (Aaronovitch 1961, p. 69).

Finance capital is the extreme form of capitalism, most notably in the United Kingdom: '. . . finance capital stands at the head of the British capitalist class, operating not merely in the United Kingdom but on an international scale, owning the principal means of production, appropriating the product, holding the reins of government and dominating the entire economy for its own greater profit' (Aaronovitch 1961, p. 158).

And it was able to exert considerable power in pursuit of its own objectives: 'Finance capital is not one interest among many which may lobby an impartial government and whose legitimate rights such a government should seek to satisfy. It is built into and controls the entire government and administration of this country for its own profit and against the wider interests of the nation' (Aaronovitch 1961, p. 158).

Although Aaronovitch sought, in *The Ruling Class*, to identify the UK as providing an example of finance capital, he drew attention to a particular, and almost unique, historical feature of British capitalism, namely its international orientation. He pointed out that, in the UK, capital funds were not channelled primarily into domestic investment during the early stages of Britain's industrial development: 'From a very early stage the financial and credit machine of Britain was not only not closely linked with British industry but was very closely linked with investment and loans overseas and the exploitation of colonial and foreign raw materials and resources' (Aaronovitch 1961, p. 398).

This separation produced conflicts between the City of London, with its overseas interests, and that section of British industrialists concerned primarily with the domestic market.

This analysis was developed in more detail in *The Political Economy of British Capitalism* (1981). The basic idea had changed slightly with the recognition that the UK had its own version of capitalism (along with the more conventional type), which could be called 'financial capital': 'What has been called here "financial capital" should be distinguished from "finance capital". The latter was the term used by Lenin to describe the fusion of banking and industrial capital. Such a fusion seems more characteristic of German or Japanese capitalism and the British pattern has been rather different' (Aaronovitch and Smith 1981, p. 29).

Freed from the attempt to show that the UK is a typical example of capitalism, Aaronovitch and Smith are able to explain its differences and discuss their consequences.

In brief, the history – which is a fairly orthodox one – runs as follows. The British were the great industrial innovators and entrepreneurs of the eighteenth and early nineteenth centuries. Their progress occurred alongside, but largely independently from, the continued success of the City of London's role as a centre for trade and finance. The City was not a major source of funds for domestic industry; instead it provided funds to finance the Government's deficit and it transferred funds overseas to finance foreign governments and industries.

There were thus two distinguishing features of economic development in the UK. First, there was greater separation of financial from industrial capital than elsewhere. Second, the focus of financial capital was overseas rather than domestic. The separation of financial from industrial capital meant that British industrialists were less financially secure (because they relied to a greater degree on short-term funds). They therefore were reluctant to accept the risks associated with long-term investment projects. Also where, as on the Continent, banks were closely involved in industry they not only took a longer-term view but were able to disseminate information from one company to another.

Not only did financial capital develop separately in the UK, it also became increasingly powerful: 'The City became very early a major economic force in its own right. As a result, the maintenance of conditions in which exported capital was safe, sterling defended, and international commercial and financial operations could freely function became the first priority in state policy' (Aaronovitch and Smith 1981, p. 61).

The conflicts between the interests of the City and the interests of domestic industry became most apparent by the late nineteenth and early twentieth centuries. In the US and on the Continent, particularly in Germany, industry had developed behind tariff walls. In the UK, funds had been transferred overseas. Thus British industry found it increasingly difficult to compete in these markets. The City responded by seeking to maintain control of its own imperial markets.

The restructuring and reorganization of UK industry not only required capital funds, it also required a degree of state intervention which British capitalists were not prepared to accept for fear that it would be used to harm their interests. They also feared that control of trade and capital movements would endanger their freedom to pursue profitability on a world scale and might harm their existing overseas investments. Thus, the dual character of the British industry became established during the period between 1905 and 1914: 'While British capital was a dynamic and expanding force, servicing the development of imperialism and operating profitably on a global level, domestic production failed to develop on the same scale. To the British multi-national companies and international institutions the fact that the British industrial structure decayed as a result of the policies they advocated was of little concern, since those policies also guaranteed their international profitability' (Aaronovitch and Smith 1981, p. 74).

The weaknesses of UK industry were briefly concealed by the disruption of the First World War but soon revealed themselves again in the inter-war years. Matters were made worse by the decision to return to the Gold Standard in 1925: 'The return to gold at the pre-war parity was a City policy, based on their international financial interests; on their desire to discipline the working class; and on their political perception of Britain's world role. The cost of the policy was domestic stagnation, great damage to British industry, and high unemployment'. (Aaronovitch and Smith 1981, p. 75).

In the post-war period, they argue, Britain's industrial weakness and lack of competitiveness caused chronic problems with the balance of payments, particularly during the period of fixed exchange rates. The prolonged struggle to defend the exchange rate and thereby adopt policies inimical to British industry was itself a response to the City's power: 'At almost every critical moment, economic growth within the UK was sacrificed to measures thought necessary to defend Britain's world financial and political position' (Aaronovitch and Smith 1981, p. 69).

Not only could the City exercise its power through its role in the political process, it could also, by its actions, generate balance of payments and sterling crises and thereby directly discipline wayward politicians.

Under this Marxist analysis, the UK has witnessed the familiar class struggle: 'The working class are concerned with advancing employment, income, and social policies; capitalists with advancing profits, maintaining movement of capital and trade, and stopping anything that smacks of socialism' (Aaronovitch and Smith 1981, p. 85).

The main results, Aaronovitch and Smith conclude have been:

- a failure (or refusal) by the British state to carry through the necessary co-ordination and direction for modernizing and expanding the industrial base of the domestic economy;
- a separation of financial and industrial capital that has held back the mobilization of funds for economic growth based on long-term investment strategies;
- a pre-occupation of financial capital with a world role rather than with the UK domestic economy; and
- an insistence (by the City) that the UK was opened up to world competitive pressures, thereby imposing acute balance of payments constraints on economic policy.

We turn next to a neo-classical account of the City and of the developments stressed by Aaronovitch and Smith.

The City: a neo-classical account

How might an NC economist describe the activities of the City? Although 'it's all in Marshall', there is no entry in the index for 'banking'. In discussing money, Marshall has one of his typical moral discussions: 'The growth of a money economy and of modern habits of business does indeed hinder the accumulation of wealth by putting new temptations in the way of those who are inclined to live extravagantly. But against that it increases the opportunity to provide for one's old age and, better still, for one's descendants' (Marshall [1920] 1956, p. 188).

One might invent an NC account as follows. The activities of the financial sector are, in principle, no different from any other commercial or industrial activity. The sector provides a service of intermediation, linking lenders and borrowers. It thereby assists the process of separating expenditure from income, by allowing individuals to spend, for a time, more than they earn. Some parts of the financial sector produce, as a by-product of their activities, financial assets which can be used for transactions. That may or may not be important.

The financial sector is part of a system which produces the following macro-economic conditions. In flow terms, a level of income and pattern of expenditure and output, including a rate of saving and a balance of trade. It also produces a price level, an inflation rate, an exchange rate and a set of interest rates. In stock terms it produces a domestic physical capital stock, stocks of financial assets and liabilities, and levels of employment and unemployment. The ownership of the physical stock and of the financial assets will depend on past flows of income and expenditure and on relative prices and interest rates. So will the distribution of ownership between residents and non-residents.

Thus, non-residents may own UK real and financial assets, and UK residents may own foreign assets. The distribution of ownership is not particularly relevant for the performance of the economy except to the extent that the pattern of ownership (and the distribution of income) affects consumer choices. (This is not to deny that the mechanism for changing the control of firms when default occurs, i.e. the mechanism for dealing with bankruptcy, may be extremely important.)

The neo-classical economist will know something about relative prices, etc. when the system is in equilibrium. Those who work in the financial sector need not, in principle, own any of the funds that are intermediated by it, nor need they own any of the equity capital invested in it. If there were perfect competition in borrowing and lending, the equity capital would earn normal returns, adjusted for risk. To the extent that loans to, or deposits with, financial intermediaries were risky, the lenders and depositors would have to be compensated for this risk and the lending decisions of the intermediaries would be constrained by the depositors' preferences.

Since stocks represent past decisions, the neo-classical economist studying the current state of the City would see it as the result of a process of *ex ante* optimizing decisions taken by households and firms (domestic and foreign). The decisions may have been constrained in the past by regulations, e.g. capital controls. Subject to those constraints, the pattern of assets and loans (maturity, etc.) and the allocation of real and financial assets, between industries and between nations, will reflect the normal marginality conditions.

Thus, if the assets of the financial sector consist, to a considerable extent, of claims on overseas companies that will simply reflect preferences and opportunity in the past.

Is it inevitable that the so-called overseas orientation of the City will be harmful to the domestic UK economy – particularly to its industrialists and workers? To the NC economist the answer is clearly not. We can consider the micro-economic choices made by the agents within the economy and their macro-economic consequences. Decisions about production and consumption (and, in particular, choices between current and deferred consumption) will simultaneously determine output (and its associated level of employment), savings, investment and the trade balance. For our purposes, the crucial aggregate accounting identities show that net international financial flows (including capital movements) are equal, and with the opposite sign, to the current account of the balance of payments. That is, broadly speaking, a balance of payments surplus must be accompanied by an equal net outflow on the capital account. At the same time the trade balance (the surplus of exports over imports) must equal the surplus of aggregate savings over investment (in fixed capital and inventories).

The level of domestic output will depend on employment and the capital stock. The level of employment will tend to full employment and will (in most models) be independent of the level of the capital stock. Gross national product will exceed gross domestic product if the returns from UK investment overseas are greater than the returns from foreign investment in the UK.

We can accept, as an historical fact, that the UK was a net exporter of capital during the nineteenth century. There was a corresponding cumulative balance of payments surplus and surplus of savings over domestic investment. If this was harmful to the domestic economy we have to consider counter-factuals that would have produced a more favourable outcome. The most relevant must be one in which resources were allocated to domestic fixed investment rather than to net trade. (Exports would have been lower and/or imports would have been higher.) The higher path for capital accumulation would have been accompanied, presumably, by a higher path for domestic output; but net income from overseas assets would have been lower, so that there is no reason to believe that gross national product would have been higher. The main difference between the two cases is the extent to which the accumulated savings of the UK were invested in domestic or foreign real assets. It is not obvious, at least to the NC economist, why the accumulation of domestic fixed assets is better than the accumulation of overseas fixed assets. On the contrary, if the events of the nineteenth century occurred in a competitive environment, the NC economist is likely to argue that the chosen path was better than any other (in a Pareto-optimal sense).

Nor is it easy to see where the class struggle or the special interests of the City come into it. There is the usual conflict between the supplier of and the purchaser of labour as there is between the suppliers of and purchasers of fixed and financial capital. Suppliers will want high prices for their goods and services; buyers will want low prices. Competitive markets will resolve that issue. I have commented earlier that there is no reason why the funds that are intermediated by the City institutions should be owned by them. In a competitive market, funds must be allocated to meet the preferences of their owners. To that extent the question of ownership matters, but there is no obvious reason why funds owned by a pure rentier, for example, will be invested in a way that is more harmful to the workers than funds owned by the workers themselves. It does not matter, therefore, that, in the UK, financial capital developed separately from industrial capital.

Thus, the NC economist can observe and explain the same economic processes as the Marxist economist but may regard the outcomes as neither regrettable nor sinister.

Towards a synthesis?

We seem to have a problem of communication here. The Marxist tells a vivid story. There is the fundamental class struggle between capital and labour. In the UK there is the particular development of financial capital embodied in the institutions of the City somewhat separate for domestic industry. Its orientation is international. It finances overseas rather than domestic investment. It supports – as long as it can – British imperialism. It uses its great political power to produce policies which favour international capital rather than the domestic economy. The result, over a long period, is inadequate investment in domestic industry, a loss of world markets for UK exports and increased import penetration, leaving the economy particularly vulnerable to balance of payments crises. In general, the activities of the City go a long way towards explaining the relative decline of the UK economy.

The NC economist wonders what all the fuss is about. He notes the history of UK economic development and observes the role of the City but draws no particular conclusion from it. He does not accept that the British economy (including its workers) would have been better off if the City had been weaker. He certainly does not accept that the success of the City must have been at the expense of the rest of the economy (except in the sense that, for a given level of aggregate real income, one man's gain must be another man's loss).

Can anything be done to bring the two sides closer? Can NC economics inform the Marxist analysis, or vice-versa? Both approaches are seeking to explain and evaluate the same phenomena. NC economics combines explanation and evaluation in the way proposed by Adam Smith and considerably elaborated by later economists in the neo-classical tradition. The familiar result is that a competitive equilibrium (under restrictive conditions) is also a Pareto optimum.

Thus, in a narrow sense, the NC economist can claim not only that what is must be, but also what is is good. So the moral task of evaluating the outcome is replaced by the apparently technical task of asking whether the market conditions are met. The NC economist will recognize that the resulting distribution of income and wealth will legitimately be a subject of moral inquiry, and possibly of policy intervention, but will regard that as a separate issue. Instead of seeing the role of the City and its effects on the economy as the outcome of a class struggle, with peculiar British features, the NC economist asks whether there is market failure.

It would be absurd to suggest that Marxist economics is no more than a discussion of certain types of market failure and I am not doing so. But since, almost by definition, the NC economist can only find fault with the system if there is market failure it is worth asking how far the problems identified by Aaronovitch and Smith can be explained in these terms.

Market failure is technically defined as a breach of one or more of the requirements for the First Fundamental Theorem of welfare economics, namely:

- sufficient markets
- competitive behaviour by producers and consumers, and
- the existence of an equilibrium.

The broad requirements cover the more familiar examples of market failure, such as externalities (pollution, etc.) public goods (defence, etc.), and the existence of monopolies. Stiglitz (1994) particularly emphasizes the problem of incomplete markets. Complete futures markets, as he says, are essential for making the correct investment allocations. Without these markets there are no prices to perform the co-ordinating and information roles that are essential if the market economy is to operate efficiently. And these markets are required for all periods extending infinitely far into the future.

Stiglitz emphasizes, above all, the problem of imperfect information. He also draws attention to the paradox of the inconsistency between the assumptions of perfect information and complete markets: '. . . if there were a complete set of markets, information would be so well conveyed that investors would have no incentives to gather information'. (Stiglitz 1994, p. 38). He also shows that the idea of complete markets is inconsistent with the idea of innovation.

Stiglitz and others have demonstrated why it is wrong to believe that market economies will produce Pareto-optimal outcomes. It does not, of course, follow that if Arrow-Debreu is wrong (in the sense that the necessary conditions are not met) Marx must be right. As Stiglitz says: 'This pervasiveness of [market] failures, while it reduces our confidence in the efficiency of market solutions, also reduces our confidence in the ability of the government to correct them. Most important from our perspective neither the theory nor the practice of socialism paid any attention to these problems' (Stiglitz 1994, p. 45).

Let us re-examine the account of economic history of Aaronovitch and Smith in the light of the concept of market failure. The two features of financial capital which they particularly stress are its separation from industrial capital and its overseas orientation. Those features caused, they argue, under-investment in the domestic UK economy over long periods and that in turn contributed to the UK's relative industrial decline.

I have suggested that there is no reason, in principle, to believe that the emphasis on overseas rather than domestic investment harmed the British economy. If it was a response to efficient market prices it provided the best way of investing UK savings. However, one can recognize the possibilities of market failure both at home and overseas.

The first possibility is that the returns available on overseas investments may have been distorted by imperfect competition, caused for example by trade restrictions.[2] Even that may have been to the benefit of UK residents, even it if was sub-optimal for the world as a whole. A second possibility relates to the kind of informational problems emphasized by Stiglitz. A higher level of domestic investment might have been socially preferable for the UK economy. In fact, infant industry arguments can be seen as an example of policies designed to correct market failure, and the tariff barriers used by our competitors during their early industrial development may have been a more efficient response. The theory of endogenous growth can similarly be seen as an example of market failure (because of the externalities associated with research and development, for example), although current applications of the theory tend to play down the role of fixed capital investment as such. (See, for example, Crafts 1997.)

Thus, it is possible to write an account of UK economic history in which the activities of the City and the policies of successive governments (which the City may have influenced) may have produced a sub-optimal path of capital accumulation and pattern of industrial development. But that does not require a Marxist analysis; it can be encompassed within a neo-classical approach which has been extended to include the full range of possible market failures. (We should not forget that recent history in Eastern Europe shows that non-capitalist economies are capable of wasteful over-investment while recent history in parts of Asia suggests that capitalist economies may make similar mistakes.) The wide definition I have used can also include problems of macro-economic stability and the possibility of prolonged periods of less than full employment, possibly exacerbated by errors in policy-making.[3]

A postscript

The account of UK economic history by Aaronovitch and Smith ends around 1980 as the Thatcher experiment was getting under way. The policies proposed by Aaronovitch and Smith were part of the Alternative Economic Strategy. The measures proposed included the imposition of import controls, greater control over the activities of the City, including the extension of public ownership, and the introduction of economic planning. The Thatcher Government did almost precisely the opposite. Product markets were further de-regulated, capital controls were freed, the financial sector was de-regulated and in the major changes associated with the 'Big Bang' of 1986.

Aaronovitch and Smith illustrated the decline of Britain's economic performance by a chart showing the UK share of world exports of manufactured goods. The chart ended in 1977. Figure 10.1 brings the record up to date, but it is not claimed that this illustration proves anything. And a NC economist would be the last person to claim that the share of world exports is a relevant measure of economic performance. But it may give other readers cause for thought.

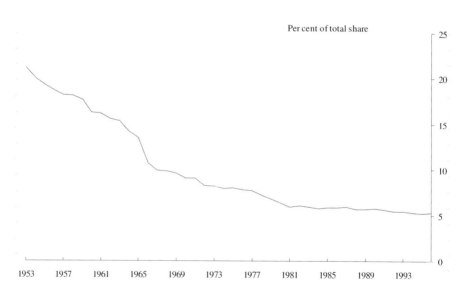

Figure 10.1 The UK's share of exports of manufactures. Source: National Institute Economic Review, Statistical Appendix Table 22,23 (1953–65), HM Treasury (1966–96)

Notes

1   The views expressed in this paper are those of the author and not necessarily of the Bank of England. It is written as a mark of appreciation for Sam Aaronovitch and in grateful recognition of snatched conversations on windy street corners. I cannot resist including a quotation from The Ruling Class: 'The top men at the Treasury move in and out of the City freely; their policies are well known to suit finance capital, and their subsequent careers show where their affinity lies'. Touché!

2   This is separate from the suspicion (which cannot quite be allayed) that the service of financial intermediation by the City is provided under conditions of imperfect competition. If that is true (and it may help to explain the high earnings of its employees) it will tend to mean that financial intermediation is under-supplied.

3   There is a separate, and potentially extremely important, question of how a government, in its conduct of macro-economic policy, chooses between price stability and output stability when it is required to do so. It is obviously possible that the City has a strong preference for price stability, and instances such as the return to the Gold Standard may demonstrate its influence on policy. That question merits more detailed study than provided in this paper.

References

Aaronovitch, S. (1961), *The Ruling Class*, London: Laurence and Wishart.

Aaronovitch, S. and Smith, R. (1981), *The Political Economy of British Capitalism*, Maidenhead: McGraw-Hill.

Crafts, N. (1997), *Britain's Relative Economic Decline 1870–1995*, London: The Social Market Foundation.

Marshall, A. (1920), *Principles of Economics*, 8th edition (1956), London: MacMillan.

Stiglitz, J. (1994), *Whither Socialism?* Boston, MA: MIT Press.

11 Profits and exchange rate instability in a capitalist world

Jan Toporowski

Summary and introduction

Since at least 1949, a number of economists have noted that devaluation may have deflationary effects on an economy (Hirschman 1949, Diaz-Alejandro 1963, Cooper 1971, Krugman and Taylor 1978). In general, this literature is based on 'elasticity pessimism', i.e. the absence of the Marshall–Lerner conditions under which a currency depreciation is supposed to improve the trade balance. These critics of devaluation argue that, in the absence of adequate expenditure-switching in response to exchange rate-related changes in prices, currency devaluation results a fall in real income, due to the rise in import costs. This paper argues that exchange rate flexibility effects changes in total output through its effect on profits. Furthermore, the effect on profits depends crucially on trade imbalances, so that the usual exchange rate fluctuations tend to squeeze profits in surplus as well as deficit countries. In the longer term, such fluctuations discourage international trade.

The elasticities approach may be disposed of by pointing out that in the real world, with all variables changing through time, any elasticities depend on the lag that is assumed to occur between the exogenous change and the change in demand supposedly 'caused' thereby. Crucially, the elasticities approach, and the above criticisms of it, depend on the presumed price effects of exchange rate changes. The main alternatives to the elasticities approach are the absorption approach, based on the national income taxonomy which identifies the difference between domestic income and expenditure with the balance of trade, and the monetary approach which identifies a deficit in that balance with a (non-Keynesian) inflationary gap caused by excess monetary expansion. Neither of these alternatives identify separately the consequences of the trade balance and exchange rates for profits, which is the channel through which one would expect changes in those variables to transmit their effects to the corporate sector.

This paper argues that exchange rate changes have, in the first instance, no price effects but only effects on profits. This may seem implausible to a generation of economists brought up to believe that prices respond to cost changes, either as factors influencing supply, or as factors entering into some cost-plus price calculations. The empirical evidence is not necessarily as convincing as it may appear. As Cooper points out, it is often convenient for suppliers to blame price increases *that would have occurred anyway* on the external *force majeure* of an exchange rate devaluation, or to time them so that such a devaluation may exonerate them (Cooper 1971, p. 27). In practice, prices are determined by the level of demand relative to productive capacity, according to the degree of competition in a market. (A model of such price setting is given in Toporowski 1998.)

Furthermore, in practice too, foreign trade is intermediated through the corporate sector, so that changes in foreign trade and terms of trade have their primary impact on profits. This is important, because the academic account of foreign trade tends to move inconsistently between, in theory, regarding such trade as exchange between households and firms, and, in its application, viewing it as exchange between a national economy organized as a firm. In this paper, the exchange rate is viewed as a 'transfer price' between the corporate sectors of particular countries. It therefore leads to a consideration of foreign trade activity in those sectors. In his published works, Sam Aaronovitch has documented the evolution of British capitalism from an identifiably British social formation dominated by local monopolists with imperial interests (Aaronovitch and Aaronovitch 1947, Aaronovitch 1955, 1981), to one that is ceding its control over the British economy to transnational and foreign monopolists with British interests (Aaronovitch 1981, Aaronovitch and Grahl 1997). This big business also dominates the foreign trade of the main industrialized countries and, even more so, that of smaller industrialized, semi-industrialized and less-developed countries (Aaronovitch and Sawyer 1975, pp. 246–59).

Profits and the exchange rate

To determine the relationship between profits and the exchange rate, it is first necessary to show how profits are determined, and the role in them of foreign trade. Equation (11.1) is the familiar Keynesian savings identity, according to which saving in an economy, S, is by definition equal to gross domestic fixed capital formation, A, plus the fiscal deficit (government expenditure, G, minus tax revenue, T), plus the foreign trade surplus (exports, X, minus imports, M):

$$S \equiv A + (G - T) + (X - M) \tag{11.1}$$

If we divide all incomes into wages and profits, P, then the above identity gives the total of saving out of both profits and wages. Deducting saving out of wages, WS, from the right-hand side of the above identity, and adding consumption out of profits, CC, gives a total profits identity, showing profits as equal to capitalists' consumption plus their saving:

$$P \equiv A + (G - T) + (X - M) + (CC - WS) \tag{11.2}$$

This is the profits equation which Kalecki puts forward (Kalecki 1971, Chapter 7). If the final term in brackets, the difference between capitalists' consumption and workers' saving is taken away, the equation shows the net financial inflow into the corporate sector and non-incorporated businesses (Toporowski 1993). Although it is an identity, Kalecki argues that in fact the right-hand side of the equation determines profits because, in practice, economic units cannot decide their income. They can only decide on their expenditure (Kalecki 1971, pp. 78–9).

The balance of foreign trade is equal to the business sector's net acquisition of foreign assets or that sector's total profits from foreign trade. It may be formally divided up into the profits derived from exports, plus the profits derived from imports. To simplify the analysis we may assume that the only effective costs of exports are domestic production costs, and the only effective costs of imports are foreign production costs. This simplification may be rooted in the structure of foreign trade. Because of the geographical scope of its transactions, foreign trade is dominated by large companies to a far greater extent than domestic trade. For large international trading companies, such as multi-national firms, the import content of their exports, and the export content of their imports will tend to cancel each other out. Smaller companies using imported materials in exports, will tend to buy them at domestic prices from the larger ones, while such companies abroad, using exported materials in their imports, will tend to buy them at foreign prices from larger companies in foreign markets. The profits from foreign trade may therefore be written as the difference between the foreign proceeds of exports converted into domestic currency, minus the domestic cost of producing the exports, plus the domestic proceeds from the sale of imports, less the foreign cost of the imports converted into domestic currency:

$$(X - M) = (x.P^f/ER - x.C^d) + (m.P^d - m.C^f/ER) \tag{11.3}$$

or

$$(X - M) = x(P^f/ER - C^d) + m(P^d - C^f/ER)$$

where x and m are the volume of exports and imports respectively; P^f is the unit price of exports abroad in foreign currency; ER is the exchange rate; C^d is the unit cost of exports in domestic currency; P^d is the unit price of imported goods in domestic currency; and C^f is the unit cost of imports in foreign currency.

Substituting Equation (11.3) into equation (11.2) gives a profits equation which shows how profits are affected by changes in the exchange rate:

$$P = A + (G - T) + (CC - WS) + x(P^f/ER - C^d) + m(P^d - C^f/ER) \tag{11.2'}$$

A devaluation of the domestic currency reduces ER. The immediate translation effect is therefore to increase the domestic currency equivalent of exports, $x.P^f/ER$, and to increase the amount of domestic currency needed to buy the same volume of imports, $m.C^f/ER$. The domestic cost of producing exports, C^d, and the foreign cost of imports, C^f, are not affected by the depreciation. These costs are determined by demand and supply in the home and foreign markets which would not be directly affected by the exchange rate. When prices do not change, but costs do, the effect is a change in the profit margin. The devaluation therefore increases the profit margin on exports, and reduces the profit margin on imports. If the economy has a trade deficit, so that imports exceed exports, then the reduction in the profit margin on imports is greater than the increase in the profit margin on exports. The devaluation then reduces profits overall. If the economy has a trade surplus, then the increase in export profits is greater than the fall in import profits, and profits overall rise. Only if foreign trade is in equilibrium is the export profits rise balanced by the import profits fall, and there is no change in total profits (c.f. Hirschman 1949).

Similarly, an exchange rate appreciation increases the profit margin on imports, and reduces the profit margin on exports. The profits of importers rise, and the profits of importers fall. If the country has a trade surplus, then the appreciation reduces profits overall. If the country has a trade deficit, then the appreciation of the currency increases total profits.

Exchange rate policy and corporate structure

This analysis has a number of policy implications. First of all, left to the foreign exchange markets or to the multi-lateral agency responsible for exchange rate stability, the International Monetary Fund, exchange rates tend move perversely from the point of view of profits. Countries with trade deficits are typically obliged to devalue their currencies, under pressure from the foreign exchange markets and the International Monetary Fund. Yet, as was shown in the previous section, this has the effect of squeezing profits overall. As a result of such devaluations, the exchange rates for the currencies of countries with trade surpluses, such as Japan and pre-unification Germany, has tended to appreciate. This appreciation then squeezes profits in those surplus countries. Exchange rate realignments in which deficit countries' currencies devalue, and surplus countries' currencies are revalued reduces profits in both countries. By contrast, a 'contrary' policy of raising the foreign exchange value of deficit countries' currencies, and devaluing surplus countries' currencies would increase profits in both sets of countries.

Exchange rate fluctuations also have to be seen in the context of the trade cycle. Unless the cycles of trading partners are synchronized, so that trading economies approach peaks and troughs in economic activity at the same time, a country's trade balance fluctuates with domestic demand. For a small number of countries, such as France in recent years for example, the trade account is balanced over the cycle. Exchange rate depreciation in a boom, with a trade deficit, would tend to decrease profits which would then be decreased further when the trade surplus in the recession causes the foreign exchange market to induce an exchange rate appreciation.

However, most countries, and the largest trading countries such as Japan, the United States and Great Britain in particular, have either chronic trade deficits which get smaller in a recession, or chronic trade surpluses which get smaller in a boom. Successive trade deficits tend to increase as an economic boom approaches its peak. At this stage, the pressure to devalue the currency of a deficit country generally increases. The squeeze on profits resulting from a devaluation would then coincide with the fall in investment that occurs at the peak of the boom and transforms it into a recession. For surplus countries, exchange rate movements at the peak of the boom are relatively more neutral in that the surplus is usually reduced in the boom, bringing more balanced trade. This would tend to balance a decline in the profitability of imports, attendant upon a devaluation, with a more equal improvement in the profitability of exports. However, a recession would tend to increase the trade surplus in a country, bringing with it pressure for exchange rate appreciation. The greater is the trade surplus, the more are profits squeezed by a given exchange rate appreciation. By contrast, a deficit country has its smallest trade deficit as a recession approaches its trough, so that any currency appreciation at this stage has a more neutral effect on the profitability of foreign trade.

In sum then, 'normal' currency fluctuations squeeze foreign trade profits most in deficit countries as their economic booms approach their peak. In chronically surplus countries, 'normal' exchange rate movements squeeze profits most as their currencies appreciate when their economic recession approaches its trough. To be realistic, it has to be admitted that the trade balances of the largest trading countries, Japan, the United States, Germany, the United Kingdom, France and Italy, are small, amounting to less than 3 per cent of Gross Domestic Product. This means that the net effect of exchange rate fluctuations on total profits in those economies is small. However, smaller open economies, such as the smaller European economies and many of the developing countries, are much more dependent on foreign trade. Their trade imbalances can reach 5 per cent and more of GDP. These smaller economies are therefore much more affected by changes in profits due to exchange rate fluctuations.

The adverse effects on profits of changes in the exchange rate are also unequally distributed among companies. Larger trading companies and multi-national firms may more easily evade the effects of exchange rate movements by spreading their purchasing and production activities across a number of countries. This enables them to off-set adverse exchange rate movements in some countries with favourable exchange rate movements in other countries. Such big businesses also hold liquid financial assets in a number of countries, using leads and lags to avoid converting payments at unfavourable exchange rates. They can also match cash inflows with payments in particular currencies, avoiding the foreign exchange market altogether. Smaller companies and indigenous companies in developing countries, tend either to be solely importers or exporters. They do not have their own international networks of trading and production activities. Exchange rate movements are much more like a lottery for such companies: If they are exporting when their country devalues its currency, they benefit. But if they are importing they lose. Their inability to off-set such gains and losses makes the existence of such companies much more hazardous than that of big business and multi-national companies.

Since the 1970s, international money capital flows have, because of their size (amounting to 20 times the value of commodity trade), determined exchange rates. While this has been the subject of much criticism, mainly due to the loss of control by central banks over exchange rates, it has also disturbed the system of perverse exchange rate effects on profits. Because of the effects on exchange rates of capital flows going through the foreign exchange markets some currencies have at times appreciated in the face of trade deficits, for example, the rise of sterling between 1992 and 1997. Other currencies have depreciated in the face of surpluses, e.g. the depreciation of the Japanese yen after 1994. Such changes in the exchange rate have the paradoxical effect of increasing profits. However, this is by no means a systematic effect in the way in which, when exchange rates were determined by trade flows, the currencies of countries with deficits tended to depreciate, and those of surplus countries tended to appreciate. The exchange rate movements that accompanied the financial crises in Mexico in 1994, and East Asia in 1997, indicate that exchange rate determination by money capital flows can be even more catastrophic than when exchange rates are affected only by trade flows.

In large measure this is because international money capital flows create foreign liabilities and assets. Again, in the case of multi-national corporations and large companies in the industrialized countries, such assets and liabilities are likely to be more or less balanced. Medium and smaller businesses in the industrialized countries tend not to use foreign capital. However, during the 1990s, the larger indigenous companies in developing and semi-industrialized countries were encouraged by prodigious capital inflows and high domestic interest rates to enter into foreign liabilities, principally denominated in US dollars, that were not balanced by assets in dollars. When substantial devaluations were forced during the Mexican and East Asian crises, in 1995 and in 1997 respectively, the value of the foreign borrowing increased in proportion to the devaluation.

In conclusion, exchange rate instability tends to squeeze profits. It does so most heavily in smaller and developing countries, and among smaller businesses. This discrimination discourages international trade which does not benefit directly big countries and big business.

Acknowledgement

I am grateful to Ilene Grabel for helpful advice at an early stage in this research and to her, Victoria Chick and Ron Smith for comments on an earlier draft. The responsibility for any errors is mine.

References

Aaronovitch, S. (1955), *Monopoly*, London: Lawrence and Wishart.
Aaronovitch, S. (1981), 'International Aspects of U.K. Capital', in Aaronovitch, S. and Smith, R. with Gardiner, J. and Moore, R. (eds), *The Political Economy of British Capitalism: A Marxist Analysis*, Maidenhead: McGraw-Hill.
Aaronovitch, S. and Aaronovitch, K. (1947), *Crisis in Kenya*, London: Lawrence and Wishart.

Aaronovitch, S. and Grahl, J. (1997), 'Building on Maastricht', in Anderson, P. and Gowan, P. (eds), *The Question of Europe*, London: Verso.

Aaronovitch, S. and Sawyer, M. C. (1975), *Big Business: Theoretical and Empirical Aspects of Concentration and Mergers in the United Kingdom*, London: Macmillan.

Cooper, R. N. (1971), 'Currency devaluation in developing countries', *Essays in International Finance*, No. 86, June 1971.

Diaz-Alejandro, C. F. (1963), 'A note on the impact of devaluation and the redistributive effect', *Journal of Political Economy*, December 1963, Vol. 71, pp. 577–80.

Hirschman, A. O. (1949), 'Devaluation and the Trade Balance: A Note', *Review of Economics and Statistics*, No. 31, pp. 50–3.

Kalecki, M. (1971) *Selected Essays on the Dynamics of the Capitalist Economy 1933–1970*, Cambridge: Cambridge University Press.

Krugman, P., and Taylor, L. (1978), 'Contractionary Effects of Devaluation', *Journal of International Economics*, Vol. 8, pp. 445–56.

Toporowski, J. (1993), 'Profits in the U.K. Economy: Some Kaleckian Models', *Review of Political Economy*, Vol. 5, no. 1, pp. 40–54.

Toporowski, J. (1998), 'The Capital Stock and the Phillips Curve', mimeo.

12 Globalization, regionalism and national economic policies[1]

Philip Arestis and Eleni Paliginis

Introduction

Globalization is the buzz word of the 1990s. The exponential rise of multi-national corporations in recent years, the extent, movement and accessibility of international finance capital and the consequent interdependence of countries, raised questions about the sovereignty, autonomy and future of the nation state. Sam Aaronovitch devoted a great deal of his working life in helping us to understand these type of developments at both the national and local spheres. His work represents an attempt to probe the forces making for structural changes in advanced capitalist economies, but especially in the UK.[2] This essay attempts to extend a particularly important aspect of it.

The present pattern of world economic activity is in sharp contrast to the pattern that evolved after the Second World War in the developed economies. The post-war period was marked by an increasing concentration of political and economic power in the hands of governments. Heavy and successful regulation during the war years, together with hopes and expectations for a better future, legitimised this new role of the State. Stabilization, re-distribution and regulation became the core functions of the capitalist state, with varying degrees of emphasis in different countries. Fordist mass production and mass consumption in the USA and the core European countries led to the economic 'emancipation' of the working force. Macro-economic stabilization policies aimed at full employment and price stability. Growth was driven first by the buoyancy of the domestic market and, second, by international trade. Redistributive policies brought social justice. The Bretton Woods agreement provided a framework of fixed exchange rates and external stability.

The end of the golden age of capitalism in the early 1970s, marked by a fall in the rate of profit and the collapse of the Bretton Woods agreement, led to the search for alternative forms of capital formation and operation (Glyn *et al.* 1990). Both international trade and international production increased at very fast rates, involving both developing and developed countries. The ideological changes of the 1980s, the liberalization of capital movements, the newly introduced flexibility in the labour market, the abolition of exchange controls as well as the de-regulation of both industrial and finance capital had serious impacts on the new restructuring of global markets. The internationalization of production, unregulated capital movements as well as the ensuing economic integration among countries, decreased the effectiveness of state macro-economic policies. A new world order emerged, where financial markets and global movements of capital could affect employment and growth rates but were outside the control of individual countries. The lack of new regulatory institutions implied that there was little to protect a country from 'contagion', and the overall system from global instability.

The move towards the globalization of the markets was linked with a parallel, but not independent, increase in regional formations. From the 1980s onwards there was a new wave of regional blocks, qualitatively different to previous blocks (Grilli 1997). The most advanced and dynamic regional formation is the European Union. Within the EU, European institutions aim to substitute for national ones, creating a stronger and more competitive basis for European capital. The creation of the European Central Bank (ECB), the operating arm of the independent European System of Central Banks (ESCB), provides the strongest example of European regulation.

We see this formation as the result of two rather inconsistent tendencies. One, which emanates from globalization, places the ECB at the apotheosis of the power of financial markets seeking independence from political control. The second emanates from regionalism which we see as an attempt at deeper integration within the EU – a development which does not sit comfortably with the proposed institutional arrangements. We wish to argue that these institutional arrangements do not resolve the inconsistencies we have just identified. We suggest alternatives which we see as more congenial than globalization and regionalism and which are designed to achieve and maintain full employment. The rest of the paper discusses the 'Globalization' thesis and the role of macro-economic policies in a globalized world, the new wave of regionalism and issues arising out of the creation of the ECB. We then discuss the inconsistencies referred to above, before we conclude with proposals for the creation of an alternative institution within the EU.

The internationalization of capital since the 1980s

Globalization refers to the increasing inter-dependence between economies as a result of increasing international trade and international capital flows. Under the Bretton Woods agreement, and in an effort to control exchange rates, there was control of capital both for foreign direct and portfolio investment. The focus of economic activity was the nation state. The collapse of Bretton Woods in the early 1970s, together with the international crisis of this period, started off the changing pattern of international operation. Further, the liberalization of capital movements, implemented in the UK in 1979 and completed in most major countries by the beginning of 1990s, accelerated this process.

Foreign Direct Investment (FDI) grew rapidly between 1967 and 1980, followed by a dramatic increase in the following 15 years. The stock of FDI reached almost $3.2 trillion in 1996, rising from $2 trillion in 1993 and $1 trillion in 1987, while sales and assets of Transnational Corporations (TNCs) grew faster than world GDP, exports and gross fixed capital formation (United Nations 1997). Growth of FDI in the period 1980 to 1996 was three times higher than domestic investment, while in the same period FDI more than doubled as a percentage of world GDP (United Nations 1997). The stock of outward FDI, for some of the leading developed economies, is depicted in Figure 12.1. Developed economies accounted for 60 per cent of total inflows and 80 per cent of total outflows of FDI in 1996 with the USA, the EU and Japan representing 90 per cent of the total of inflows and outflows of the developed economies for this period.

Although several explanations were put forward for the geographical distribution of FDI, their concentration in pockets of the world has led to a new pattern of development, with a selected group of developing economies experiencing a greater accessibility to capital funds than others. In 1996, inward FDI reached $80 bn in South, East and South-East Asia, $39 bn in Latin American countries, but only $5 bn in Africa (United Nations 1997). In 1996, the least developed countries absorbed only 0.5 per cent of total FDIs flows (op. cit.).

The concentration of foreign investment into the developed economies did not preclude funds going to a selected group of emerging markets. In 1996, their share of world inward FDI rose to 28 per cent with China being the most favoured destination, followed by South-East Asia (Figure 12.2).

Sales from foreign affiliates are becoming increasingly more important, outweighing exports for the developed economies. In the latter, sales of foreign affiliates increased from $1770 bn in 1982 to $4528 bn in 1994, while the ratio

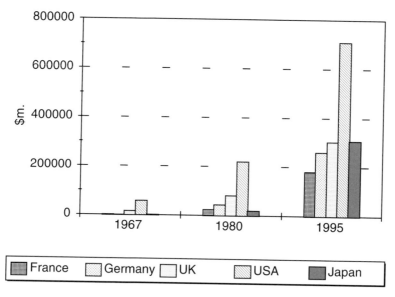

Figure 12.1 Outward Foreign Direct Investments (FDI), 1967–95. Source: United Nations (1997)

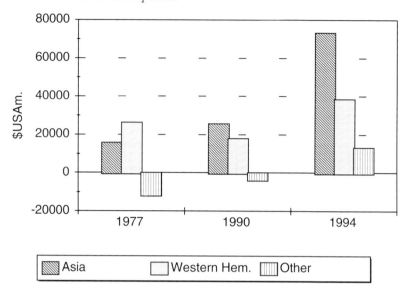

Figure 12.2 Total net capital inflows: emerging economies. Source: IMF (1995)

of sales of foreign affiliates to exports increased from 1.61 to 1.65 respectively (United Nations 1997).

This increase in international production was met by an equivalent increase in international financial movements. In the 1950s and 1960s, fixed exchange rates necessitated controls of capital movements. Since the collapse of Bretton Woods, capital movements became easier and, within the last decade, as a result of neo-liberal reforms, they experienced an exponential rise. The daily turnover of foreign currency in New York, London and Tokyo rose from $190 bn in 1990 to $1.2 trillion in 1995 while private capital flows into emerging markets increased from $50 bn in 1990 to $336 bn in 1996 (*The Economist*, 25 October 1997).

The 'unprecedented' nature of these transactions is nonetheless questioned when comparisons are made with the last 50 years preceding the First World War. This also was a period of large capital movements from some of the most developed countries to a selected number of destinations. In 1914, stocks of outward investment represented over 80 per cent of GDP in the Netherlands, and over 60 per cent in the UK, compared with values for 1996 of over 40 per cent and 30 per cent respectively (*The Economist*, 18 October 1997). However, although the exposure of a selected number of countries to international production was more extensive in 1914 than today, the number of countries involved was very small. In absolute terms, the UK, Netherlands, France and Germany (in that order) were the main investors, while the main recipients were mainly countries rich in natural resources. Further, the end of the nineteenth century was characterized by a large movement of labour. It is estimated that approximately 60 million people migrated from Europe to the USA in the second half of the nineteenth century. Today, globalization is characterized by movements of capital, with labour (particularly unskilled) being rather immobile. Labour migration is limited and, to a large extent, of an illegal nature. The internationalization of production brings capital to labour. This, it seems, is in line with workers' preferences. Cultural links and linguistic barriers hinder labour mobility, and when workers are not compelled by economic or political forces to migrate, they express their strong preference for remaining at home (Faini and Venturini 1994).

From the internationalization of capital to globalization

The present internationalization of production and the mobility of finance has led to heated debates over the substance of these changes and their implications for individual countries. It is conceivable that, within a Keynesian environment, the government could influence the level of employment, the rate of growth of output and external balance through the use of fiscal and/ or monetary policies.[3] Further, redistribution of income and the creation of a welfare state were feasible because of the ability of the government to increase taxation to finance expenditure. Are we therefore experiencing the collapse of these achievements? Does capital, in its pursuit of higher profits, move to countries where labour is cheaper and/or taxation lower, creating unemployment in the developed economies and undermining their welfare system? As markets become global does the national state lose its ability to control and regulate?

There is a large literature on this subject but we will concentrate on two important contributions. In an interesting discussion of the present changes Hirst and Thompson (1996) reject the 'globalization' thesis. Comparing recent trends with the pre-1914 flows of international capital, goods and labour they argue that in some respects present economies are less open than in the period 1870–1914. Trade, investment and financial flow are concentrated in Europe, USA and Japan, leaving the Third World largely untouched. The concentration of these flows in the developed countries implies, according to them, that governance is feasible. The domination of international production not by foot-loose trans-national companies (TNCs) but by multi-national companies (MNCs) with a national base mainly in the developed economies, implies that national governments are still able to regulate these companies (Hirst and Thompson 1996). National states are still powerful and could operate both at national and international level.

In contrast to these views, the extreme 'globalization' thesis, as expressed by Ohmae (1985, 1990), sees the world dominated by TNCs in an Interlinked Economy (ILE) centred in the USA, Japan and Europe. TNCs respond to varying demands by locating their production in specific regional markets. Information, through the electronic highways, creates a new environment of interaction between producers and consumers. In this context, national governments have lost their ability to deliver economic policies. Their power is reduced to that of municipal authorities. Their role is seen as directed merely at the facilitation of the requirements of global capital. Other interventionist policies are considered as an interference with the demands of global capital, creating distortions and thus being counter-productive. Regulation, from this point of view is both undesirable and not feasible.

Neither Hirst and Thompson nor Ohmae have captured fully, however, the changes that have occurred in recent years. On the one hand, contrary to the views of Hirst and Thompson, international production in the form of TNCs or MNCs has actually created a new dimension for policy. The liberalization of capital movements and the dramatic growth of both international productive and financial capital over the past decade have created pressures on the domestic policies of individual governments. The nation state may not have lost all its governing and regulatory power as Ohmae argues, but it has experienced a serious weakening of its macro-economic policies. In an environment of an 'open' economy with limited capital flows and fixed but adjustable exchange rates, the control of the economy through fiscal and monetary policy is arguably feasible. The post-Second World War long boom (roughly 1945–1973) provides plenty of evidence in support of this proposition. That era was by no means free of any problems, but it did deliver a long period of healthy growth. The institutional picture since that period has changed dramatically, and the economic performance of the world economy with it. Those institutions which provided the muscle of that period have either disappeared or been substantially weakened.

Liberalization of the real, the monetary and the foreign sectors has resulted in a growing economic integration of goods, services and capital markets. There is completely free movement of capital in an environment of nearly flexible exchange rates. As this new environment began to unfold since the early 1970s, two problems have become apparent in terms of economic policy. First, monetary policy is no longer under the firm grip of central banks, notwithstanding the independence they have received recently, because financial markets have assumed a great deal more power than hitherto. Second, fiscal policy lost its potential by virtue of the fact that governments have become increasingly concerned with the rise of public deficits, prompted by fear of their potential impact on the financial markets. Full employment has ceased to be the cornerstone of domestic policies and was substituted by the quest for the enhancement of competitiveness. Labour markets are becoming more flexible and the welfare state came under pressure as a result of new social problems and insufficient funding. The new objectives became: 'to promote product, process, organizational and market innovation in open economies in order to strengthen as far as possible the structural competitiveness of the national economy by intervening on the supply side; and to subordinate social policy to the needs of labour market flexibility and/or the constraints of international competition. In this sense it marks a clear break with the Keynesian welfare state as domestic full employment is downplayed in favour of international competitiveness and redistributive welfare rights take second place to a productivist reordering of social policy' (Jessop 1994, p. 263).

Globalization has created both fiscal and employment pressures. Regarding the former, large companies through relocation, transfer pricing and tax havens could easily influence the level of their taxation. With respect to employment, it was argued that, as MNCs concentrate their operation in the developed economies, there was no transfer of jobs from the developed to the developing world. While this argument is partly true, there is plenty of evidence which suggests that the internationalization of capital had an uneven effect on the level of employment, creating unemployment among the unskilled workers of the developed economies (Wood 1994). As Boyer states: 'At the very moment when post-Second World War institutions are being reassessed and partially reformed under the pressures of deregulation, foreign competition and anti-Keynesian political programmes, the sophistication of modern economic theory warns about the numerous market failures which would affect societies devoid of any complementary or alternative co-ordinating mechanisms. The state remains the most powerful institution to channel and tame the power of markets. In the absence of countervailing regulation, economic analysis shows that persisting unemployment, recurring financial crises, rising inequalities, under-investment in productive activities such as education and research, cumulative asymmetry of information and power, are some possible outcomes of a complete reliance on pure market functioning' (Boyer 1996, p. 108).

Hirst and Thompson (1996) see the world operating on a basis of regional blocks, a Triad (North America, Japan and EU), able to control and regulate the operation of MNCs as well as the activities of financial capital. This argument presupposes unanimity in the three regions with respect to regulation, and disregards tensions and differences between them. Tensions arise out of the antagonistic and competitive nature of capital and the effort of each block to enhance the interest of its 'domestic' capital. For example, a serious imbalance between Japan and the rest of the Triad both with respect to their inward/outward FDIs and the level of exports/imports was the basis of continuous tensions and conflicting demands for regulation.

Regionalism

National governments, faced with different possible choices in the 1980s, decided to liberalize their financial system (Heilleiner 1994). Globalization was the result both of technological changes and of a clear choice of governments to de-regulate the markets and allow the free movement of productive and financial capital. The latter was helped by the rise of international liquidity caused by the accumulation of Euro-dollars due to the USA trade deficits, OPEC surpluses and pension fund diversification (Toporowski 1993). By doing so, governments let the 'Genie out of the bottle' and, in the process, globalization acquired its own dynamic. Countries could not be sure that they could reap the benefits of de-regulation while they were under the constant fears of global instability. This created tension between the national state and international capital. Regionalism was a response to that tension.

Regionalism, defined as 'the tendency of a select group of countries to liberalise trade amongst themselves while discriminating against the rest of the world' (Grilli 1997, p. 194) actually preceded the present globalization. Even the creation of Germany back in 1870 was the outcome of a Deutscher Zollverein, a German Customs Union (Grilli op. cit.). In the post-war period, a first wave of regionalism was short-lived but a new wave appeared in the 1980s.[4] This new form was based on an enlargement and deepening of regional formations. The old North–North, South–South blocks were increasingly replaced by North–South ones. Old formations reappeared and new ones sprang up in all five continents. Among the most significant developments was the changed position of the USA as, for the first time, it entered into a Free Trade Area (FTA) initially with Canada and then with both Canada and Mexico in NAFTA. In Latin America, the MERCOSUR represented an FTA between Argentina, Brazil, Paraguay and Uruguay; in North Africa, a Maghreb area involved Tunisia, Morocco, Algeria and Mauritania. Grilli points out that 'According to the Director General of the GATT at the beginning of 1994 almost all of the 115 contracting partners were members of at least one preferential trade agreement (Grilli 1997, p. 194). In 1991 intra-regional trade represented 34.5 per cent of world trade, up from 17 per cent in 1960 (Grilli op. cit.).

The qualitative difference between the first and second waves of regionalism was that the new wave was intended not only to by-pass high tariff walls but to respond to the internationalization of production and to corresponding capital movements. The reduction of tariffs weakened the original rationale for FTAs. Between 1947 and 1979 the average US tariffs had come down by 92 per cent and by the mid-1980s the average US tariff was 5 per cent and the EC 6 per cent (De Mello and Panagariya 1995). The new response involved first a strategic expansion and acquisition of markets and secondly a deepening of integration through the creation of new institutions.

Enlargement now takes place through the integration not only of North/North but also of North/South countries. The removal of tariff and, in some cases, non-tariff barriers allows the exploitation of economies of scale and scope and permits dynamic companies to capture markets and increase their global competitiveness. Strategic mergers and acquisitions enhance this process. This new form of wider, less homogeneous, regional integration has its own difficulties. Integration among unequal partners may involve losses for the less developed of them (Arestis and Paliginis 1995), unless sufficient transfers are made from North to South, as compensation for losses or assistance to convergence. We argue elsewhere that they are not sufficient (Arestis and Paliginis op. cit.).

A second characteristic (not common in all of them) was the deepening of integration. The weakening of regulation at national level called for the gradual transfer of decision making from the state to the regional block. New institutions sprang up to express the new emerging balance of political and economic power. Within the EU a number of institutions from the European Court to the expected creation of a European Central Bank, are manifestations of this deeper integration. This transfer of sovereignty is not smooth. It involves tensions between the region and member states arising out of conflicting interests. In the following sections we will further analyse these tensions by concentrating on the

EU and in particular on (probably) the most significant regulatory development, the European System of Central Banks.

The independent European System of Central Banks

The proposed independent European System of Central Banks (ESCB) comprises two important institutions: the national central banks and the European Central Bank (ECB). National central banks will not be abolished in the monetary union. They will become part of the ESCB and are expected to be independent from the national governments. It is envisaged that such an institution would be accountable to the European Parliament through regular monitoring of its performance, and in that way democratic accountability is expected to be retained. The key points in the ESCB mandate are the following. First, to maintain price stability, using whatever monetary policy will be necessary regardless of the costs involved, in unemployment and lost output. Second, to support the general economic policies of the EC, provided that it does not interfere with the objective of price stability. Third, to act in accordance with the free market economy principles. Fourth, to set interest rates, to conduct foreign exchange operations and to manage member states foreign exchange reserves. Fifth, to ensure smooth functioning of the payment system which links banks across the EU.

A country's membership of the ESCB system requires the fulfilment of certain criteria.[5] These convergence criteria are very stringent and will have severe implications for the European Union's unemployment prospects. Most countries – especially those in the periphery, such as Greece, Portugal, Spain – will find them extremely difficult, if not impossible, to meet. These countries are already experiencing high and increasing unemployment partly as a result of their attempts to meet the Maastricht criteria. The glaring omission from the convergence conditions is any mention of output or employment considerations. They suggest that price stability is to be pursued through the free-market mechanism rather than through positive interventionist measures to encourage economies to absorb rising costs by productivity increases and not by higher prices. There is no allowance for the clear differences in inflationary tendencies in the member countries.

For the peripheral countries, the cost of monetary union is likely to be high, in view of the public-sector deficits, due to their inefficient public sectors and their high levels of tax evasions, and their higher inflationary tendencies. To the extent that they try seriously to meet the criteria despite the high cost, they will find their economies plunging into deep economic crises and diverging even more from those of the more advanced core countries (Arestis and Paliginis 1993, Bain 1995). Attempts to control inflation through deflation suppresses growth. In turn, lower growth tends to worsen the government budget position which, under the Maastricht conditions, would lead to further deflation in an attempt to restrain the budget deficit. Some countries will inevitably be left out of the European monetary system. Once a country is outside this system, the credibility of any promises to achieve convergence in future will be low, thereby making the cost of convergence even higher and the chances of eventually joining the Economic and Monetary Union (EMU) substantially lower.

There is another problem with these monetary arrangements, arising from the crucial assumption that appointed central bankers are to be trusted more than elected governments. But since central bankers see themselves as the custodians of international capital, the formation of monetary policy will be geared more to the interests of international financial capital rather than to those of the EU (see Coakley and Harris 1983).

This analysis clearly indicates that the institutional arrangements within the EU may very well emanate from globalization pressures, but by no means promote deeper integration among the EU member states. Globalization entails EU institutions which promote the interests of international financial capital but weaken EU economic integration. In the rest of the paper we propose certain institutional arrangements which could resolve this problem.

Alternative institutional arrangements

The purpose of this section is to enquire into possible alternatives to the Maastricht Treaty. Such alternatives are based on the thesis that institutional arrangements supportive of high levels of aggregate demand are required to underpin full employment, but that at the same time the supply side of the economy must be allowed to provide sufficient capacity to employ the work force. One alternative attempts to build on the Maastricht criteria, along the lines suggested by Arestis and Sawyer (1998). Another alternative may be the creation of a European Clearing Agency as in Arestis (1993) (see also Arestis and Sawyer 1997). This alternative has some similarities with Keynes's Clearing Union proposals at the Bretton Woods conference. The rest of the paper outlines and comments on those alternatives.

Redefining the Maastricht criteria

The problem with the Maastricht criteria is that to achieve them, high unemployment rates would have to be tolerated within the EU, and in the EMU in the future, for a long time, if not for ever as a consequence of the pursuit of the deflationary policies required by those crieria. It is therefore important to include unemployment as one of the criteria for convergence and thus relax the other criteria. Convergence and a common currency can only work if all countries are reasonably near to full employment. To achieve such a state of affairs, control of aggregate demand at the pan-European level is necessary along with other economic policies to enhance the supply side of the economy, especially in deprived areas of the Union. It is not difficult to demonstrate that low levels of unemployment are not unthinkable, even at this stage of the EU development. The experience of Luxembourg and the Netherlands shows that they are possible. A very important requirement in this respect is centralized European fiscal management alongside European monetary management. Clearly, though, if the goal of full employment is in conflict with the 3 per cent of GDP budget deficit limit and the 60 per cent government debt limit, it becomes necessary for these criteria to be relaxed.

Such a proposal strengthens EU considerably. It reinforces the argument for a Federal European state which would be in a better position to pursue Keynesian policies, including support for welfare institutions and social security, than the Maastricht Treaty institutional arrangements. Support for such a state of affairs, however, is not very strong at the moment. It may, therefore, be the case that the whole EU and EMU project should be halted until such time the inclination and support for a truly Keynesian European state can be created before a common European currency is implemented.

A European Clearing Agency

This proposal draws heavily upon the views expressed in the 1940s by Keynes (1980) and Kalecki and Schumacher (1943), and more recently by Davidson (1992/93). The main ingredients of this proposal can only be summarized briefly (for full details, see Arestis 1993, Arestis and Sawyer 1997). The main objective is the achievement of and maintenance of full employment in all EU economies. Other objectives, such as low inflation, are seen as secondary. This entails symmetrical and reciprocal rights and responsibilities between surplus and deficit countries, both of which should be responsible for balance of payments imbalances, so that there is not a deflationary bias in the correction of imbalances as deficit countries reduce their purchases of imports.

This proposal envisages the establishment of a European Clearing Agency (ECA), with personnel appointed by national governments reporting to a democratically elected body. The ECA would issue a European Clearing Unit (ECU) to serve as a medium of exchange and reserve asset. The ECA would issue ECUs in return for gold, dollar, and other reserves of member central banks. ECUs should be held only by central banks, and in more general terms the ECA would operate as an institution that would periodically settle outstanding balances between central banks. The ECA would, therefore, be a 'double-entry book-keeping clearing institution', providing overdraft facilities so that unused credit balances could be mobilized effectively. It would be committed, along with its member central banks, to guaranteeing one-way convertibility from ECU deposits to domestic money. Alongside and under the aegis of the ECA there should be a European Investment Agency (EIA), with two specific aims. These are to provide finance for long-term investment, especially to the peripheral countries that need to industrialize in a way that does not increase dependency on the core economies, and to provide long-term lending facilities to enable countries to avoid foreign exchange difficulties.

This latter aspect of the proposal relies on the notion that European countries are at different stages of banking and economic development and as such they do not run continuously balanced current and capital accounts. The exchange rate system would be a fixed but adjustable one. Changes in parities can take place when money wages and profit margins relative to productivity are permanently out of line, or when countries experience chronic difficulties in their balance of payments for other reasons. This provides a means of adjustment that is not necessarily deflationary. In the case of the peripheral countries, transfer of credit balances from surplus countries should be a requirement, but only to the extent that peripheral countries are prepared to undertake positive steps toward developing their economies, raising capacity and skill levels.

Summary and conclusions

In this paper we discussed the changes that have taken place since the early 1980s. In this period de-regulation and greater reliance on market forces were considered as the main means for the achievement of fast economic growth and development. As a result, the internationalization of production was accelerated and the liberalization of the financial markets led to ever larger movements of capital, creating a strong interdependence between countries. This is what we see as 'globalization', a rather new phenomenon, emasculating the governing power of the national state, while possessing tremendous capability to influence rates of growth, development as well as employment.

Regionalism was a parallel movement at the time, addressing some of the issues of globalization. The new wave of regional formations is fuelled by economic and political considerations. They intended to guarantee market access, to enhance the international bargaining power of the group, and to provide new forms of regulatory power. Contrary to some neo-liberal theories, the internationalization of production, far from requiring a lesser regulatory environment, necessitates stronger regulation. The weaker ability of the nation states to control or take advantage of the movements of capital and regulate them led to an enhancement of regulation at a supra-national level. New institutions arise with the intention to exercise this control at a supranational level, but this is not a smooth process. In the EU, the most notable regulatory institutions with potentially the most significant micro-economic and macro-economic effects on the Community is the independent ECB. This is an example of the transfer of power and control from the nation states to the regional block, and it expresses the triumph of banking capital over 'old' values such as the creation and maintenance of full employment. The alternative institutional proposals put forward in this paper stand a much better chance than the Maastricht policies now in place to achieve this employment objective, however 'old'. They are proposals that Sam Aaronovitch would applaud, especially as they fit comfortably with the proposals he has put forward over the years for capital controls.

Notes

1   We are grateful to Sam Aaronovitch, Iraj Seyf, Jan Toporowski and Mike Walsh for helpful comments.

2   Examples of his work relevant to issues of this essay include: Aaronovitch (1955, 1961), Aaronovitch and Smith (1981) and Aaronovitch and Sawyer (1975).
3   The extent to which Keynesian policies could influence the level of employment, the rate of growth and other magnitudes is by no means a settled issue. For a recent contribution see Arestis and Sawyer (1998).
4   A first wave of regionalism in the late 1950s and 1960s covering a number of regions such as EEC and EFTA in Europe, the Latin America Free Trade Area (LAFTA), the Arab Common Market (ACM) in the Middle East, etc. was intended mainly to circumvent tariff walls. By the 1970s most of them with the exception of EEC have ceased to function. Viner and subsequently Lipsey, showing that Free Trade Agreements (FTAs) differ from free trade as they led to both trade creation and trade diversion, had a serious impact on both economists and policy makers (Viner 1950, Lipsey 1957). Regionalism could not guarantee the enhancement of global welfare.
5   Four criteria were agreed at Maastricht in 1995: (i) a high degree of price stability, with an inflation rate within 1.5 per cent of the three-best performing member states; (ii) 'healthy' government finance, defined as a maximum ratio of 3 per cent government deficit to GDP at market prices, and a maximum ratio of 60 per cent of government debt to GDP at market prices; (iii) observance of the normal ERM fluctuation margins for at least two years without any devaluation among the member state currencies; and (iv) long-term interest rate levels that do not exceed two percentage points from the nominal long-term government bond rates of the three best-performing member states in terms of price stability.

References

Aaronovitch, S. (1955), *Monopoly. A Study of British Capitalism*, London: Lawrence and Wishart.

Aaronovitch, S. (1961), *The Ruling Class. A study of British Finance Capital*, London: Lawrence and Wishart.

Aaronovitch, S, and Sawyer, M. (1975), *Big Business. Theoretical and Empirical Aspects of Concentration and Mergers in the UK*, London: Macmillan.

Aaronovitch, S. and Smith, R. (1981), *The Political Economy of British Capitalism*, Maidenhead: McGraw-Hill.

Arestis, P. (1993), 'An Independent European Central Bank: A Post-Keynesian Perspective', Paper delivered at the 11th Keynes Conference, University of Kent, 19 November.

Arestis, P. and Paliginis, E. (1993), 'Financial Fragility, Peripherality and Divergence in the European Community', *Journal of Economic Issues*, Vol. 27, no. 2, pp. 657–65.

Arestis, P. and Paliginis, E. (1995), 'Divergence and Peripheral Fordism in the European Union', *Review of Social Economics*, Vol. LIII, no. 2, pp. 261–83.

Arestis, P. and Sawyer, M. (1997), 'Unemployment and the Independent European System of Central Banks: Prospects and Some Alternative Arrangements', *American Journal of Economics and Sociology*, Vol. 56 No. 3, pp. 353–68.

Arestis, P. and Sawyer, M. (1998), 'The Single European Currency: Prospects and an Alternative Proposal', paper presented at the annual meeting of the Allied Social Sciences Association, Chicago, 3–5 January, 1998.

Bain, K. (1995), 'European Monetary Integration and Unemployment in the Periphery', in Arestis, P. and Marshall, M. (eds), *The Political Economy of Full Employment: Conservatism, Corporatism and Institutional Change*, Cheltenham: Edward Elgar.

Boyer, R. (1996), 'State and Market. A New Engagement for the Twenty-First Century' in Boyer, R. and Drache, D. (eds) *States Against Markets. The Limits of Globalization*, London and New York: Routledge.

166 *Finance and the New Capitalism*

Coakley, J. and Harris, L. (1983), *The City of Capital*, Oxford: Basil Blackwell.

Davidson, P. (1992/93), 'Reforming the World's Money', *Journal of Post Keynesian Economics*, Vol. 15, no. 2, pp. 154–79.

De Mello, J. and Panagariya, A. (1995), 'Introduction', in De Melo, J. and Panagariya, A. (eds), *New Dimensions in Regional Integration*, Cambridge: Cambridge University Press.

Faini, R. and Venturini, A. (1994), 'Migration and Growth: The Experience of Southern Europe', CEPR Discussion paper No. 964.

Glyn, A., Hughes, A., Lipietz, A. and Singh, A. (1990), 'The Rise and Fall of the Golden Age', in Marglin, S. and Shor, J. (eds), *The Golden Age of Capitalism*, Oxford: Oxford University Press.

Grilli, E. (1997), 'Multilateralism and Regionalism: A still Difficult Coexistence', in Faini, R. and Grilli, E. (eds), *Multilateralism and Regionalism after the Uruguay Round*, London: Macmillan.

Helleiner, E. (1994), *States and the Remergence of Global Finance: From Bretton Woods to the 1990s*, New York: Cornell University Press.

Hirst, P. and Thompson, G. (1996), *Globalization in Question*, Cambridge: Polity Press.

Jessop, B. (1994), 'Post Fordism and the State', in Amin, A. (ed.), *Post-Fordism: A Reader*, Oxford: Blackwell.

Kalecki, M. and Schumacher, E. F. (1943), 'International Clearing and Long-Term Lending', *Bulletin of the Oxford Institute of Statistics*, Vol. 5, Supplement (August) pp. 29–33.

Keynes, J. M. (1980), *The Collected Writings of John Maynard Keynes*, Vol. 25, London: Macmillan.

Lipsey, R. (1957), 'The Theory of Customs Unions: Trade Diversion and Welfare', *Economica*, Vol. 24.

Ohmae, K. (1985), 'Putting Global Logic First', in Ohmae, K. (ed.), *The Evolving Global Economy: Making Sense of the New World Order*, Boston: Harvard Business School Publishing.

Ohmae, K. (1990), *The Borderless World*, London: Collins.

The Economist (1997), Articles on globalization, 18 and 25 October.

Toporowski, J. (1993), *Economics of Financial Markets and the 1987 Crash*, Aldershot: Edward Elgar.

United Nations (1997), World Investment Report.

Viner, J. (1950), *The Customs Union Issue*, New York: The Carnegie Endowment for International Peace.

Wood, A. (1994), *North–South Trade, Employment and Inequality*, Oxford: Clarendon Press.

13 Big banks, small business and the regions in bankers' Europe

Victoria Chick

This paper touches on three of Sam Aaronovitch's economic preoccupations: the prosperity of local economies, the structure of financial institutions, and the fate of the underdog. These concerns have not, as far as I know, appeared in Sam's work in the combination at issue in this paper: the paper examines the potential of the European single market in financial services, reinforced by a single currency, to disadvantage the small, local business and regional autonomy and to privilege the large, pan-European or global company.

The theoretical groundwork for this proposition has already been laid in Chick and Dow (1988, 1995) and Dow (1990) and the references cited therein. A summary of the argument of those pieces follows.

The rhetoric of the European Commission (1990) and most economist commentators is concentrated on the benefits of competition, in which banking is analysed in the same way as any other business. Thus, attention has concentrated on price competition: the expected micro-economic benefits of lower costs to borrowers in the form of lower lending rates and charges and higher returns on deposits. With the exception of these factors, the effects of competition have gone largely unexamined; it has, rather, been assumed that competition can only produce good results. Sheila Dow and I (1995) have called this competition-optimism.

By contrast, we are competition-pessimists. This stance is the result of analysing the structural changes which competition in banking are likely to bring about in a de-regulated and liberalized single market for financial services. We are conscious of the problems of local monopoly power and of startling differences nationally in the efficiency of operation of banking systems, so we easily sympathise with the somewhat exasperated reaction to our paper of one seminar participant: 'As an Italian I welcome *any* competition in banking!' But while we welcome the effects of competition in improving efficiency, the structural changes which we argued would ensue we thought would be likely to have some very unfortunate consequences.

At the core of our competition-pessimism are two propositions:

1   Financial markets are not like other businesses and competition cannot be expected to produce results similar to those in ordinary business; in particular competition is likely to lead to concentration in banking.

2   The chief importance of banking is its relationship with other businesses; if banking becomes more concentrated, large, multi-national companies will tend to be favoured recipients of loans and other services and small, regional companies will tend to be squeezed out.

We proposed that there was a natural tendency of banks to combine into larger units to take advantage of the law of large numbers in reducing the risk of cash drain and improving asset diversification. On that basis, we predicted that once barriers to cross-border banking were removed, a period of consolidation of national banking systems and cross-border alliances and mergers between the big banks would ensue. These developments would centralize banking within countries of the EU and provide internationalized services for enterprises which operated Europe-wide. The knowledge base between banks and enterprises at the regional level would suffer, and small and medium-sized businesses would be likely to be seen by the new bigger banks as not quite worth their trouble. Furthermore, we doubted that medium-sized banks would enter into pan-European competition and did not anticipate a rapid emergence of a pan-European retail banking system. The competitive pressures initiated by the removal of capital controls in the Exchange Rate Mechanism were intensified by the measures in the White Paper on Completing the Internal Market (Commission for the European Communities 1985) and subsequent Banking Directives. The institution of a common currency will remove another important barrier to cross-border competition.

Prior to 1993, institutions seeking entry into another EU state were required to comply with the regulations of the host country, and rules governing banking differed in many ways between each pair of countries (for examples see Cordero 1990, pp. 98–102). Considerable effort had been devoted to harmonize banking law, but this effort met with little success, given the diversity of banking law across EU countries and each country's strong attachment to its own ways of doing banking business. (For example, variable-rate mortgages, the most common form of mortgage contract in the UK, are illegal in Belgium.) Thus, in addition to barriers of language, information, currency and custom, there were still formidable legal obstacles to cross-border banking. Despite these problems, considerable cross-border activity did take place under this regime as some banks sought to strengthen their position on an EU-wide basis. The complexity of establishing cross-border banking under these rules tended to restrict such activity to banks which had the resources necessary to overcome the set-up costs.

The 'log-jam' was broken in the Single European Act, which recognized that harmonization should be abandoned and adopted instead the principles of: (i) mutual recognition of the regulatory regimes of other countries; and (ii) home country control. Together, these principles allowed institutions authorized in one member state to set up branches or offer services in another without seeking the authority or following the regulatory rules of the host country. The Second Banking Directive implemented this provision for banking as of January 1993, with the additional requirement that all banks engaging in cross-border activity, even banks of countries not participating in the Bank for International Settlements (BIS), must adhere to the capital adequacy guidelines of the Basle Agreement (BIS 1987). In addition, these banks are required to maintain a minimum capital of ECU 5 million (Hoschka 1993, p. 43). Authorization in one country provides the so-called 'financial services passport' to operate on home-country rules in any other EU country.

Gardener and Molyneux (1990) and Hoschka (1993) have documented the cross-border activity,[1] including cross-border mergers and alliances, which took place in anticipation of the single market. The first wave, motivated by the relaxation of exchange controls within the European Monetary System, consisted mainly in opening up lending and deposit-taking across national boundaries. This phenomenon was particularly strong in the British banks (Hoschka 1993, Figures 2.1–2.3, pp. 39–41) but was a general feature of the period roughly between 1977 and 1984 (as identified in *The Banker*, August 1992, p. 9). This is the activity which should have brought about the benefits anticipated by the EC, and there is indeed some weak evidence of success (see Gardener and Molyneux 1990 and Hoschka 1993), though nothing on the scale that perhaps was expected. Data recently compiled by Chaplin (1996) shows no persistent improvement continuing into the 1990s.

In any case, Dow and I consider these price effects to be minor in comparison with the structural implications, with which the bulk of this paper is concerned. In the rest of this paper I consider the structural changes which have taken place, starting with a summary of already-published findings and then carrying them forward. I then evaluate the predictions of our earlier paper in the light of this evidence.

The evidence up to 1989

The article in *The Banker* cited above distinguished four further phases of change in European banking after the phase of expansion of cross-border lending and deposit-taking: (i) 1984–6, in which capital-market diversification was important; (ii) 1986–8, the period of pan-European expansion; (iii) 1988–90, when alliances were forged between banks and insurance companies; and (iv) 1991–3, in which restructuring was the prime activity. (Although the article was published in 1992, enough was known of banks' plans to project to 1993.)

Thus, the period analysed by Gardener and Molyneux (1990) and Hoschka (1993) comprises the first wave of cross-border mergers and alliances in the EU. Clearly, the very prospect of the single market focused the minds of some EU bankers on positioning their institutions for the competition to come, despite the barriers and legal difficulties alluded to earlier.

Hoschka discusses the variety of means by which banks can expand across national borders. In increasing order of integration of EU financial services, one can distinguish five levels of activity: (i) strategic alliances between existing institutions, usually supported by minority shareholdings, co-operating to market each others' products; (ii) the export of services from home-based banks; (iii) the joint venture, forming a legally independent entity owned by two or more parent companies; (iv) merger or acquisition, involving the purchase of a controlling share; and (v) *de novo* entry, by branch or subsidiary, into a foreign country under the home bank's own name. This last method is comparatively rare: Hoschka accounts for 59 new openings and five upgrades between 1986 and 1992; he remarks that almost none of these is in retail banking. No *de novo* entries have been reported in Gardener and Molyneux or in the primary sources I have consulted, though a retail branch of Deutsche Bank was sighted in Milan, and branches of Banque National de Paris and BBV in Kensington, where the Royal Bank of Scotland also trades in alliance with Banco Santander. ABN-Amro has about 40 branches in Europe (*The Banker* July 1998, p. 121), but these are business-oriented. There is a need for much more information on this point.

The data of Gardener and Molyneux (Table 12.3) distinguish only three categories of cross-border activity: alliances (non-predatory minority interests), blocking or strategic minority interests, and acquisitions. These are documented from 1982 to 1989, but the majority took place in 1987 and 1989. Of the 69 events involving EU banks, 57 took place across borders and only 12 were national mergers. Fourteen of the cross-border events were alliances, eight involved a strategic or blocking minority interest, and two were listed as mergers to create supranational groups. The bulk, 33 events, were cross-border acquisitions. What is most striking about the table is that the active agent in the cross-border events was, by 1990, always among the top 10 banks within their own country, and in all but five instances they were in the top five (measured by Tier 1 capital, as defined in the Basle Agreement; *The Banker*, October 1990). In terms of European ranking, all but five, again, were among the top 60, a fact which Gardener and Molyneux also remark. So our prediction that it would be the big banks which would forge cross-border alliances seems to be borne out by the facts.

The mergers and acquisitions and strategic minority interests listed in Gardener and Molyneux by home country of the active bank and the target are analysed in Table 13.1. It can be seen that the main activity involved French, German, Spanish and British banks, with German banks the chief 'aggressors' and British banks the most frequent targets. This observation goes against the prediction in Chick and Dow (1995), that British banks were amongst the strongest (with some obvious exceptions) and thus more likely to be the 'aggressors' in take-overs. Although there are signs that the polar types of universal banking and a 'market based' system are converging in any case, this merger activity may have implications for the type of financial system which emerges as dominant in Europe.

If universal banking is to be the norm, this may favour small firms in the sense that it provides them with long-term lending, but it will work against those who go to the banks for working capital only, for the universal banks work on the basis of long-term involvement and may not wish to be bothered with the comparatively small loans which this business generates. From the point of view of the health of the regions, the expansion of the big German banks may not be so

Table 13.1 Participation by country in bank mergers and acquisitions, 1981–9. Data from Gardener and Molyneux 1990, Table 12

Country	As acquirer	As target
Belgium	4	6
Denmark	1	2
Finland	1	2
France	10	7
Germany	12	3
Ireland	1	0
Italy	6	4
Netherlands	2	4
Norway	0	1
Portugal	0	3
Spain	9	8
Sweden	5	1
UK	3	12

damaging: they have a tradition of leaving local managers to run even those branches which they have taken over, in order to benefit from local expertise. This was noted in comments on the handling by Deutsche Bank of their take-over of the Banca d'America e d'Italia. The expansionary intentions of the big German banks is not in doubt.

Size is also likely to be inimical to the interests of small business, and the location of large banks' head offices in financial centres militates against regional lending. Another indicator of the average size of banks involved in mergers and acquisitions is provided in tables appearing in the EC Competition Reports. These data over the years 1986–7 to 1991–2 are summarized in Table 13.2. The years covered by Gardener and Molyneux are 1982–1990 – not the same years, but a larger number of years than are covered by the EC data. Since the EC data list 510 events in comparison with the 67 data shown by Gardener and Molyneux, and since the data I have collected show no bulge in 1990–2, we can conclude without doubt that the Gardener and Molyneux data miss out a substantial number of events. (The same must surely be said of my data, summarized in the next section.)

Table 13.2, especially the analysis by percentage of row and column totals, shows clearly that the average size of majority acquisitions is significantly higher in the case of mergers across national borders within the EU as compared with intra-national mergers. Furthermore, while in each size category 'international' mergers – that is, mergers between an EU bank and a non-EU bank – accounted for roughly the same proportion of the total, smaller mergers were more important intra-nationally and larger ones across EU borders. The same pattern emerges from looking at participation in the horizontal totals.

These data were not repeated in the same form in later Competition Reports because of a change in the EC's source of data. In any case, data have only been

Table 13.2 Size distribution of majority acquisitions (including mergers) in banking, 1986–7 to 1991–2. (Combined turnover >1, 2, 5 and 10 bn ecu)*

	>1	>2	>5	>10	Total
National	102	79	46	25	252
EU	57	52	39	22	170
International	33	28	17	10	88
Total	192	159	102	57	510

Proportions of column and row totals (%)

% of column total \ % of row total	>1	>2	>5	>10
National	40.5	31.3	18.3	9.9
	53.1	49.7	45.1	43.8
EU	33.5	30.6	22.9	12.9
	29.7	32.7	38.2	38.6
International	37.5	31.8	19.3	11.4
	17.2	17.6	16.7	17.5

*Note: Presumably the size categories are exclusive, i.e. '>1' means '>1 and <2'

Source: EC *22nd Competition Report*, 1992, Annex IV, Table 2, p. 495

given for one further year, here repeated as Table 13.3. This table does not discriminate between national and EU mergers, but it is interesting that mergers in this joint category involve a higher percentage of the largest known mergers as compared with 'international' mergers, and account for a smaller percentage of the really small mergers. These results, coupled with the results from Table 13.2, are somewhat surprising: one might expect that the difficulties to be overcome in the case of international mergers would be greater than for intra-EU mergers (even given the difficulties of the latter as explained above), and therefore that international mergers would only be justified by the largest 'catches'. That this is not the case suggests either that large EU banks are giving strong priority to establishing cross-EU-border links rather than expanding outside the EU, or that the hurdles within the EU in this period are as strong as the international barriers – or both.

Table 13.4 includes other forms of cross-border alliances in addition to majority acquisitions, but gives only the number of events in each category; there is no indication of size. Nor are the tables compatible, even for single years in the original data. The table shows that majority acquisitions and mergers are more important nationally and minority acquisitions more numerous in intra-EU activity. Joint ventures are comparatively rare at all levels but are most common between EU banks.

Table 13.3 Distribution of majority acquisitions and mergers in banking, by size of bid-value (ecu, m.), 1992–3

	National and EU		*International*	
Value unknown (% of total)	469	*(64%)*	129	*(66%)*
Bid-value		*% of known*		*% of known*
>10 m.	143	55.2	28	45.2
>50 m.	59	22.7	21	33.9
>100 m.	24	9.3	8	12.9
>200 m.	25	9.7	4	6.5
>500 m.	6	2.3	4	6.5
>900 m.	2	0.8	0	
<900 m.	0		0	
Total	728		191	

Source: EC, *23rd Competition Report*, Annex IV, Table 7, p. 538

Note: In 1992/3 the final sources of data changed and are therefore not comparable with earlier years

Table 13.4 Acquisitions of majority holdings (including mergers), minority holdings and joint ventures in banking involving EU banks, 1986–7 to 1991–2

	Majority acquisitions and mergers	*Minority acquisitions*	*Joint ventures*	*Total*
National	315	185	61	561
EU	84	119	40	243
International	82	91	26	199
Total	481	395	127	1003

% of row total / *% of column total*	*Majority acquisitions and mergers*	*Minority acquisitions*	*Joint ventures*
National	56.1 / 65.5	33.0 / 46.8	10.9 / 48.0
EU	34.5 / 17.5	48.9 / 30.1	16.4 / 31.5
International	41.2 / 17.0	45.7 / 23.0	13.1 / 20.5

Sources: EC, *20th Competition Report* 1990, Tables 14–16, pp. 233–5; *22nd Competition Report*, 1992, Table 1, p. 494, Tables 9 and 10, p. 507

Results after 1989

A list of mergers and alliances involving EU banks since 1989 has been compiled from footnotes to the annual compilation of the world Top 1000 banks in *The Banker* (July issues), country articles and news notes published in the same source, and the European Commission's *Competition Reports*. Although mergers and alliances with banks in other continents have been excluded, activity between EU banks and Switzerland has been included. These data include intra-national mergers as well as cross-border activity and include both Swiss and Norwegian activity to serve as 'controls' as European non-EU countries. The two lists are too long to be published here but can be obtained from the author on request.

Table 13.5 summarizes these data. The data on mergers from the *Competition Reports* cannot be reported on the same basis as the material from *The Banker*, and are reported separately. They do, however, serve as a good check, for there are important mergers missing from the search of *The Banker*, due almost certainly to my oversight.

Table 13.5 Country analysis of mergers, 1990–7

Country	Cross-border mergers		Alliances and joint ventures	Intra-country mergers	Cross-border mergers in CR*
	Acquirer	Target			
Austria	0	0	0	6 + 3 (CR)*	0
Belgium	0	2	0	1 + 1 (CR)	0
Denmark	0	0	0	7	0
Finland	0	0	0	4	0
France	0	2	2	7 + 3 (CR)	5
Germany	4	0	1	13 (+ 1000)** + 1 (CR)	0
Italy	2	1	1	33	0
Luxembourg	1	0	0	0	0
Netherlands	3	0	0	3	2
Portugal	2	3	2	8	1
Spain	2	3	2	6 + 1 (CR)	2
Sweden	1	0	0	7	0
UK	0	7	4	3 + 3 (CR)	6
Switzerland	1	1	0	9 (+ 50)** + 1 (CR)	1
Norway	0	0	0	6	0

Notes:
* CR = data from *Competition Reports* not otherwise recorded. Data in last column do not differentiate between acquirer and target
** These numbers refer to reports of mergers of small savings banks

Sources: Columns 1–4: *The Banker*, various issues from January 1990 to February 1998; a few data also came from *The Economist* and one issue of *Il Sole – 24 Ore*, but there was no systematic search except of *The Banker*; additions to column 4, and column 5: European Commission *Competition Reports* 1991–6

Although the aforementioned article from *The Banker* (August 1992) designates the beginning of our period as one of restructuring, there was still important cross-border activity. This may partly be explained by the wave of privatizations which have taken place since 1990, making open to take-over some banks which earlier were protected by their public status. The number of mergers was fewer than that reported by Gardener and Molyneux for an equivalent period, but in terms of their importance for the future shape of European banking they were significant. Most prominent perhaps were the connections forged between Crédit Local de France and Hypo Bank Berlin; the troubled Crédit Lyonnais and BfG (Germany) and Generale Bank (Belgium); Banesto (Spain) and Banco Totta e Açores (Portugal); and the purchase of three British investment banks by ING, Dresdner and SBC and of Banque Brussels Lambert by ING (Netherlands).

As before, almost all the banks involved in cross-border deals are in the top 60 European banks and the acquirers, though not always the targets, are in the top 10 in their country. Again as before, Germany, France and the UK are the most active, with the UK most often the target and Germany a prime acquirer. This is, again, surprising, for UK banks have shown the strongest performance in terms of both Tier 1 capital/assets and pre-tax return on capital. They are clearly in a position to expand but are choosing not to.

The outstanding feature of these new data, however, is the rash of intra-country mergers. The sheer numbers are impressive (Table 13.5, column 4). They encompass two separate phenomena: mergers at the very top and a rather drastic re-organization of the smaller banks, especially regional savings and other popular banks. Mergers at the top are, of course, more fully documented, especially since we have used the footnotes to the Top 1000 as a main source. They include the merger of Crédit Agricole and Banque Indosuez (1st and 12th) in France and after merger first in Europe (now second to HSBC, which changed its registration to the UK); the take-over of Banesto by Banco Santander to become Spain's second-largest bank (Europe's 29th); the formation by merger of Bank Austria, now Austria's largest bank and Europe's 52nd; the merger of Finland's top two banks to form Merita, 60th in Europe; the merger of Cariplo with Banco Ambrosiano Veneto (1st and 16th in Italy) to form Banca Intesa; the merger of ABN and Amro to form Europe's sixth-largest bank; the formation of Argentaria from five Spanish state-owned banks to become Spain's third largest, 31st in Europe. Drastic change in life at the top is not, however, restricted to the Single Market: the merger of Switzerland's first- and third-largest banks, UBC and SBC (3rd and 8th in Europe), has recently been announced.

As Table 13.5 indicates, a drastic consolidation of savings banks has occurred in Germany and Switzerland (1000 and 50 mergers, respectively). A similar trend has occurred in Italy, though among quite large savings banks as well as the 'minnows'; this restructuring accounts for a substantial amount of the Italian list. Perhaps the most important of all these, from the point of view of sheer size, is the recent creation of Banca Intesa. But even more important from the structural point of view is the merger of Bayerische Vereinsbank and Bayerische

Hypotheken und Wechselbank to become Germany's second largest bank (BHV), in 1997. Commentators made the point that this completely changes the clear structure of the German banking system, as this new bank is Germany's second-largest, up in the ranks of the *Gross-banken* with no intention of taking on that role and giving savings and mortgage activity a higher profile than everywhere else but Italy. Both in Germany and (to a greater extent) in Italy, these mergers cut across regional lines. In Switzerland this has not happened, because the local banks are linked to their cantons.

The widely publicized mergers amongst the largest banks have raised the average size of the important banks and brought home the need for consolidation to banks further down the scale; in particular, there has been rationalization among all but the top Danish bank and a 'consolidation frenzy' (*The Banker*'s phrase) in Portugal. The Danish experience is to some extent mirrored by the Norwegian, though the former has been more far-reaching.

So important has the restructuring been almost everywhere, that the constituents of the banks included in the European Top 500 have in most cases changed radically. Table 13.6 measures the level of turnover of this list between 1990 and 1996, in two different ways: column 5 simply records the new entrants to the list as a proportion of the total; column 6 adds the entrants to the 1996 list to the 'exits' from the 1990 list and deflates this by the average of the total number of banks each country has in the list in each year. The numbers need careful interpretation: they are a measure of activity, not of concentration, though this clearly has increased also. Italy, despite all the entries in the overall list, does not head the list judging by column 6: it is tied with Austria but more active have been Norway, Spain, the Netherlands, Germany and Denmark. Switzerland is close behind. Belgium is, by this measure, a model of structural stability. Small and fluctuating denominators obviously distort the results, but the numbers give some feeling for the tremendous changes which have been taking place even without going further down the size range. The restructuring has been profound.

The restructuring has resulted in the creation of more powerful, larger banks at the top and amalgamations and consolidations among the smaller banks. It has also, in many cases, blurred the functional distinction between investment and commercial banking at the top and ordinary retail banking and saving, mortgage and girobanking further down the scale.

Conclusions

What will this restructuring mean for the regions and for small business? – the question with which we began. One should not be too dogmatic, for there are many mergers where the local character of the acquired bank is respected, but the general drift is toward cross-border activity by the really big players and a response by the small banks which also entails concentration for them. In particular, the regional character of the lower layer of banking has been to some extent lost. Both this loss of regional character and the increased size is in general inimical to the interests of regional robustness and independence and to the

Table 13.6 Numbers of banks in European Top 500: 1996 and 1990 compared

Country	1996		1990		Turnover 1: 1996 new entrants/ 1996 total	Turnover 2: entrants and exits/totals 1996 + 1990
	Total	New entrants	Total	of which, not in 1996 list (exits)		
Austria	23	10	22	9	43	84
Belgium	10	0	11	1	0	9
Denmark	8	2	16	10	25	100
Finland	4	0	7	3	0	55
France	24	5	31	12	21	62
Germany	98	60	105	52	61	103
Greece	9	5	6	1	56	60
Ireland	4	2	2	0	50	67
Italy	98	45	116	73	46	85
Luxembourg	4	0	5	1	0	22
Netherlands	14	9	12	5	64	108
Norway	13	10	8	5	77	143
Portugal	10	3	11	4	30	67
Spain	45	32	38	25	71	137
Sweden	6	1	12	6	17	78
Switzerland	36	17	36	17	47	94
UK	32	9	36	11	28	59
Total	438		474			
Total EU	389		430			

Note: Figures may not 'add up' as some merged institutions are counted as having 'stayed'. Figures for Germany and Italy may not be accurate, because of the difficulty of scanning the large numbers involved.

Participation in Top 500:	1996	1990
EU + Switzerland + Norway/ All banks	87.6	94.8
EU/All banks	80.4	87.6

interests of small and medium-sized firms. The creation of a single market for financial services may produce a bit of an improvement in 'efficiency' – in some cases quite a large improvement – but the net result is the creation of a banking system which is well organized to serve the pan-European or multi-national firms and less able and/or willing, for a given level of efficiency, to support small and more local enterprises.

One has to wonder, however, how important the creation of the single market has been in this process. The inclusion of Norway and Switzerland in the data-base makes it clear that the same process that we have documented for the EU is in train in those countries also. It is also going on in the United States. If anything, the single market may be a response to the pressures of globalization rather than an initiator of structural change, whether in banking or in industry. 'Bankers' Europe' may just be conforming to a pattern begun elsewhere, responding to forces rather than creating them. Here, the roles of optimist and pessimist are reversed: the pessimist reckons that these forces are just too big to be resisted; the optimist deplores and wishes to set up barriers to the same forces. I began as a pessimist, but I end as an optimist, as befits an essay in honour of one of the most optimistic people I have had the pleasure to know.

Note

1   Canals (1994) has a list of mergers almost identical to that in Gardener and Molyneux, though from a different source.

References

Canals, J. (1994), *Competitive Strategies in European Banking*, Oxford: The Clarendon Press.

Chaplin, G. E. (1996), *European Retail Banking under the Single Market and EMU: Regional Implications*, MSc Dissertation, London: University College.

Chick, V. and Dow, S. C. (1988), 'A Post Keynesian Perspective on the Relation between Banking and Regional Development', *Thames Papers in Political Economy*, Spring, pp. 1–22. Reprinted in Arestis, P. (ed.) (1988), *Post Keynesian Monetary Economics: New Approaches to Financial Modelling*, Edward Elgar, pp. 219–50.

Chick, V. and S. C. Dow, (1995), 'Wettbewerb und die Zukunft des europäischen Banken- und Finanzsystems' (Competition and the Future of the European Banking and Financial System), in Thomasberger, C. (ed.), *Europäische Geldpolitik zwischen Marktzwängen und neuen institutionellen Regelungen (New Institutions for European Monetary Integration)*, Metropolis-Verlag, Marburg, 1995, pp. 293–321. Shorter version published in Smithin, J., Hagemann, H. and Cohen, A. (eds) (1997), *Money, Financial Institutions and Macroeconomics*, Boston: Kluwer, pp. 253–70.

Commission for the European Communities (various years) *Competition Report*, Brussels.

Commission for the European Communities (1985), 'Completing the Internal Market', *White Paper* from the Commission to the European Council of Milan, 28–29 June, COM (85) 310 final, 14.6.85.

Commission for the European Communities (1988), *The Cost of Non-Europe* (the Cecchini Report), Brussels.

Commission for the European Communities (1990), 'One Market, One Money: An Evaluation of the Potential Benefits and Costs of Forming an Economic and Monetary Union', *European Economy*, Vol. 44, October.

Cordero, R. (1990), *The Creation of a European Banking System: A Study of its Legal and Technical Aspects*, New York, Peter Lang.

Di Tommasi, E. (1993), 'Banks and Enterprises: A New Commitment in favour of Local Realities', *Journal of Regional Policy*, Vol. 13(3–4), pp. 413–28.

Dow, S. C. (1990), *Financial Markets and Regional Economic Development: The Canadian Experience*, Aldershot: Avebury.

Gardener, E. P. M. and Molyneux, P. (1990), *Changes in Western European Banking*, London: Routledge.

Hoschka, T. C. (1993), *Cross-Border Entry in European Retail Financial Services*, Macmillan.

The Banker (various issues), London: Financial Times Publishing.

14 ESOP's fable

Golden egg or sour grapes?

Ben Fine

Introduction

In the early 1990s, I was asked to assess the significance of Employee Share-ownership Plans, ESOPs, for South African workers. At that time, as apartheid moved through what was to prove to be its final stage, large South African conglomerates were putting forward proposals to woo the trade union movement. More recently, ESOPs have come to the fore once more as the African National Congress government embarks upon a privatization programme, or 'restructuring of state assets', on a scale that would have been inconceivable earlier, in view of the ANC's fierce opposition to free market capitalism. Workers are being offered ESOPs as a palliative although, in South Africa, an extra twist is added by the simultaneous goal of empowering what will inevitably be an élite within black business.

This essay, drawing upon a report prepared for the South African trade union movement, assesses the position of ESOPs.[1] The first part addresses conceptual issues, while later sections discuss the historical record of ESOPs and examines some of the theoretical literature. Finally, the literature for the more recent empirical evidence is reviewed. Overall, it is found that ESOPs have become a management strategy not only to incorporate workers but also to gain tax, financial and other advantages useful in takeover battles. The last part of the chapter examines the trade union involvement around ESOPs and finds that they have proved an inadequate vehicle for working class advance, even in the most favourable circumstances provided by Swedish social democracy.

Conceptual issues

ESOPs raise strategic issues for the labour movement as well as problems of detail. How are they to be understood? At one extreme, there are those who argue that they are simply a different form in which wages are paid, obscuring the fundamental conflict between capital and labour by misleading the latter into believing it has a stake in the firm or economy, other than as a wage-labourer. At the other extreme, ESOPs are considered to have turned workers into capitalists, to have given them a genuine stake in the system, and to have created a share-owning democracy or people's capitalism.

The truth is undoubtedly closer to the first version. There are many different ways of remunerating workers, and the difference in these methods should not lead us to consider that something fundamental has changed. Consider, for example, the British coal industry at the end of the nineteenth century. Then wages were on a 'sliding scale', going up and down on the basis of a pre-determined formula with the price of coal. Accordingly, the wages were higher in periods of prosperity (when the price of coal tended to rise) and lower in depressions. Sharecropping involves the division of output between the producer and the non-productive landowner according to pre-determined proportions. Feudal society was characterized by similar divisions of produce. The church used to receive a tithe, for example, the old English word for one-tenth of income. Similarly, payments by piece-rates means that wages vary with performance. Consequently this has similar characteristics to an ESOP or Profit-Related Pay (PRP) in that extra work leads to extra pay and to extra profit. Much the same is true of the premium paid for overtime.

Yet, these different ways of paying wages are not particularly associated with a favourable or novel development for working people. Formally, much the same is true of the ESOP and PRP schemes. For the worker remains tied to employment irrespective of the forms in which wages are paid. At various times, for reasons of incentives and of control as much as for ideological reasons, capitalists find it convenient to vary the way in which wages are assessed and paid. Significantly, employee profit-sharing logically entails a profit share to non-employees, the preservation of the underlying capitalist relations. As such there is no qualitative transformation in the relations between employer and employee.

Whether there is a quantitative change or not is not pre-determined. ESOPs make it appear as though wages are supplemented by the added element listed as a profit share. But it may well be that the pre-profit wage will be driven down to compensate for the other elements making up wages. This is well understood in other circumstances. Increases in wage taxes, for example, may lead to compensating claims for higher negotiated settlements to restore take-home pay levels. More dramatically, for piece rates, short run increases in overall wages may well be adjusted back to previous levels through increases in the norm or reduction in the payment per piece. The net result is harder work for the same or even less pay – speed-up at no extra cost to the capitalist.

More generally, profit-sharing is intended to make leading employees identify with their company and have an added incentive to provide for its success. The idea is to persuade them to work harder for some, but not all, of the profits, to moderate conflict between management and labour, and to pose ESOP and PRP as alternatives to trade unionism and industrial conflict and, in the longer term, as alternatives to the social ownership of the means of production. As President Reagan crudely put it, 'Could there be a better answer to the stupidity of Karl Marx than millions of workers individually sharing in the means of production?'. (This comment has to be set against the distribution of share ownership in the United States where the wealthiest 1 percent of the population own 50 per cent of shares and the wealthiest 6 per cent own 80 per cent.) Even so, worker share ownership can induce a feeling of corporate loyalty. One study even showed that this was induced even among workers *not* included in the ESOP scheme.[2]

As a form of paying wages and of commanding workforce loyalty and co-operation, ESOPs are far from new. It is worth emphasizing that various forms of profit-sharing have been around for a long time, going back 150 years or more in the UK. Its apparent recent discovery and promotion as a form of people's capitalism, able to solve economic problems, has been tried and tested – and has failed – many times in the past. Matthews reviews the British evidence and concludes, 'To sum up then, although some historians have viewed profit-sharing as the work of philanthropic employers, the historical experience suggests that it was usually a management strategy of labour discipline by profit-maximizing companies. It is evident that interest in profit-sharing has fluctuated with the problems in labour relations; in the long run the bonus was set by management as a relatively fixed proportion of wages, not profits, while even the most outwardly altruistic employers refused to cede significant control of their companies' (Matthews 1989, p. 461).[3]

Realistically, like many others, he suggests that the frequent re-appearance of the idea through history is probably a consequence of the sporadic, altruistic impulses of the occasional employer (or the egalitarian champion of the free market and capitalism). Its re-appearance may also be due to the difficulty of isolating its exact effects from other more important factors in explaining economic performance so, 'the fact that the effects of profit-sharing are so difficult to quantify may have been a factor in preserving its credibility for so long' (Matthews op. cit. p. 462).

In modern times, the philanthropic or calculating sponsors of such schemes are no longer confined to the ranks of the idiosyncratic entrepreneur. In addition, governments have been prepared to offer tax relief or other subsidies to convince employees of their commitment to, and stake in, some form of people's capitalism. Consequently, ESOPs have flourished over the past two decades, providing a much sounder basis on which to judge their impact.

ESOP theory

The recent literature on ESOPs has gone through a number of stages. Initially, there was a theoretical literature, less interested in the details of the schemes involved. These could vary according to the degree of share ownership or not, the freedom of workers to sell their shares or not, who takes control of them, whether it be the individual workers or a collective agency on their behalf, the use to which the dividends may be applied, to supplement money wages or to promote worker or community welfare, and whether the ownership is offered free, at a price or as a reward for long service, skill or seniority and whether the state is supporting the scheme through offering tax relief on it, etc.

From the point of view of orthodox economics, these different schemes have small but significant differences. They place the firm along a continuum between a worker co-operative and a firm purely owned and controlled by an individual capitalist. Workers are presumed to vary the way in which they supply labour (whether in total amount or in terms of the intensity with which they work) according to the way and the extent to which they share in profits or the equity of the firm. For example, if workers share in profits, they may wish to see fewer workers offered jobs so that their share is not diluted across too large a workforce. At the same time, as they are perceived to have an interest in the performance of the firm, they have an added incentive to work harder to increase the profits from which they take a share.

As suggested, these motivations and the variations in how they can be realized have been the focus of the orthodox view of ESOPs. The London School of Economic's Centre for Labour Economics alone, for example, produced at least eight discussion papers on the issue over a two-year period at the end of the 1980s, as well as a number of published contributions across a range of journals in economics and industrial relations. This, usually abstract, theoretical analysis has also been accompanied by some assessment of the empirical results obtained and this is considered later.

Interest in ESOPs also inspired analysis at the macro-economic as well as at the micro-economic level. Would an economy function more favourably if every worker was involved in an ESOP? One of the leading exponents of ESOPs has been the US economics professor, Martin Weitzman, whose book on the subject was judged by the *New York Times* as the most important contribution to economic thought since Keynes' *General Theory*. His argument is that, at the macro-economic level, profit-sharing will lead to lower levels of unemployment. This is because it will handle supposed downward rigidities in the level of real wages, since labour's pay will fall along with profitability in a recession and make higher levels of employment less costly. This notion of dealing with inflexibility in the labour market is repeated again and again throughout the UK's Green Paper discussion document on PRP (HMSO 1986). It should be emphasized that the Weitzman employment effect consists of obtaining more jobs through the indirect acceptance of lower pay.[4]

This was also the motivation of James Meade, the Nobel Prize winner for economics. He favoured profit-sharing because, 'it removes the large element of direct conflict of interest between capital and labour'. Preferred is a scheme in which *new* employees do not share in profits, for otherwise, 'there would be a conflict between "insiders" and "outsiders". Those already in employment in any successful partnership would be required to face a reduction in pay as a necessary condition for allowing unemployed outsiders to join in the concern's useful activities'. This would impede the employment creation effects so that, for Meade, it is better to put forward a proposal that is essentially the same as taking on new workers at lower wages than those already employed and is an implicit attack on the basic principle of trade unionism – the same pay for the same job. In this context, Meade had been notable in the past for proposing taxes on wage increases as a means of controlling inflation. Keeping wages down has remained the aim, only the methods of doing so have changed.

This can be seen in another way, for one of the assumptions of the Weitzman-type analysis is the absence of trade unions. This ought, perhaps, to be seen the other way around, in that PRP is designed to nullify the effects of the presence of trade unions by making wages more flexible (downwards in recession as profits fall) and, with Meade, allowing new workers to be hired at lower wages than incumbents. All of this is a far cry from the ideology of higher pay (in the form of higher profit) and participation through share ownership that is the image offered by people's capitalism! Despite all of this grand theory, PRP in the UK was inspired by the government of Mrs Thatcher with a deeply embedded hostility to trade unions and, in the event, her period of office over the 1980s witnessed a dramatic worsening of income distribution. In the UK, PRP and ESOP were encouraged by various tax incentives. Assets involved increased from £1.5 to £2 billion between 1987 and 1985/86, covering 1.5 million workers.[5]

The ESOP record

The second phase of literature concerned with ESOPs has addressed the issue of the impact upon performance, especially productivity. This poses certain problems of method since it is necessary to make a judgement about what would have happened in the absence of a scheme. Should ESOP firms be compared with non-ESOP? Or should firms be examined for comparative performance before and after introduction of an ESOP? Even if all the necessary information is available, determining the effects is, in any case, extremely difficult since what differences there are may be the result of other factors unrelated to the ESOP, such as a boom or recession in market conditions. ICI, for example, has had a scheme in place in the UK since 1954. But to measure the impact of this scheme would require the existence of an equivalent ICI without the scheme and, as it is the overwhelmingly dominant chemicals company in the UK economy, this is impossible. Nor can comparisons be made with similar companies deriving from other countries, since national and accounting differences are liable to swamp any of the effects arising out of the presence of such schemes.

It could even be that any differences in economic and other characteristics across companies are the cause rather than the consequence an ESOP. If a firm is failing, it might launch an ESOP to persuade workers to take lower wages in return for shares. In doing so, it would hardly be fair to compare such a firm with one without an ESOP that is not in trouble. Similarly, it is known that large-scale companies are more likely to have ESOP schemes than small businesses. They are also more likely to be unionized and have a developed system of industrial relations. This may lead to bargaining for higher wages in the form of profit-sharing while productivity increase may arise independently out of the economies of scale enjoyed by the large company. Interestingly, however, the evidence appears to suggest that, where there is a strong union, PRP is less likely than where there is a weaker union present (although the absence of unionization makes PRP least likely). This is because the stronger union is able to prevent the company from setting workers' profits against wages. But this just confirms that wages tend to be higher where unions are stronger, irrespective of the form in which those wages are paid. A final point concerns the survival of firms with ESOPs. In any study at any particular time, surviving firms with ESOPS will be the only ones left to be recorded, so that failed ESOP firms will be excluded. This may bias assessment in ESOP's favour, although the same is true of non-ESOP firms. In effect, all firms have to meet commercial criteria to survive so that they will tend to have a degree of uniform performance, with the presence or not of an ESOP being compensated by other non-observed factors.[6]

Putting these considerations aside, the evidence on ESOPs is conclusive in denying any significant effect. In the case of the UK, in an early study, Blanch-flower and Oswald (1988) report that the impact of ESOPs is unproven. This is confirmed by Duncan (1988). Wadhwani and Wall conclude after looking at micro-data: 'Nevertheless, if our results were correct, they would suggest that much of the recent debate on profit-sharing has been "much ado about nothing"!' (Wadhwani and Wall 1990, p. 16). Similarly, Aitken and Wood conclude that: 'There is limited evidence that such plans will produce improvements in the employee motivational states and organizational performance' (Aitken and Wood 1989, p. 166).

Two studies that do find a relationship between profit-sharing and productivity are those of Cable and Wilson (1989) and Cable (1988). The first is for the UK and the authors conclude that, 'estimates of productivity differentials between firms practising profit-sharing in the UK engineering industry and those without profit-sharing indicate overall gains of between 3 and 8 per cent' (Cable and Wilson 1989, p. 372). But they explain that this is not a simple relation: 'more is involved than a simple shift . . . due to increased work effort or "cooperation" in some broader sense. Rather the effect is entwined with the firm's choice of technology, internal organization and labour force character-istics. It follows that, contrary to what might be inferred from previous work . . . the introduction of profit-sharing *ceteris paribus* will not necessarily have productivity enhancing effects; accompanying changes in other dimensions of organizational design are likely to be required'. (Cable and Wilson op. cit. p. 373). Thus, the productivity effect is dependent upon the presence of other factors which are generally in themselves associated with better performance and in which a strong component of workers participation in decision-making is liable to be important.

In a later study updating the earlier study for West Germany, Cable (1988), and drawing comparisons with the UK, Cable and Wilson find a much more significant impact: 'New estimates for West Germany indicate overall produc-tivity differentials of 20–30 per cent in favour of firms practising profit-sharing. These compare with estimates of 3–8 per cent for comparable British firms. . . . Like the UK results, they reveal evidence of important interactions between profit-sharing and other aspects of the firms' organization and operation. However, it appears that in Germany profit-sharing is being used in a different way, by different kinds of firms, than in the United Kingdom. Our previous general conclusion – that the effect of profit-sharing is intimately related to firms' choices of technology, internal organization and labour-force characteristics, and that profit-sharing is to this extent an integral element of overall organizational design – is therefore reinforced by the new results, but with an important additional insight: that there is evidently no uniquely appropriate context and role for profit-sharing' (Cable and Wilson 1990, p. 554).

In short, where profit-sharing has succeeded, it requires particular types of firms, typical of the more progressive West German engineering firms in terms of technology, organization and skill composition of the labour force. In addition, such schemes must not be simply tacked onto the existing wage-payment systems but must be an integral part of the management and industrial relations system. A similar conclusion can be drawn from the work of Jones and Kato (1993a,b) for Japan. They observe that the Japanese approach has been undeservedly ignored. By 1984, 90 per cent of firms quoted on the Japanese stock exchanges were running ESOPs, applicable to over 50 per cent of their workforce. The Japanese schemes have certain notable features which reinforce the workers' legendary loyalty to their employers – they are not granted tax relief, they are subsidised by the firms themselves, they are skewed towards benefiting the lower ranks in the workforce, there is limited opportunity for workers to sell their shares, and the workers have directors to represent their interests. The net impact appears to be a small improvement in productivity in such firms. Jones and Kato conclude: 'Our finding of the largely favorable effects on company productivity of Japanese ESOPs points to the potentially important role played by specific institutional features in accounting for the observed variation in economic effects of ESOPs. Specifically, given the presence in most Japanese firms of mechanisms designed to encourage employee participation, our findings support the conclusion of . . . others that both decision and financial participation are needed in order for improvements in business performance to be realized'. (Jones and Kato 1993a, p. 366).

A much more extensive literature on productivity and ESOPs is to be found for the USA, not least because the ESOP movement has continued to prosper there for longer. ESOPs flourished in the 1920s, there having been 300 at the beginning of the century, with one of the first originating with the retailer Sears Roebuck in 1916. But 90 per cent of these ESOPs were wiped out by the crash of 1929 and the Great Depression. In the 1950s, Louis Kelso, a US lawyer wrote a book entitled, *The Capitalist Manifesto: How to Turn Eighty Million Workers into Capitalists on Borrowed Money*. In a preface to a publication from the right-wing laissez-faire Adam Smith Institute (Taylor 1988), he claimed to have invented ESOPs in 1956. His history is as poor as his logic for he claims to be able to, 'broaden the ownership of capital without invading the private property of anyone'. This reflects the desire to avoid any fundamental shift in economic power or the redistribution of wealth; this being freely admitted in the form of seeking a 'populism without Robin Hood'! From 1975 to 1992, the number of plans in the USA rose from 1,601 to 9,764 with the number of employees growing from 248,000 to over 11 million (Gianaris 1996, p. 134).

The study of Blinder (1990) was a relatively early confirmation of the positive impact of profit-related pay on productivity when it is combined with workforce participation in decision-making. More recently, Doucouliagos (1995) has undertaken a meta-analysis (or compilation) of 43 studies, mainly for US firms, of the relationship between worker participation and productivity. He finds the productivity effects overall are positive but small, and dependent upon worker participation in decision-making in firms not wholly owned by the workers themselves. This is confirmed by Kaufman and Russell: 'Insufficient attention has been given to coupling worker participation with ESOPs. The best research on ESOPs repeatedly has found that greater worker participation in decision-making is an indispensable ingredient in the design of successful ESOPs' (Kaufman and Russell 1995, p. 46).

The most sophisticated study of the impact of ESOPs, in the US context, is provided by Kruse (1996), drawing upon a sample of 275 US firms (with a response rate of 61.6 per cent). Unlike other studies, he employs panel data (observations on the different firms over time) so that the evolution and performance of firm behaviour can be charted chronologically. He finds that profit-sharing may have been adopted to raise productivity, with the older companies having higher R&D expenditure (suggesting collaboration between workforce and management), more job-enrichment and worker participation programmes, and higher capital:labour ratios.

A weakness in Kruse's interpretation of his results is that he takes outcomes, such as those reported in the previous paragraph, as indicative of motives. This reflects the passage to a new phase in the academic literature. It has become less concerned with the results of ESOPs and more concerned with why they are adopted. In this, the literature on the USA has been particularly prominent. This is because the productivity motive for ESOPs has become overtaken by other priorities unrelated to worker participation as such.

Consider the dramatic increase in ESOPs in the USA in the late 1980s. Scholes and Wolfson (1989, p. 25) find that there were 4,028 plans in 1978; this had risen to 8,046 in 1986 and 9,500 in 1988. Corresponding numbers of employees covered were 2.8, 7.8 and 9.5 million, respectively, the latter making up more than 10 per cent of the workforce. The reason for this huge increase is to be found in the company legislation for the state of Delaware, where 179,000 companies are incorporated, including 56 per cent of the *Fortune* top 500 companies and 45 per cent of those quoted on the New York Stock Exchange. According to Delaware state law, ESOPs legally expand the category of shareholders to include employees, all of whom have to be taken into account in voting for approval to change control. A wait of three years is necessary for a takeover unless 85 per cent of shareholders vote in favour. Polaroid, for example, in early 1989 took out 14 per cent of its shares for an ESOP in order to obstruct a hostile merger, and were backed by the courts in their strategy. So Scholes and Wolfson regard 'the creation of impediments to changes in corporate control as the prime motivation for ESOPs' (Scholes and Wolfson 1989, p. 26).

Nor is this all. In the first six months of 1989, US corporations acquired over $19 billion of their own stock for ESOPs compared with $5.6 billion for the whole of 1988 and less than $1.5 billion per annum from 1974 to 1987. This was partly to take advantage of tax allowances favouring ESOPs, but also to raise capital through leveraged loans out of the implied future earnings on the employee-owned stock, $9 billion being borrowed in this way in 1989 up to 10 May. The company is, as it were, borrowing against the future dividends of its employees – similar to the use of pension funds for speculative purposes. This all serves to confirm the point that ESOPs, far from shifting control to workers, may even act as a way of consolidating and redistributing corporate control among and between the managerial elite.

So important has become the tax motive for engaging in ESOPs that the issue has now become the regular subject of discussion in academic journals such as *Journal of Financial Economics, Journal of Corporate Taxation, Banking Law Journal, Journal of Banking and Finance, Financial Management, Journal of Accountancy, Journal of Taxation, Securities Regulation Law Journal* and *Journal of Accounting and Economics*. In discussing ESOPs, these journals are primarily concerned with examining tax law and how it can be turned to the advantage of corporate managers. Even so, following the Polaroid ruling, Dhillon and Ramirez (1994) find that ESOPs have primarily been adopted for yet another motive unconnected to workers' interests, that is as a defensive measure against hostile take-over.

Apart from tax and anti-merger strategy, perhaps the most significant aspect of the more recent wave of ESOPs is that they have involved companies under threat of bankruptcy, the Chrysler motor company, for example, and airlines that suffered under deregulation such as the Eastern, Pan Am and Republic airlines. In negotiating employee share ownership, the *quid pro quo* has been wage cuts or restraint. At Chrysler, the US Government guaranteed a loan of $1.5 billion dollars to support an ESOP. But employees had to give up $585 million dollars in pay increases over the next three years in return for equity valued at $165 million. In return for $35 million in shares, 23,000 unionized employees at Pan Am had to suffer a 10 per cent wage cut and a 15-month pay freeze. Under such conditions, the granting of union representation on the Board could only be of limited, more accurately limiting, significance to the workforce. At Eastern, salary cuts of between 18 per cent and 22 per cent were the cost of a 25 per cent employee share ownership. Put together a loss of $290 million in wages, and a subsequent net profit of $190 million, of which workers' pro rata share would be less than $50 million. It would not need worker managers to calculate a net loss to employees of over $240 million!

The introduction of an ESOP for a company in trouble is designed to allow for labour market flexibility under the guise of share ownership. It can involve redundancies and loss of wages but also other forms of flexibility. It is possible that the workers' pension funds become dedicated to speculation in the corporation's prospects. Even more disturbing is the willing erosion of working conditions on the part of employees whose remunerations depends upon it. Grunberg *et al.* draw the following conclusion from their study of the safety records in timber mills: 'Our findings are very disappointing for those who see employee ownership as a way to improve the quality of work life. The producer cooperatives had similar accident and injury experiences to the conventional mills but a worse days missed record. The ESOP did worse on all measures of safety. It is also clear that employee ownership does not necessarily translate into changes in the work process to make it less hazardous or into greater worker participation over shopfloor safety and working conditions. The picture is not improved when we look at levels of worker satisfaction and morale. Workers perceive working in these types of mills as particularly distressful' (Grunberg *et al.* 1996, p. 235).

Not surprisingly, in his study of ESOPs, Kruse (1996) finds that the motives for adopting ESOPs have been mixed, between the search for productivity, flexibility, anti-merger strategy, and tax benefits.[7] For him, 'In sum, profit-sharing or employee ownership may be implemented in order to: (1) enhance workplace cooperation and productivity . . . (2) increase compensation flexibility . . . (3) discourage unionization, or gain concessions from unions; and/or (4) gain tax incentives, have easy access to capital, or avoid takeovers in the USA' (Kruse 1996, p. 518).

Whatever the historical and specific motives that informed the formation of ESOPs, they have become more and more heavily embroiled in the general process of corporate strategy, with limited actual and potential deference to the interests of employees. The broader context within which schemes have operated in the USA has been one of widening pay differentials between the rich and poor, with high levels of unemployment and casualized service sector employment for the poor. A weak position in the more general labour market has encouraged a threatened workforce to accept wage cuts rather than redundancies, taking government tax hand-outs to smooth the process.

Trade union responses

Not surprisingly, in view of the history and underlying principles of ESOPs, trade unions have generally been hostile to these initiatives. As the British TUC reported in 1974, 'First, such schemes do not in reality provide for any real control over the managerial decisions. . . . Second, there is no advantage to workpeople tying up their savings in the firm since this doubles the insecurity . . . (third) they do little or nothing to reduce the inequality of wealth'. (Quoted in Baddon *et al.* 1989, p. 43.)

Furthermore, the TUC observed that such schemes exclude those who do not create commodities, thereby leaving out the majority of those who work in the public sector and also those in smaller scale and casualized or disadvantaged employment in the private sector. In Britain, for example, one way in which equal pay legislation has been avoided is through tying bonus payments predominantly to those jobs occupied by male employees, and much the same applies to the greater use of profit-sharing and discounted share offers to those who are placed higher up in the job hierarchy. Workers may also rarely be able to afford to keep the shares that they receive, rather selling them for cash when allowed to do so to supplement wages and buy essentials or tide over emergencies.

Matthews points to: 'unpopularity of shares as opposed to cash. Until recently, most workers were not sufficiently well off to afford to save, especially in the form of shares. Indeed, holding shares of one company, particularly one's own employer, is simply unwise speculation. Therefore, for good reason, given the choice, workers would take a cash bonus, but given shares these would usually be sold immediately. If this were forbidden the shares were looked upon as 'dead money' . . . 80 per cent of employees free to choose between shares or cash took the money' (Matthews 1989, p. 461).

In the USA, trade union opposition to ESOPs and other forms of share ownership has mellowed. In part, this is a matter of economic necessity – trade unions are faced with negotiating with employers who only offer continuing employment on the basis of an ESOP. On the other hand, whether through pensions or other sources of funds, trade unions appear to have the potential to influence the level and composition of investment. Gianaris (1996, p. 143) estimates that ESOPs had accumulated $150 billion in stock by the 1990s, but this is totally dominated by the further $4.8 trillion which is held in workers' pension funds. These are, however, managed as financial assets with little attention paid to using the ownership power that this might allow, with as much as $140 billion being held in foreign equities (Gianaris 1996, p. 155).

The difficulties of taking control over the economy through worker ownership is best illustrated by the Swedish experience, where the strongest attempt has been made. Within Sweden itself, although the influence of the labour movement was declining,[8] the conditions for success could not otherwise have been more favourable for the following reasons. First, Sweden has had a strong trade union movement with high density of union membership, customary rights to participate in policy formation, and intimate links with the Social Democratic Party.

Second, the latter has formed the Government in power in all but six years over the period from 1932 until the 1990s. It is perceived to have introduced the most enlightened form of the welfare state and has overseen rapid economic growth. Employers have also been highly unified in policy, partly reflecting the high degree of concentration of ownership, and the economy's success has depended upon competitiveness in international markets, given the small scale of the domestic market.

During the early 1970s, support in the labour movement was won for a proposal that 20 percent of the annual profits of large firms should be owned by trusts representing the interests of wage earners as a whole. The reforms were proposed by the Meidner Committee in 1976 and were specifically linked to a fundamental shift in the balance of economic power, as quoted by Pontusson: 'We want to deprive the capitalists of the power that they exercise by virtue of ownership. All experience shows that it is not enough to have influence and control. Ownership plays a decisive role . . . we cannot fundamentally change society without changing its ownership structure' (Pontusson 1987).

Assisted by unusual economic and political circumstances, the Meidner Plan gained widespread support and was adopted as policy. Ultimately, however, legislation to bring the workers' fund into being was only introduced in 1983. It was on a much smaller scale than originally planned and geared towards sustaining investment and subsidising pensions as part and parcel of an austerity programme. With the absolute opposition from employers, redistribution was at most confined to newly created wealth. No attempt was made to extend the democratic rights of workers in economic decision-making.

The reasons for this failure in terms of the original conception and in shifting the balance of economic power in favour of working people is not of direct concern here, although worsening economic conditions and unified opposition from capital were clearly of enormous importance, along with the export of capital.[9] Rather, the example of Sweden serves to illustrate what limited change has been achieved even in the society which is arguably conceived to have travelled furthest and most successfully along the road of welfare capitalism.

Conclusion

Like ESOPs, pensions have been used to argue that workers have become share owners and are a factor in the creation of a people's capitalism. This is incorrect for similar reasons to those that prevent ESOPs from transferring corporate ownership to workers. Pensions do not turn workers into rentier capitalists; they merely pay back to the working class, in a particular form, a portion of the revenue that it has itself produced. In other words, pensions are a form of wages which are paid, after delay, to workers for their subsistence during retirement.

Moreover, pension funds are generally administered by and on behalf of the banking system that controls them, whether directly or indirectly. They have given workers little control over the economy. According to the estimate by Minns (1982), well over 75 per cent of pension fund investments in the UK are looked after by banks, insurance companies and stockbrokers. For this reason, socialist literature is occasionally awash with schemes to employ pension funds to regenerate British industry, and for more modest schemes that put planning and need before profitability. But such are the legal and financial powers of the City's financial institutions that progress has been limited. Even attempts to withdraw investments from South Africa as a protest against apartheid proved difficult against the legal requirements that pension funds should maximize financial returns.[10]

At the time of writing, the ideology of ESOPs, and of people's capitalism more generally, had become prominent in South Africa as the apartheid regime drew to a close. But it would be a mistake to see the ideology as a simple and inevitable product of hard times, in a capitalist crisis, or a political transition as in South Africa or eastern Europe. While it might be argued that workers can deploy such participation as a basis for further gains, experience suggests otherwise as goals and practices become subordinated to, and incorporated into, the logic and dynamic of capitalism.

Notes

1 For discussion of the implications for South Africa, see the report mentioned, Fine (1997).
2 See Tucker *et al.* (1989).
3 See also Church (1971) and Hatton (1988).
4 For a discussion of Weitzman in historical perspective, see Outram (1985). Mitchell (1995) sees wage flexibility as just one of only three factors in favour of ESOPs, the other two being either to internalize transactions costs between owners and workers or to reduce informational costs in the valuation of a firm's assets. Note that Benner and Jun use the latter as a device to explain ESOPs in terms of worker and entrepreneur strategies: 'Owners of relatively unprofitable firms will tend to sell out for low prices instead of paying high wages, whereas owners of profitable firms will prefer pay high wages over receiving low firm prices; the buy-out serves as a screening mechanism. The probability of an employee buy-out decreases with the employees' outside options and increases with owners' outside options' (Benner and Jun 1996, p. 502). See also Outram (1987).
5 For discussion of the details for the UK both here and below, see Smith (1986), Bradley and Gelb (1986), Estrin and Wadhwani (1986), Blanchflower and Oswald (1987), Poole (1988) and Pryce and Nicholson (1988).
6 McElrath and Rowan (1992) report that of 50 buy-outs by workers since 1975, only 32 were still operating.
7 Kruse, however, employs the notion of flexibility in a slightly different way, as the sharing of risk with employees over fluctuating corporate fortunes (Kruse 1996).
8 See Standing (1988, Chapter 6).
9 See also Meidner (1991), Pontusson (1994) and Minns (1996).
10 See also Minns (1996).

References

Aitken, M. and Wood, R. (1989), 'Employee Stock Ownership Plans: Issues and Evidence', in Baddon *et al.* (eds), *People's Capitalism: A Critical Analysis of Profit-Sharing and Employee Share Ownership*, London: Routledge.

Anderson, P. and Camiller, P. (eds) (1994), *Mapping the West European Left*, London: Verso.

Baddon, L. *et al.* (eds) (1989), *People's Capitalism: A Critical Analysis of Profit-Sharing and Employee Share Ownership*, London: Routledge.

Benner, A. and Jun, B. (1996), 'Employee Buy-Out in a Bargaining Game with Asymmetric Information', *American Economic Review*, Vol. 86, no. 3, pp. 502–23.

Blanchflower, D. and Oswald, A. (1987), 'Profit-Sharing – Can It Work', *Oxford Economic Papers*, Vol. 39, no. 1, pp. 1–19.

Blanchflower, D. and Oswald, A. (1988), 'Profit-Related Pay: Prose Discovered?', *Economic Journal*, Vol. 98, September, pp. 720–30.

Blinder, A. (ed.) (1990), *Paying for Productivity*, Washington: Brookings.

Bradley, K. and Gelb, A. (1986), *Share Ownership for Employees*, London: Public Policy Centre.

Cable, J. (1988) 'Is Profit-Sharing Participation? Evidence on Alternative Firm Types from West Germany', in Estrin *et al.* (eds), 'Employee Share Ownership, Profit-sharing and Participation', Special Issue of *International Journal of Industrial Organization*, Vol. 6, no. 1, March, pp. 121–38.

Cable, J. and Wilson, N. (1989), 'Profit-Sharing and Productivity: An Analysis of UK Engineering Firms', *Economic Journal*, Vol. 99, June, pp. 366–75.

Cable, J. and Wilson, N. (1990), 'Profit-Sharing and Productivity: Some Further Evidence', *Economic Journal*, Vol. 100, June, pp. 550–5.

Church, R. (1971), 'Profit-Sharing and Labour Relations in England in the Nineteenth Century', *International Review of Social History*, Vol. XVI, pp. 1–16.

Dhillon, U. and Ramirez, G. (1994), 'Employee Stock Ownership and Corporate Control – An Empirical Study', *Journal of Banking and Finance*, Vol. 18, no. 1, pp. 9–26.

Doucouliagos, C. (1995), 'Worker Participation and Productivity in Labor-Managed and Participatory Capitalist Firms – A Meta-Analysis', *Industrial and Labor Relations Review*, Vol. 49, no. 1, pp. 58–77.

Duncan, C. (1988) 'Why Profit Related Pay Will Fail', *Industrial Relations Journal*, Autumn, pp. 186–200.

Estrin, S. and Wadhwani, S. (1986), *Will Profit-Sharing Work?*, London: Employment Institute.

Estrin, S. *et al.* (eds) (1988), 'Employee Share Ownership, Profit-sharing and Participation', Special Issue of *International Journal of Industrial Organization*, Vol. 6, no. 1.

Fine, B. (1997), 'ESOP's Fable: Golden Egg or Sour Grapes?', NIEP Occasional Paper Series, no. 9, Johannesburg: National Institute for Economic Policy.

Gianaris, N. (1996) *Modern Capitalism: Privatization, Employee Ownership, and Industrial Democracy*, Westport, CT: Praeger.

Grunberg, L. *et al.* (1996), 'The Relationship of Employee Ownership and Participation to Workplace Safety', *Economic and Industrial Democracy*, Vol. 17, no. 2, pp. 221–41.

Hatton, T. (1988), 'Profit-sharing in British Industry, 1865–1913', in Estrin et al. (eds), 'Employee Share Ownership, Profit-sharing and Participation', Special Issue of *International Journal of Industrial Organization*, Vol. 6, no. 1, pp. 69–90.

HMSO (1986), *Profit Related Pay: a Consultative Document*, London, Cmnd 9835.

Jones, D. and Kato, T. (1993a), 'The Scope, Nature, and Effects of Employee Stock Ownership Plans in Japan', *Industrial and Labor Relations Review*, Vol. 46, no. 2, pp. 352–67.

Jones, D. and Kato, T. (1993b) 'Employee Stock Ownership Plans and Productivity in Japanese Manufacturing Firms', *British Journal of Industrial Relations*, Vol. 31, no. 3, pp. 331–46.

Kaufman, R. and Russell, R. (1995), 'Government Support for Profit-Sharing, Gain-sharing, ESOPs, and TQM', *Contemporary Economic Policy*, Vol. 13, no. 2, pp. 38–48.

Kruse, D. (1996), 'Why Do Firms Adopt Profit-Sharing and Employee Ownership Plans', *British Journal of Industrial Relations*, Vol. 34, no. 4, pp. 515–38.

Matthews, D. (1989), 'The British Experience of Profit-Sharing', *Economic History Review*, Vol. XLII, no. 4, Nov, pp. 439–64.

McElrath, R. and Rowan, R. (1992), 'The American Labor Movement and Employee Ownership – Objections to and Uses of Employee Ownership Plans', *Journal of Labor Research*, Vol. 13, no. 1, pp. 99–119.

Meade, J. (1986), *Alternative Systems of Business Organization and of Workers' Remuneration*, London: Allen and Unwin.

Meidner, R. (1991), 'Why Did the Swedish Model Fail?', *Socialist Register*, London: Merlin Press.

Minns, R. (1982), *Take Over the City*, London: Pluto Press.

Minns, R. (1996), 'The Social Ownership of Capital', *New Left Review*, no. 219, pp. 42–61.

Mitchell, D. (1995) 'Profit-Sharing and Employee Ownership – Policy Implications', *Contemporary Economic Policy*, Vol. 13, no. 2, pp. 16–25.

Outram, Q. (1985), 'Weitzman in Historical Perspective', University of Leeds, Discussion Paper Series, no. 144, April.

Outram, Q. (1987), 'Profit Related Pay and Asymmetric Information', University of Leeds, Discussion Paper Series, 87/6, March.

Pontusson, J. (1987), 'Radicalization and Retreat in Swedish Social Democracy', *New Left Review*, no. 165, September/October, pp. 5–33.

Pontusson, J. (1994), 'Sweden after the Golden Age', in Anderson, P. and Camiller, P. (eds), *Mapping the West European Left*, London: Verso.

Poole, M. (1988), 'Factors Affecting the Development of Employee Financial Participation in Contemporary Britain: Evidence from a National Survey', *British Journal of Industrial Relations*, Vol. 26, no. 1, March, pp. 21–36.

Pryce, V. and Nicholson, C. (1988), 'The Problems and Performance of Employee Ownership Firms', *Employment Gazette*, June, pp. 346–50.

Scholes, M. and Wolfson, M. (1989), 'Employee Stock Ownership Plans and Corporate Restructuring', *NBER Working Paper*, no. 3094, September.

Smith, G. (1986), 'Profit-Sharing and Employee Share Ownership in Britain', *Employment Gazette*, September, pp. 380–85.

Standing, G. (1988), *Unemployment and Labour Market Flexibility: Sweden*, Geneva: ILO.

Taylor, I. (1988), *Fair Shares for all the Workers*, London: Adam Smith Institute.

Tucker, J. *et al.* (1989), 'Employee Ownership and Perceptions of Work – The Effect of an Employee Stock Ownership Plan', *Work and Occupations*, Vol. 16, no. 1, pp. 26–42.

Wadhwani, S. and Wall, M. (1990), 'The Effects of Profit-Sharing on Employment, Wages, Stock Returns and Productivity: Evidence from UK Micro-Data', *Economic Journal*, Vol. 100, March, pp. 1–17.

Weitzman, M. (1984), *The Share Economy: Conquering Stagflation*, Cambridge, MA: Harvard University Press.

A bibliography of the writings of Sam Aaronovitch

Compiled by Jan Toporowski

'Agriculture in the Colonies' *Communist Review*, July 1946, pp. 21–6.

with Kirstine Aaronovitch, *Crisis in Kenya*, London: Lawrence and Wishart, 1947.

'The Communist Party and the Battle of Ideas' Report to the National Cultural Conference, *Communist Review*, May 1948, pp. 148–52.

'Imperialist Plans and the African National Movement – I', *Communist Review*, November 1948, pp. 349–52.

'Imperialist Plans and the African National Movement – II', *Communist Review*, December 1948, pp. 381–84.

'New Political Economy Textbook' a review of J. Eaton's *Political Economy A Textbook*, *Communist Review*, August 1949, pp. 638–40.

'Imperialist Heart-Searchings', a review of R. Hinden's *Empire and After*, *Communist Review*, November 1949, pp. 730–1.

'Comment on Dr S. Lilley's Review of Professor V. G. Childe's Book *History*' *Modern Quarterly* 1950, Vol. 5, no. 1, pp. 81–5.

'To Start You Reading', a review of T.A. Jackson's *Old Friends to Keep: Studies of English Novels and Novelists*, *Communist Review*, January 1951, pp. 31–2.

'Capitalist Reaction against Socialist Realism', in *Essays on Socialist Realism and the British Cultural Tradition*, Arena Publications, undated.

co-author, *The American Threat to British Culture*, Arena Publications, undated.

'The Party's Cultural Work', *Communist Review*, July 1952, pp. 216–24.

'Using the Power of Marxism', *Communist Review*, August 1953, pp. 245–51.

Monopoly: A Study of British Monopoly Capitalism, London: Lawrence and Wishart, 1955.

The Ruling Class: A Study of British Finance Capital, London: Lawrence and Wishart, 1961.

'Sociology, Class and Power' and 'Reply to Discussion', *Marxism Today*, June 1964, pp. 170–8.

Economics for Trade Unionists: The Wage System, London: Lawrence and Wishart, 1964.

'Forward or Back: Prospects for the Movement', *Marxism Today*, January 1967, pp. 6–12.

'Perspectives for Class Struggle and Alliances: A Contribution to the discussion of Communist Strategy', *Marxism Today*, March 1973, pp. 68–77.

'The Next Stage', *Marxism Today*, August 1974, pp. 236–40.

with Malcolm Sawyer 'The Concentration of British Manufacturing', *Lloyds Bank Review*, 1974, no. 114.

with Malcolm Sawyer, *Big Business: Theoretical and Empirical Aspects of Concentration and Mergers in the United Kingdom*, London: Macmillan, 1975.

'Theories of the Firm' in Green, F. and Nore, P. (eds), *Economics: An Anti-Text*, London: Macmillan, 1975.

with Malcolm Sawyer, 'Mergers, Growth and Concentration', *Oxford Economic Papers*, 1975, Vol. 27.

'Eurocommunism: A Discussion of Carillo's *Eurocommunism and the State*', *Marxism Today*, July 1978, pp. 222–7.

'The Working Class and the Broad Democratic Alliance', *Marxism Today*, September 1979, pp. 289–92.

'Unemployment – Halting the Slide', *Marxism Today*, May 1981, Vol. 25, no. 1, pp. 6–11.

The Road from Thatcherism: The Alternative Economic Strategy, London: Lawrence and Wishart, 1981.

with Ron Smith, Jean Gardiner and Roger Moore, *The Political Economy of British Capitalism, A Marxist Analysis*, Maidenhead: McGraw-Hill, 1981.

with Malcolm Sawyer, 'Price Change and Oligopoly', *Journal of Industrial Economics*, 1981, Vol.30, no. 2, December, pp.137–47.

with Paul Levine, 'Financial Characteristics of Firms and Theories of Merger Activity', *Journal of Industrial Economics*, 1981, Vol. 30, no. 2, December, pp. 149–72.

'Recipe for Defeat', *Marxism Today*, April 1982, Vol. 26, no. 4, pp. 15–19.

with Malcolm Sawyer and Peter Samson, 'The Influence of Cost and Demand Changes on the Rate of Change of Prices', *Applied Economics*, April 1982, Vol. 14, no. 2, pp. 195–209.

'Redrawing the Political Map: Has Thatcherism Changed British Politics', a discussion between Peter Jenkins, Stuart Hall and Sam Aaronovitch, *Marxism Today*, December 1982, Vol. 26 no. 12, pp. 14–19.

with Peter Samson, *The Insurance Industry in the Countries of the EEC. Structure, Conduct and Performance*, Luxembourg: Office for the Official Publications of the European Communities, 1985.

'The Alternative Economic Strategy: Goodbye to All That?', *Marxism Today*, February 1986, Vol. 30, no. 2, pp. 20–6.

with John Grahl, 'Controversy – EMU: Join, but not yet', *New Economy*, 1997, Vol. 4, no. 3.

with John Grahl, 'Building on Maastricht' in Gowan, P. and Anderson, P. (eds), *The Question of Europe*, London: Verso, 1997.

with John Grahl 'EMU and the Blair Government', *Renewal*, 1997, Vol. 5, no. 2, pp. 27–33.

Index

Emminger, Otmar 91
Employee Share-ownership Plans
    (ESOPs) 179–90
employment: agricultural sector 124;
    European unity 91, 96; full 23, 24, 25,
    30, 36, 42; trajectory of capitalism 11;
    unequal exchange 103–4; United
    Kingdom 140
'empty chair' policy 90
endogenous growth (EG) 104–12: market
    failure 143
Engels, Friedrich 80: agrarian question
    116; changing perceptions 4; Classical
    Marxism 7; military technology 83;
    scientific developments, interest in 9
Engels' Law 120
Europe: conflict theory of inflation 33, 34,
    35, 37; military expenditure 84; new
    socio-economic context 41–2
European Central Bank (ECB) 87: and
    European economic government 95;
    globalization 154, 161, 164; interest
    rates 96; new socio-economic context
    45; regionalism 154; Werner Report
    90
European Clearing Agency (ECA) 163–4
European Clearing Unit (ECU) 163
European Cohesion Fund 89
European funds for monetary
    cooperation (EFMC) 90
European Investment Agency (EIA) 163
European Monetary System (EMS) 95,
    97: conflict theory of inflation 29;
    establishment 89; European System of
    Central Banks 161–2; German
    obstruction 91–2; termination 94
European Reconstruction Programme
    (Marshall Plan) 41, 52
European Regional Development Fund
    89
European single currency: banking 168;
    conflict theory of inflation 23;
    institutional change 54; new socio-
    economic context 44–5; positive-sum
    games 55, 56
European System of Central Banks
    (ESCB) 154, 161–2
European Union: banking 168–78;
    budget 91; conflict resolution 82;
    economic government 87–9, 90, 95–6,
    97; global food trade 120;
    globalization 154; institutional change
    47; new socio-economic context 47;
    positive-sum games 55, 56, 59;

regionalism 160; regional policy 89;
    share of world GDP 100
European unity 87–97
exchange rate instability 146–51
Exchange Rate Mechanism (ERM) 93–4:
    conflict theory of inflation 23
exogenous growth 104–5
expectations, inflationary 23, 25, 27

'fair trade' 112
fascism 11
Federal Reserve Bank 92
fertilizer consumption 125
feudalism 9, 180
Fian, Antonio 60n.6
finance capital 136–7
financial capital 137–9, 141, 143
financial services passport 169
firm, definition of 69
First World War 9, 85: globalization 79,
    80; institutional change 52
fiscal policy 43
fixed exchange rates: conflict theory
    of inflation 23, 29; European
    Monetary System 90; Keynes's
    General Theory 17
floating exchange rates 17, 149
Ford 84
foreign affiliates, sales of 155–6
foreign direct investment (FDI): agrarian
    question 117, 118, 122;
    internationalization of capital 154–5;
    new socio-economic context 43; UK
    140
foreign-owned enterprises 69
France: agrarian question 122; banking
    170, 175; European Community,
    views on 82; European unity 87–8, 90,
    92–6, 97; exchange rates 149, 150;
    foreign direct investment 155;
    internationalization of capital 156;
    military expenditure 78, 81, 84;
    neo-liberal policies, response to 94;
    peace, interest in 81
franchising 69
Frank, R. 71
Frankfurt School 13n.1
freedom of association 13
free speech 13
full employment: conflict theory of
    inflation 23, 24, 25, 30, 36; new
    socio-economic context 42
fuzzy logic 18
fuzzy sets 18